Authors and Owners

Authors and Owners

The Invention of Copyright

Mark Rose

Harvard University Press
Cambridge, Massachusetts
London, England
1993

This book is printed on acid-free paper, and its binding materials
have been chosen for strength and durability.

Library of Congress Cataloging-in-Publication Data
Rose, Mark.
Authors and owners : the invention of copyright / Mark Rose.
p. cm.
Includes bibliographical references and index.
ISBN 0-674-05308-7 (alk. paper)
1. Copyright—Great Britain—History.
2. Copyright—United States—History. I. Title.
KD1300.R67 1993
346.4104'82—dc20
[344.106482]
92-43010
CIP

For Ted

Preface

My interest in copyright emerges from my experience as a literary "expert witness" in a number of copyright-infringement cases. The principal cases in which I have participated—a suit against a television police serial with a science-fictional gimmick (one of the cops was a robot), a suit against a made-for-television movie about a child "genius" and his experiences in college, a suit against *Raiders of the Lost Ark* by the author of a long, mystical novel about the Ark of the Covenant, a suit against a movie about the rock music industry in the 1950s, a suit against a television movie about an alien invader—are, I believe, representative of run-of-the-mill infringement cases in the film and television industry. The issues are usually access and similarity. Did the defendant have access to the plaintiff's work, and could he or she have copied that work or otherwise taken something of value from it? Is the defendant's work so similar to the plaintiff's that plagiarism is a reasonable hypothesis, or, alternatively, is the defendant's work different enough from the plaintiff's to be considered original?

The issue for the expert witness is usually similarity. In the police serial case, the robot cop in the plaintiff's story was a mechanical device that was supposed to look something like a vacuum cleaner and was conspicuously mechanical and irritating in its behavior. The defendant's cop looked like an ordinary police rookie; his true nature was unknown to everyone except his older partner. Were these two figures essentially the same? Was it relevant that a robot detective had been the central character in a well-known science-fiction novel of the 1950s and that robot police had figured in minor ways in a number of other texts?

As a legal witness, I became conscious of the contradiction between the romantic conception of authorship—the notion of the creative individual—that underlies copyright and the fact that most work in the entertainment industry is corporate rather than individual. Furthermore, many of the characteristic products of the industry—game shows, soap operas, situation comedies, police stories, spy stories, and the like—tend to be formulaic. Romantic conceptions of authorship seem as inappropriate in discussing these cultural productions as in discussing the equally formulaic productions of some older periods, ballads, say, or chivalric romances. I found these contradictions between the ideology of copyright and the actual circumstances of litigation intriguing and provocative.

Imagining that my experiences in infringement cases might make an interesting essay, my colleague Richard Helgerson suggested that I should write something about copyright. My friend Robert Burt encouraged me and suggested that I look at Lyman Ray Patterson's *Copyright in Historical Perspective*, a book to which all students of the history of Anglo-American copyright must be enormously indebted. Patterson's study in turn whetted my curiosity about the early British cases, and my interests turned historical. The first fruit of these interests was an article, "The Author as Proprietor: *Donaldson v. Becket* and the Genealogy of Modern Authorship," published in 1988. This book is an expansion and, I trust, a deepening of that article.

Suspicious as I am of romantic notions of authorship, I am keenly aware that my own work is part of a collective enterprise in which many scholars, building on the work of such older historians of literature as A. S. Collins and such recent historians of publishing as John Feather, are attempting to understand the relations between conceptions of authorship and the development of intellectual property. The claim that there is a connection between the invention of the author as original genius and the invention of copyright was prefigured by Benjamin Kaplan in *An Unhurried View of Copyright* (1967), still one of the most penetrating discussions of copyright law we have. But in its recent phase this enterprise has been stimulated by the questions about authorship raised by Roland Barthes and Michel Foucault. The first extended consideration of the interaction between aesthetic and legal developments in the eighteenth century that I know was Martha Woodmansee's important "The Genius and the Copyright: Economic and Legal Conditions of the Emergence of the 'Author'" (1984), which focused on Germany in the latter part of the century. Since then Carla Hesse has explored the legal construction of authorship in eighteenth-century France, where the political situation was very different from that in England, and Margreta de Grazia, Peter Jaszi, and Jane M. Gaines, among others, have made significant contributions to the historical enterprise. Recently the *Cardozo Arts & Entertainment Law Journal* published a special number devoted to "Intellectual Property and the Construction of Authorship," which contains essays from the important conference on this subject organized by Peter Jaszi and Martha Woodmansee at Case Western Reserve University in April 1991.

I am keenly aware, too, of the many institutional and personal debts I have incurred in writing this book. I am grateful to the Santa Barbara and Irvine campuses of the University of California for providing funds for research and to Shannon Miller and Ruth Warkentin for their excellent assistance at different stages in my work. I am grateful as well to the National Endowment for the Humanities for a Research Fellowship and to the Board of Governors of the University of California Humanities Research Institute for allowing me to take a six-month leave of absence from my duties as director in order to accept the fellowship. The Harvard Center for Literary and Cultural Studies provided a wonderful refuge in which to work.

Many friends and colleagues have been generous with their time and support. I am particularly indebted to Ann Bermingham, Robert Burt, Marjorie Garber, Paul Geller, Peter Haidu, Richard Helgerson, Alvin Kernan, Robert Post, and Everett Zimmerman. I am also grateful to James Boyle, Cynthia Brown, Robert Folkenflik, Paul Hernadi, David Lieberman, James Oldham, Roberta Rosental, Ted Rose, Bert States, Maud Wilcox, and to the readers for Harvard University Press, whose reports were genuinely helpful to me. Debra Massey and the fine staff at UCHRI have been understanding and supportive beyond the call of duty.

Sections of this book were presented at the Interdisciplinary Humanities Center at UC Santa Barbara, the Stanford Humanities Center, the Center for Literary and Cultural Studies at Harvard, and the Case Western Reserve conference on intellectual property and authorship. In every instance I profited from the discussions that followed. My thanks are also due to the Regents of the University of California for permission to reprint material that originally appeared as "The Author as Proprietor: *Donaldson v. Becket* and the Genealogy of Modern Authorship," *Representations* 23 (1988): 51–85, and to Oxford University Press for permission to reprint material that originally appeared as "The Author in Court: *Pope v. Curll* (1741)," *Cultural Critique* 21 (1992): 197–217.

A few words about procedures are in order. I have preserved the spelling and punctuation in quotations from original materials, but I have silently expanded abbreviations and ignored the complexities of eighteenth-century typefaces—small capitals and such—except for preserving italics. I have regularized the capitalization in book titles and normalized dates to conform with present practice (for example, the date of the Statute of Anne is listed as 1710 rather than 1709). Bibliographical information for authors and works referred to in the text can be found in the list of works cited. Sources for law cases and standard references for statutes can be found in parentheses after the listing in the index. I have attempted to keep the apparatus simple and unobtrusive. British cases are cited, when possible, to the standard set of *English Reports*. Direct quotes from American cases are cited to the page on which the quote appears. The following abbreviations are used throughout: *CJ* for *Journal of the House of Commons; LJ* for *Journal of the House of Lords;* and *ER* for *English Reports.*

Contents

I thought of a sudden that I was hurried away to the realms of *Parnassus* . . . The greatest part of these regions is portioned out by *Apollo* into different tenures, some of them conveyed to the person for ever, others for life, and many for a shorter duration. There are mansion-houses built on many of these estates, and the great genius's, who have made a figure in the world, have here fixed their residence . . . The ancient Patriarchs of Poetry are generous, as they are rich: a great part of their possessions is let on lease to the moderns. *Dryden,* besides his own hereditary estate, had taken a large scope of ground from *Virgil.* Mr. *Pope* held *by copy* near half of *Homer's* rent-roll. Mr. *Dryden* spent most of his time in writing Prefaces and Dedications to the great men of *Parnassus:* Mr. *Pope* was retired to his own house, on the banks of the river already mentioned. His grounds were laid out in the most exquisite taste . . . The great *Shakespeare* sat upon a cliff, looking abroad through all creation. His possessions were very near as extensive as *Homer's,* but in some places, had not received sufficient culture. But even there spontaneous flowers shot up, and in the *unweeded garden, which grows to seed,* you might cull lavender, myrtle, and wild thyme . . . *Aristotle* seemed to lament that *Shakespear* had not studied his Art of Poetry, but *Longinus* admired him to a degree of enthusiasm. *Otway, Rowe,* and *Congreve* had him constantly in their eye. Even *Milton* was looking for flowers to transplant into his own Paradise.

—Arthur Murphy, *The Gray's-Inn Journal,* 11 November 1752

1

◦·◦·◦

The Question of Literary Property

What is an author? As Roland Barthes, Michel Foucault, and others have emphasized, the notion of the author is a relatively recent formation, and, as a cultural formation, it is inseparable from the commodification of literature. The distinguishing characteristic of the modern author, I propose, is proprietorship; the author is conceived as the originator and therefore the owner of a special kind of commodity, the work. This book, then, is concerned with the relationship between origination and ownership, and with the way these notions are incorporated in what Foucault calls "the solid and fundamental unit of the author and the work" (101).

The author and the work. The autonomous creator and the distinct literary object, unitary, closed, and caught up in relations of ownership. The author-work relation is embedded in library catalogues, the indexes of standard literary histories, and such basic reference tools as *Books in Print.* It is pervasive in our educational system, where students are typically taught from the canon of major works by major authors. It is also institutionalized in our system of marketing cultural products. Joyce Carol Oates, Saul Bellow, Zane Grey, Pablo Picasso, Leonard Bernstein, Stephen Spielberg, Clint Eastwood: the name of the author— or artist, conductor, director, or, sometimes, star, for in mass culture the authorial function is often filled by the star—becomes a kind of brand name, a recognizable sign that the cultural commodity will be of a certain kind and quality. No institutional embodiment of the author-work relation, however, is more fundamental than copyright, which not only makes possible the profitable manufacture and distribution of books, films, and other commodities but also, by endowing it with legal reality, helps to produce and affirm the very identity of the author as author.

Copyright is founded on the concept of the unique individual who creates something original and is entitled to reap a profit from those labors. Until recently, the dominant modes of aesthetic thinking have shared the romantic and individualistic assumptions inscribed in copyright. But these assumptions obscure important truths about the processes of cultural production. As Northrop Frye remarked many years ago, all literature is conventional, but in our day the conventionality of literature is "elaborately disguised by a law of copyright pretending that every work of art is an invention distinctive enough to be patented."

> This state of things makes it difficult to appraise a literature which includes Chaucer, much of whose poetry is translated or paraphrased from others; Shakespeare, whose plays sometimes follow their sources almost verbatim; and Milton, who asked for nothing better than to steal as much as possible out of the Bible. It is not only the inexperienced reader who looks for a *residual* originality in such works. Most of us tend to think of a poet's real achievement as distinct from, or even contrasted with, the achievement present in what he stole, and we are thus apt to concentrate on peripheral rather than on central critical facts. For instance, the central greatness of *Paradise Regained*, as a poem, is not the greatness of the rhetorical decorations that Milton added to his source, but the greatness of the theme itself, which Milton *passes on* to the reader from his source.

"Poetry can only be made out of other poems; novels out of other novels," Frye continues. "All this was much clearer before the assimilation of literature to private enterprise concealed so many of the facts of criticism" (96–97).

Frye's comments about the disparity between "the facts of criticism" and the assumptions underlying copyright were made well before the poststructuralist transformation of the literary landscape. At the time Frye was writing, the dominant mode of critical thinking with its concern for the integrity of the individual work as an aesthetic artifact—the well-wrought urn of Cleanth Brooks's famous title—was committed to the same mode of thinking, the same problematic, as the legal system with its concern for property rights. The characteristic form of interpretive criticism in this period, the "reading," was typically a demonstration of the coherence of structure and meaning in a work. Likewise, textual study was typically committed to establishing what an author *really* wrote (as if there were always a single theoretically determinable literary object), and source study consisted of a quasi-judicial process in which the scholar was seen as determining the extent of one author's indebtedness to another. But today the gap between copyright and literary thinking is striking. Copyright depends on drawing lines between works, on saying where one text ends and another begins. What much current literary thought emphasizes, however, is that texts permeate and enable one another, and so the notion of distinct boundaries between texts becomes difficult to sustain. Indeed, in what sense does the literary work exist objectively at all? Many critics reject any notion of the text as a stable, independent object, insisting on the centrality of the reader's role in reproducing the text. Many critics, too, reject any sense of the text as an object that exists apart from the culture that produced it or the succeeding cultures that have appropriated and, for their own purposes, reproduced it. Thus the concept of the historically transcendent masterpiece, the notion of the work that speaks to us directly, person to person, across the ages disappears, and along with it goes the notion of the creative genius, the autonomous author.

Discussions of copyright not infrequently regard intellectual property as an "ancient and eternal idea" (Prager 106) or "a natural need of the human mind" (Streibich 2). But copyright—the practice of securing marketable rights in texts that are treated as commodities—is a specifically modern institution, the creature of the printing press, the individualization of authorship in the late Middle Ages and early Renaissance, and the development of the advanced marketplace society in the seventeenth and eighteenth centuries. As Elizabeth Eisenstein remarks in *The Printing Press as an Agent of Change*, the "game of books and authors" depends on printing technology:

> The wish to see one's work in print (fixed forever with one's name in card files and anthologies) is different from the desire to pen lines that could never get fixed in a permanent form, might be lost forever, altered by copying, or—if truly memorable—be carried by oral transmission and assigned ultimately to "anon." Until it became possible to distinguish between composing a poem and reciting one, or writing a book and copying one; until books could be classified by something

other than incipits; how could the modern game of books and authors be played? (121)

Before authors could become professionals, however, a certain level of production and consumption of printed materials had to be attained, and this, as Terry Belanger among others has emphasized, did not occur until the eighteenth century. Politically, socially, and economically, eighteenth-century Britain was the most advanced country in Europe, and it was there that the world's first copyright statute was enacted in 1710. Accordingly, it is on eighteenth-century Britain that my book is centered; more specifically, it is centered on the long legal struggle known at the time as "the question of literary property."

At the start of this struggle stands this first copyright law, the Statute of Anne. This act was, in part, a legislative extension of the long-standing regulatory practices of the Stationers' Company, the ancient London guild of printers and booksellers. Yet there were two major innovations: the statute limited the term of protection (the guild copyrights were perpetual), and authors were legally recognized as possible proprietors of their works (previously only members of the guild could hold copyrights). In 1710, however, authors' primary economic relations were still typically with patrons rather than with booksellers; it was not until 1754 that Samuel Johnson's famous letter rejecting Lord Chesterfield's belated gesture of patronage in connection with the *Dictionary*—a document that Alvin Kernan calls "the Magna Carta of the modern author" (105)—signaled that circumstances were changing and that professional authorship was becoming both economically feasible and socially acceptable. In the Statute of Anne, the author was established as a legally empowered figure in the marketplace well before professional authorship was realized in practice.

The "question of literary property" was essentially a commercial struggle, a battle between two groups of booksellers. At its heart was the limitation of the copyright term, an issue of little consequence to authors who normally sold their works outright to the booksellers. Did the statute determine the whole extent of protection, or did it merely supplement an underlying common-law right of property? The London booksellers, who dominated the English book trade since the early days of the Stationers' Company, sought to maintain their position by establishing that, despite the statute, copyright was perpetual. Their rights, they argued, derived not from the statute but from the common-law rights of property transferred to them by authors. They were challenged by booksellers and printers of the provinces—and in particular by Scottish booksellers who were seeking an independent role for themselves as reprinters of popular titles—who denied that any protection existed beyond the term provided by the statute. Was there an author's common-law right? This question had to be resolved in the courts. It was litigated without resolution in *Tonson v. Collins* (1760), and then again in *Millar v. Taylor* (1769) when the Court of King's Bench, the highest common-law court in England, ruled that literary property was indeed a common-law right and that copyright was perpetual. But then in the great case of *Donaldson v. Becket* (1774) the House of Lords reversed the King's Bench decision and declared that copyright was limited in term.

Significantly, the parties in these cases were all booksellers, not authors; nevertheless, in the course of the litigation, the representation of the author as proprietor was elaborated and promulgated. This representation was dependent on the classical liberal discourse of property as represented, most famously, by John Locke's notion of the origins of property in acts of appropriation from the general state of nature.[1] The key to Locke's thought was the axiom that an individual's "person" was his own property. From this it could be demonstrated that through labor an individual might convert the raw materials of nature into private property. The familiar passage from the *Two Treatises of Government* (1690) is worth quoting:

> Though the Earth, and all inferior Creatures be common to all Men, yet every Man has a *Property* in his own *Person*. This no Body has any Right to but himself. The *Labour* of his Body, and the *Work* of his Hands, we may say, are properly his. Whatsoever then he removes out of the State that Nature hath provided, and left it in, he hath mixed his *Labour* with, and joyned to it something that is his own, and thereby makes it his *Property*. (305–306)

1. C. B. Macpherson's well-known account of Locke as the self-conscious ideologist of the new bourgeois order has been challenged from many different points of view in the last thirty years—for example, by John Dunn and James Tully, who emphasize the religious dimensions of Locke's thought. But what Locke may have meant is of less concern here than how his writings came to be used to articulate a certain discourse of property.

The act of appropriation thus involved solely the individual in relation to nature. Property was not a social convention but a natural right that was prior to the social order. Indeed, the principal function of the social order was to protect individual property rights. Extended into the realm of literary production, the liberal theory of property produced the notion put forward by the London booksellers of a property founded on the author's labor, one the author could sell to the bookseller. Though immaterial, this property was no less real and permanent, they argued, than any other kind of estate.

With its concerns for origins and first proprietors, the liberal discourse of property blended readily with the eighteenth-century discourse of original genius. As David Quint has shown, the notion of originality had roots in Renaissance literature, but the representation of originality as a central value in cultural production developed, as M. H. Abrams' classic study reveals, in precisely the same period as the notion of the author's property right. As late as 1711 Alexander Pope could still evoke the idea of the poet as the reproducer of traditional truths, speaking of *"True Wit"* as *"Nature* to Advantage drest, / What oft was *Thought,* but ne'er so well Exprest" (*Poems* 1:272–273). Seven years earlier, however, John Dennis made originality the basis for his praise of Milton (1:333–334), and in 1728 Edward Young was also insisting on its importance:

> Above all, in this, as in every work of genius, somewhat of an original spirit should be at least attempted; otherwise the poet, whose character disclaims mediocrity, makes a secondary praise his ultimate ambition; which has something of a contradiction in it. Originals only have true life, and differ as much from the best imitations as men from the most animated pictures of them. ("On Lyric Poetry" 414)

By the 1770s the doctrine of originality was orthodox, and Samuel Johnson in his "Life of Milton" (1779) could state flatly, "The highest praise of genius is original invention" (*Lives* 1:194).

Thus the representation of the author as a creator who is entitled to profit from his intellectual labor came into being through a blending of literary and legal discourses in the context of the contest over perpetual copyright. The literary-property struggle generated a body of texts—parliamentary records, pamphlets, and legal reports—in which aesthetic and legal questions are often indistinguishable. What constitutes a literary work? How is a literary composition different from any other form of invention such as a clock or an orrery? What is the relationship between literature and ideas? The debate over these issues engaged many of the leading jurists of the day, including Lord Mansfield and William Blackstone, and in it one can observe the emergence of legal and literary problems that are still with us.

Let me emphasize that the focus of my discussion of authorship is not on *subjectivity* but on *discourse.* I am not concerned with the production of the author as a consciousness so much as with a representation of authorship based on notions of property, originality, and personality.[2] The production of this representation involved, among other things, the abstraction of the concept of literary property from the physical book and then the presentation of this new, immaterial property as no less fixed and certain than any other kind of property. "There is nothing which so generally strikes the imagination, and engages the affections of mankind, as the right of property," wrote Blackstone in a famous passage in his *Commentaries,* after which he proceeded to define property as "that sole and despotic dominion which one man claims and exercises over the external things of the world, in total exclusion of the right of any other individual in the universe" (2:2). The paradigm of property for Blackstone, as for other eighteenth-century jurists, was land, and it was on the model of the landed estate that the concept of literary property was formulated.

The passage from Arthur Murphy's *Gray's-Inn Journal* that I use as an epigraph is a spectacular example of the attempt to represent literary property as analogous to real estate. Journalist, playwright, and member of the Johnson circle, Murphy was also a practicing lawyer involved as counsel in both *Millar v. Taylor* and *Donaldson v. Becket.* Here in a kind of dream vision, Murphy supposes himself transported to Mount Parnassus, the realm of the Muses, which he finds "portioned out by *Apollo* into different tenures, some of them conveyed to the person for ever, others for life, and many for a shorter duration." Thus the ancients such as Homer and Virgil and the greatest of the moderns—specifically Shakespeare—are imagined as the owners of vast freehold estates, while others such as Dryden and Pope, translators of ancient texts, are

2. In "Lessons from the 'Literatory': How to Historicise Authorship," David Saunders and Ian Hunter challenge the attempt to make connections between the legal and the aesthetic spheres and, more generally, raise questions about treatments of authorship that are, they claim, "subject-centered."

imagined as holding the largest part of their possessions from the ancients by lease. Murphy's fantasy recasts the ubiquitous ancient-modern distinction into an anatomy of various kinds of land tenure. The production of poetry becomes the production of property.

The goal for Mansfield, Blackstone, and the other eighteenth-century lawyers engaged in the project of stabilizing the concept of literary property was to establish copyright as an absolute right of property, a freehold "grounded on labour and invention" (Blackstone 2:405). If an author created a work, then why should he not have "sole and despotic dominion" over it? But this effort, strenuously pressed though it was, never succeeded. In refusing to affirm perpetual copyright, whatever their reasons, the House of Lords bore witness to the radical instability of the concept of the autonomous author. After all, authors do not really create in any literal sense, but rather produce texts through complex processes of adaptation and transformation. Literary property is not fixed and certain like a piece of land. Indeed, not even the notion of landed property—as Arthur Murphy's vision of Parnassus with its complex scheme of overlapping poetical tenures might be used to indicate—is ever simple or certain. All forms of property are socially constructed and, like copyright, bear in their lineaments the traces of the struggles in which they were fabricated.

The story that I tell ends—or should be understood to end—in irresolution. The eighteenth-century lawyers sought to fix the notion of literary property, and that project continues today in the vast legal literature devoted to such problems as exactly where to draw the line between idea and expression or exactly how to define the nature of "fair use." The argument of this book suggests that all such attempts are both futile and necessary. Futile because the concept of literary property is itself finally an oxymoron. But necessary because the institution of copyright is deeply rooted both in our economic system and in our conception of ourselves.

2

⚬ ⚬ ⚬

The Regime of Regulation

In the Middle Ages the owner of a manuscript was understood to possess the right to grant permission to copy it, and this was a right that could be exploited, as it was, for example, by those monasteries that regularly charged a fee for permission to copy one of their books (Putnam 2:481–483). Perhaps this practice might be thought to imply a form of copyright, and yet the bookowner's property was not a right in the text as such but in the manuscript as a physical object made of ink and parchment. Moreover, the rights of the bookowner had nothing to do with authorship. True copyright is concerned with rights in texts as distinct from rights in material objects, and its historical emergence is related to printing technology. A manuscript could be produced by one man with a pen and a supply of parchment. Printing an edition of a book, however, required a much more substantial investment of capital than the production of a manuscript, and it resulted not in a single precious object, which often would have been commissioned in advance, but in multiple copies that had to be distributed over time. Printers needed assurance that they would be able to recoup their investment, and so some system of trade regulation was necessary if printing was to flourish.

The earliest genuine anticipations of copyright were the printing privileges, which first appeared in fifteenth-century Venice.[1] "Privileges"

1. On the early printing privileges in Venice, see H. Brown 50–82, Gerulaitis 31–56, and Chavasse. For a general discussion of the early system of privileges, their relationship to patents, and their spread throughout Europe, see Bugbee 12–56. Armstrong's treatment of the development of book privileges in Europe does not emphasize Venice, as other scholars have (1–20).

were exclusive rights granted by the state to individuals for limited periods of time to reward them for services or to encourage them in useful activities. Earlier in the century, the practice of protecting mechanical inventions with privileges had become common in Venice, and many of the book-related privileges were also what we would today call patents. The first and most famous privilege was a monopoly on printing itself granted in 1469 for a term of five years to John of Speyer, the man who probably introduced printing to Venice. Later grants were less comprehensive, including, for example, exclusive rights to use particular types or to print in designated languages. Thus in 1496 Aldus Manutius received a twenty-year grant for all works printed by him in Greek, and grants were also awarded to print in Arabic, Syriac, and other languages.

Most privileges were issued to printers, but some were issued to authors and others to translators or editors. The first author's privilege was one granted in 1486 to Marc' Antonio Sabellico, the historian of Venice, for his *Decades rerum Venetarum*. According to the grant, Sabellico could choose which printer would publish his book, and any other printer who published it would be fined 500 ducats. Other privileges issued to authors included one in 1492 to Petro Francesco da Ravenna for *Foenix*, a pamphlet designed to improve the memory, and one in 1515 to Ariosto, who received lifetime rights in his *Orlando furioso* with a penalty for infringement set at 1000 ducats. The variety of recipients of privileges—authors, editors, translators, printers—suggests that traces of the medieval conflation of writing and the reproduction of writing under the general conception of "making books" persisted in fifteenth-century Venice.[2]

By the early sixteenth century, so many printing privileges had been issued and often in such general terms that the situation was unmanageable. In 1517, therefore, the Venetian Senate issued a remedial decree revoking all existing privileges in books and stating that henceforth privileges were to be granted solely for "new books and works" ("libri et opera nova") or for works never yet printed (H. Brown 74). But in the following decades the practice evidently arose of claiming that a few corrections, alterations, or additions made a work "new," and in

2. On the medieval conflation of writing and the reproduction of writing, see the account of St. Bonaventura's distinction between four ways of making books in Eisenstein 121–122.

1537 the Senate felt compelled to reaffirm the literal sense of the law of 1517: a new work was one that had not been previously published. A "new work," in other words, was a "new work." Even in the early days of printing regulation, then, we can see the potential for the appearance of the kind of problem that figures in copyright infringement to this day. Where does one draw the line between texts? When is a text new?

A further development in Venice at this time was the intertwining of the privilege system with censorship. The practice of seeking an imprimatur for a title from the Council of Ten had developed in the late fifteenth and early sixteenth centuries in a haphazard way along with the development of the privilege. In fact the imprimatur was at first sought as part of the process of bolstering the case for a privilege. In 1526, however, legislation required that every book published receive an imprimatur from the Council of Ten, and in 1543 a further censorship law reaffirmed the need for an imprimatur and prescribed harsh penalties for those who published without one. Finally, in the middle years of the century, a guild of printers and booksellers was organized as an instrument for government surveillance of the press.

The Venetian system of printing privileges was adopted in other European states in the sixteenth century, including England where privileges first appear in 1518 (Siebert 33–40). As in Venice, printing privileges and other kinds of grants, both based on the royal prerogative and known as "patents," were difficult to distinguish. Most of the English privileges were issued to printers, but, as in Venice, a number also went to authors, the first of these being the seven-year patent awarded in 1530 to the royal chaplain, John Palsgrave, for a textbook on the French language. Grants to individual authors for particular titles continued into the seventeenth century, as when King James granted Samuel Daniel a ten-year exclusive right to print his *History of England*. But by the middle of the sixteenth century, the most important English grants were not for particular titles but for classes of books such as lawbooks, catechisms, bibles, ABCs, and almanacs. The most powerful members of the book trade were those who secured these broad patents. (We can note in passing that the printing monopolies led in the late sixteenth century to a trade struggle that in some respects foreshadowed what was to come in the eighteenth century over copyright. As in the later struggle, the fight was between those who controlled the trade through the right to print the most valuable works and those excluded from power who resorted to what the monopolists termed "piracy.")

A second and ultimately more important system of trade regulation developed in England under the aegis of the Stationers' Company, which administered a guild system in which the right to print a book was established through entry in the company's register. The traditional stationers' term employed in the register was "copy," a word that referred both to the original manuscript—even as printers today speak of manuscript as "copy"—and to the right to make copies of it. Once secured, the right to print a particular book continued forever, and thus a "copy" might be bequeathed or sold to another stationer or it might be split into shares among several stationers. But only members of the guild—that is, booksellers and printers, not authors—might own copies. It was the guild that authorized the system and also administered it. Claims of infringement and other contentions about copyright were handled not in law courts but by the company's Court of Assistants (Blagden, *Stationers' Company* 54–55).

In early modern England, then, there were two parallel systems of press regulation: the printing patents, based on the royal prerogative, and the Stationers' Company system, based on the by-laws of the guild. But the stationers' system also derived its authority ultimately from the crown through a royal charter of 1557 which granted the guild a monopoly on printing: only members of the guild or others holding royal printing patents were permitted to practice "the art or mistery of printing" (Arber 1:xxxi). The primary interest of the state in granting this monopoly was not, however, the securing of stationers' property rights but the establishment of a more effective system for governmental surveillance of the press. The preamble to the Stationers' Company charter is explicit about the royal purpose:

> Know ye that we, considering and manifestly perceiving that certain seditious and heretical books rhymes and treatises are daily published and printed by divers scandalous malicious schismatical and heretical persons, not only moving our subjects and leiges to sedition and disobedience against us, our crown and dignity, but also to renew and move very great and detestable heresies against the faith and sound catholic doctrine of Holy Mother Church, and wishing to provide a suitable remedy in this behalf. (Arber 1:xxviii)

So begins the charter, which was issued by Philip and Mary as part of their campaign for reinstituting religious orthodoxy and which was quickly confirmed by Elizabeth, despite her very different allegiances, when she ascended the throne in 1558. Thus in England as well censorship and trade regulation became inextricable, and this was a marriage that was to endure until the passage of the Statute of Anne in 1710.

The point to be stressed is the difference between the system of cultural production and regulation characteristic of the sixteenth and seventeenth centuries and the later system that developed based on the idea of authorial property. For one thing, in the early modern period it was usual to think of a text as an action, not as a thing. The emphasis in Sidney's *Defence of Poetry,* as in most sixteenth- and seventeenth-century discussions of the function of poetry, falls on what the poet *does,* his "representing, counterfeiting, or figuring forth" of "notable images of virtues, vices, or what else" in order to teach and delight (79–81). Texts might serve to ennoble or immortalize worthy patrons and, in the process, perhaps to win office or other favors for their authors; they might move audiences to laughter or tears; they might expose corruptions or confirm the just rule of the monarch or assist in the embracing of true religion, in which case their authors were worthy of reward. Alternatively they might, as the preamble of the 1557 charter indicates, move men to "sedition and disobedience" or to "detestable heresies," in which case their authors deserved punishment. Thinking of texts as actions, valuing them for what they could do, was commensurate with the regulatory system in which censorship and the privileges of booksellers were conflated, just as, later, treating texts as aesthetic objects was commensurate with a system of cultural production and regulation based on property.

Another aspect of the older system of cultural production is noted by Natalie Zemon Davis in her study of the circulation of books as gifts in early modern Europe. Davis points to the continuation of the medieval conception of learning as a gift from God. As the transmitters of a divine gift, books were regarded as special objects, indeed as objects in which God himself might be understood to have some rights. Despite the fact that book production was one of the most capitalistic of early industries, the book itself "continued to be perceived as an object of mixed not absolute property, of collective not private enterprise." The book was a "privileged object that resisted permanent appropriation and which it was especially wrong to view only as a source of profit" (87).

Tudor and Stuart booksellers, then, entered titles in the Stationers' Register, but they did not quite "own" works in the sense of property articulated by Locke. Rather, they participated, as guildsmen of various kinds had done for hundreds of years, in a community defined in terms of reciprocal rights and responsibilities. Lyman Ray Patterson has analyzed the entries in the Stationers' Register between the mid-sixteenth and mid-seventeenth centuries and has concluded that the legal basis for stationers' copyright remained essentially the same throughout this period. Copyright did not protect a work itself but rather a stationer's right to publish a work. In granting a copyright, the wardens of the company were giving permission to a stationer to publish a particular title and were assuring the stationer of protection if any other member of the company attempted to publish the same title (*Copyright* 51–55). Such a system was commensurate with the guild as a community of members with mutual rights and responsibilities.

Patterson observes an evolution in the form of the entries in the Stationers' Register. The earliest entries consisted of a license to print granted by the company to an individual member: for example, "Owyn Rogers ys licensed to prynte a ballett Called *have pytie on the poore*" (Arber 1:96). Alternatively, an entry might be a notation of the fee received for such a license: "Recevyd of lucas haryson for his lycense for pryntinge of *a generall pardon forever*" (Arber 1:150). Gradually, though, the form of entry evolved away from one that emphasized the action whereby the company granted exclusive rights toward one that emphasized the member's proprietorship. By the seventeenth century, the accepted form was to say that a certain "book or copy" was entered as belonging to a particular member: "Entred for his copie under the hands of Master Roger Le Strange and Master Luke Fawne warden a booke or coppie intituled *Birinthea, a Romance* written by J. B." (Eyre 2:331). Patterson notes that whatever the form of the entry, the underlying legal basis for copyright before the passage of the statute remained the same: it was a grant from the company to a member. The point is well taken. Nevertheless, the evolution in the form of entry indicates that a subtle conceptual change was occurring and that booksellers had begun to think more explicitly of their "copies" or "books" as private property.

What I want to suggest is that in the seventeenth century a gap was beginning to develop between the institution of stationers' copyright, which was based upon a traditional conception of society as a community bound by ties of fidelity and service, and the emergent ideology of possessive individualism. The regime in which stationers' copyright was born was what we might call a regime of regulation rather than a regime of property. The guild was concerned with the regulation of the book trade, and the state was concerned with the regulation of public discourse. Since both copyright and censorship were understood in terms of regulation of the press, it was difficult even to think about them as separable practices.

All through the seventeenth century, the booksellers were among the strongest proponents of censorship. In 1641, for example, the book trade was thrown into what many contemporaries saw as chaos by the abolition of the Court of Star Chamber, the instrument of authority behind both licensing and the Stationers' Company's monopoly on publishing. Suddenly anything could be printed, and anyone with access to a press, legal or surreptitious, could print (Siebert 165–178). Deeply threatened, the booksellers published a pamphlet entitled *The Humble Remonstrance of the Company of Stationers to the High Court of Parliament* (1643), which begins with a discussion of the value set on printing and learning in the "civill" countries of Europe:

> Neverthelesse, it is not meere Printing, but well ordered Printing that merits so much favour and respect, since in things precious and excellent, the abuse (if not prevented) is commonly as dangerous, as the use is advantagious. *Germany* had the happy Sagacity to invent Presses . . . yet now, for want of reglement, her reputation is lost in those Manufactures . . . In the United-Provinces also, there are not above three or foure Eminent and rich Printers by reason of ill order . . . And commonly where Printing droops, and Printers grow poor by neglect of Government, there errors and heresies abound. (Arber 1:584)

Thus the stationers reproduce the traditional early modern discourse of the state as a well-ordered commonwealth and plead for the reinstitution of licensing and the restoration to the company of the power to limit the number of presses and apprentices. Embedded in what we might call the discourse of regulation, however, is an emergent discourse of property, for, in addition to pleading for the revival of regulations, the booksellers raise the issue of "their ancient Right, Propriety of Copies," arguing that if stationers cannot secure their properties they will lack "encouragement to make them active and alacrious in the service of the state" (Arber 1:586).

It would be possible to insist that the petitioning stationers were at bottom concerned only with property, that the invocation of the good of the commonwealth and of the general need for regulation was merely the pious cant of, as John Milton put it a year later in *Areopagitica*, "some old patentees and monopolizers in the trade of bookselling" (Hughes 749). But just as it is important to note in connection with the sixteenth- and seventeenth-century entries in the Stationers' Register both that the legal basis for copyright remained that of a regulatory grant from a corporate authority and that, at the same time, the booksellers had begun to think in terms of private property, so it is important in connection with the stationers' petition of 1643 not to miss the complexities and contradictions generated in the process of cultural change. The stationers at this moment evidently thought *both* in terms of property and in terms of regulation. For them to argue for the restoration of press regulation as well as for the securing of their own properties was not necessarily hypocritical. Eventually the discourse of property would become dominant, and then a distinction between copyright and censorship became possible. In 1643, however, nearly a half century before the publication of John Locke's two *Treatises of Government*, the separation of copyright and censorship that occurred with the passage of the Statute of Anne lay well in the future.

Let us turn now to the relation of authors to their texts in the early modern period. Before the evolution of the advanced marketplace society of the late seventeenth and eighteenth centuries, the major relations of exchange for authors occurred within a traditional patronage system in which, through a complex set of symbolic and material transactions, patrons received honor and status in the form of service from their clients and in return provided both material and immaterial rewards. Just as the concept of a bookseller owning property rights in a text did not quite fit the guild system and the institution of stationers' copyright, so the concept of an author owning a work did not quite fit the circumstances of literary production in the traditional patronage system. Even the printing privileges sometimes granted to authors as well as to guildsmen are best understood as versions of patronage rather than of ownership. Significantly, just as he was granted the sole right to publish his *Decades rerum Venetarum,* Marc' Antonio Sabellico was appointed librarian of San Marco with an annual stipend of 200 ducats. The joining of the grant with the appointment suggests that the Venetian Signoria regarded the privilege less as a right due an author than as a special reward for his service to the state in producing a history of the republic (Gerulaitis 36). Likewise, when the republic granted Ariosto a privilege in his *Orlando furioso* or a century later when King James granted Samuel Daniel a patent for his *History of England,* the actions of the republic and the king are perhaps best understood in terms of "honor" and "reward" rather than "property." In making these grants, the republic and the king were acting as patrons of worthy individuals.

The practice of rewarding authors for state service by granting them special printing privileges in their own work continued in England at least into the period of the civil wars. Thus in 1642 the Long Parliament established monthly fast days of public prayer for the parliamentary cause, a practice that included a pair of sermons to be preached on the fast day before the assembled house at St. Margaret's, Westminster. Parliament rewarded the preachers by granting them a special privilege in their texts. According to N. Frederick Nash, who has studied the fast-day sermons, the parliamentary vote of thanks to Mr. Bolton and Mr. Cheynall, two puritan ministers, on 25 March 1646 is typical:

> Ordered, That Mr. Holles and Sir Peter Wentworth do, from this House, give Thanks to Mr. Bolton and Mr. Cheynell, for the great Pains they took in the Sermons they preached this Day, at the Intreaty of this House, at St. Margarett's, Westminster, it being the Day of Publick Humiliation; and to desire them to print their Sermons: And they are to have the like Privilege in Printing of them, as others in the like Kind usually have had. (qtd. in Nash 182)

Clearly, Parliament was providing a reward for service, not a recognition of a preexisting property.

Authors may not have owned their texts, but they did of course own their manuscripts, the physical objects they had made with their own hands or caused to be made, and for these objects both the booksellers and the theatrical companies provided a market. The author's claim, however, ceased with the transfer of the manuscript. As G. E. Bentley remarks, a playscript after it left the playwright's hands was no more the author's property "than the cloak that he might have sold to the actors at the same time" (82). Once purchased, a script, like a cloak, might be shortened or lengthened or refurbished entirely according to the needs of the company and without consulting the author. And yet to say that authors owned nothing more than the ink and paper of their manuscripts is not to say that they had no literary interests at all. In the early modern period, in connection with the individualization of authorship, the transformation of the medieval *auctor* into the Renaissance *author*, there developed a general sense that it was improper to publish an author's text without permission. The acknowledgment of an author's interest in controlling the publication of his texts is not necessarily the same as the acknowledgment of a property right in the sense of an economic interest in an alienable commodity.[3] In practice, however, the right to control publication has economic implications, and it sometimes becomes difficult to distinguish what we might call matters of propriety from matters of property.[4]

The first cases of which I am aware in which authors' claims were legally asserted occur in France in the early sixteenth century. On 5 March 1504 Guillaume Cop, a well-known medical doctor who put together an annual almanac, obtained an order from the Parlement of Paris, which at this time functioned as a court of first instance, against the bookseller Jean Boissier who had attempted to have copies of Cop's almanac printed for him without Cop's authorization. According to the

3. Thus European copyright law has developed the concept of *droit moral*, the notion that along with the author's property rights there exists a separate body of personal rights, including the right to control first publication, the right to be acknowledged as the author, and the right to be assured that the integrity of the work will be preserved. Nineteenth-century French judges first granted systematic relief for moral rights, well after late eighteenth-century French legislators enacted authors' property rights. My argument suggests that the author was recognized as an individual with an interest in the status of his name and reputation before he was recognized as a fully empowered figure in the marketplace. On *droit moral* see Roeder and Strauss.

4. I use this terminology with some hesitation since "propriety" was often used to refer to what we now call "property"—as in the booksellers' *Humble Remonstrance* (1643) quoted above—but I cannot think of better terms. In fact, the breadth of the term "propriety" in early usage is instructive because it suggests the way that matters of "ownness" flow into matters of "ownership" in the early modern period.

court's order, Boissier was forbidden to sell any copies of the almanac that Cop had not authenticated with his signature. Thus Cop established control of his almanac, though not precisely through securing a privilege. As Elizabeth Armstrong remarks, almanacs sold particularly well when the name of a person of repute was attached to them: "Cop may indeed have thought of his signature on an almanac upon which the public relied for correct information on the phases of the moon, hours of day-light etc., as being like a signature on a medical prescription, that is, a guarantee of professional authority" (35–46). In a sense, then, what Cop was securing was as much a right having to do with the use of his name as a right to a text.

One month later, the Parlement of Paris was dealing with another case involving an author and a publisher. On 30 April 1504 the poet André de La Vigne petitioned for an injunction against the printer Michel Le Noir to prevent him from reprinting the *Vergier d'honneur*, an anthology containing poetic works by La Vigne and others. On 11 May the court issued a preliminary ruling that permitted Le Noir to complete his printing but temporarily forbade him to put the books up for sale. Finally on 3 June 1504 the court ruled in favor of La Vigne, granting him the exclusive right to print and sell the collection until 1 April 1505. At the same time, the Parlement of Paris also granted La Vigne exclusive rights over a second work, *Le Regnars traversans*, written by Jean Bouchet (Armstrong 36).

What were the circumstances that led to this case and in particular to the curious double judgment in which La Vigne was granted a brief privilege both for the collection and for Bouchet's text? Cynthia Brown, who has studied the case closely, suggests that La Vigne played a direct role in two previous printings of the *Vergier d'honneur* by Pierre Le Dru and that he had an economic interest in the work. As for the second title, *Le Regnars traversans*, Brown notes that Le Noir had also published an unauthorized edition of this text, and that it is plausible to suppose that La Vigne called Bouchet as one of his witnesses against Le Noir. But Bouchet was leaving Paris, and Brown speculates that it was perhaps because Bouchet would be absent that the court gave La Vigne the authority to supervise the printing of his text as well. What did the Parlement of Paris understand itself to be doing in granting La Vigne these privileges? Probably the recognition of some kind of author's interest was involved, but how strictly the court was thinking in such terms is difficult to say, since La Vigne was granted rights over both his own and others' texts.[5]

Much clearer is the claim made on behalf of the author toward the end of the century, in connection with the work of the French poet and scholar Marc-Antoine Muret. After Muret's death his friends initiated a project to print an annotated edition of Seneca that he had prepared. Meanwhile Nicolas Nivelle obtained a royal privilege to print this same work. Muret's friends challenged the legality of this grant in the Parlement of Paris, arguing that the king's privilege could not take precedence over the author's wishes. By a common instinct—so their argument went—men recognize that each person is the lord of what he has made, invented, and composed, even as God is the lord of the universe because it is his creation:

> In the same way, the author of a book is wholly its master, and as such he can freely do with it what he wills; even keep it permanently under his private control as he might a slave; or emancipate it by granting it common freedom; giving that freedom either purely and simply, without holding back anything, or else imposing some limits, by a kind of right of patronage, so that no one but he will have the right to print it except after a certain time.[6]

The Parlement of Paris accepted this argument on behalf of the author's claim to mastery over his text and on 15 March 1586 issued a judgment annulling the royal privilege (Dock 79).

The Parlement of Paris was not unique in its recognition of the author's interest in controlling publication of his text. Some forty years earlier on 7 February 1545, the Venetian Council of Ten issued what was in all likelihood the first public edict in Europe designed specifically to

5. I am indebted to Cynthia Brown for allowing me to see her work in progress on the transition from manuscript to print culture in sixteenth-century France. In this important study she reconstructs the activities in the first decade of the century of a group of poet-historians, the Rhétoriqueurs, as they struggled to establish their rights over their texts against printers. For an essay related to Brown's larger study, see her "Du manuscrit à l'imprimé en France: le cas des Grands Rhétoriqueurs."

6. "De manière qu'à cest exemple l'autheur d'vn liure en est du tout maistre, et comme tel en peut librement disposer; mesme le posséder tousjours sous sa main priuee, ainsi qu'vn esclaue, ou l'emanciper, en luy concedant la liberté commune: et la luy accorder ou pure et simple, sans y rien retenir, ou bien à la reseruation, par vne espece de droiet de patronage, qu'autre que luy ne pourra l'imprimer qu'après quelque temps" (*Muret v. Nivelle*, cited in Dock 78–79). For help in translating this passage I am grateful to Marie-Christine Helgerson.

protect authors. In this decree the council accused greedy printers of printing books without the authors' knowledge or consent. Henceforth no book was to be printed or sold unless the printer secured documentary proof of the consent of the author or his heirs. Books printed without such consent were to be confiscated and burned, and the offending printers were to be fined a ducat and imprisoned one month for each author and book injured (H. Brown 79–80).

I know of no early English cases analogous to the sixteenth-century French suits in the Parlement of Paris. Perhaps the closest approximation to an English judicial decision involving authorial rights in the sixteenth and seventeenth centuries was an order issued on 3 May 1619 by the Stationers' Court of Assistants—this was of course the guild court, not a court of law—forbidding printing of any of the King's Men's plays without the permission of representatives of the players (Jackson 110). The court took this action after consideration of a letter from William Herbert, the lord chamberlain, written on behalf of the King's Men, who were concerned to prevent the publication of a collection of Shakespeare's plays planned by the bookseller Thomas Pavier. Herbert's letter does not survive, but its substance is recapitulated in a lord chamberlain's letter of 1637 which explains that the action was taken both because publication would be damaging to the players and because "the bookes much corruption" would lead to "injury and disgrace of the Authors" (Greg 24). It is interesting that the lord chamberlain, who was the court official with authority in theatrical matters, in making the King's Men's case to the Stationers' Company thought it worthwhile to mention that the author would be "disgraced" by Pavier's collection—but it is also important to emphasize that the case involved neither an author as plaintiff nor a regular court of common law.

But even if authorial rights were not litigated in England, the evidence suggests that in the sixteenth and seventeenth centuries genuinely unauthorized publication was rare. Sixteenth- and seventeenth-century English books frequently include prefatory statements indicating that the author had not consented to publication, but in fact a claim of unauthorized publication was often little more than a device whereby a writer concerned with what J. W. Saunders calls "the stigma of print" might publish and yet preserve his status as a gentleman. In "Author's Copyright in England before 1640," Leo Kirschbaum has argued that unauthorized publication was commonplace, but most scholars agree that by and large English booksellers seem to have acknowledged an obligation to secure an author's permission before publishing and to pay him "copy money" if payment was appropriate.

The first English affirmation of any kind of authorial interest seems to be a parliamentary edict of 29 January 1642 that recalls the Venetian decree of a century earlier. According to this edict, which was part of Parliament's initial response to the flood of anonymous publication that followed the abolition of Star Chamber in 1641, the master and wardens of the Stationers' Company were required to take special order "that the Printers do neither print or reprint any thing without the Name and Consent of the Author" (CJ 2:402). If any printer failed to secure the author's consent and to identify him on the title page, the printer would be treated as if he himself were the author. Issued in a moment of anxiety at the prospect of an uncontrolled press, the edict was primarily intended to hold authors and printers responsible for books deemed libelous, seditious, or blasphemous; it was not primarily a declaration of authorial rights. And yet Parliament was aware that an unscrupulous printer might publish an offending book against the author's wishes. The insertion of the clause requiring the author's consent made it possible for an author to suppress questionable writings. What was at issue, then, was a matter related more to the definition of criminal liability than to economic interest. Merely to set libelous or seditious thoughts down on paper was not equivalent to making them public through the press.

The parliamentary edict of 1642 was only briefly in force, and what other legal standing an English author might have had to take action against a bookseller prior to the Statute of Anne is unclear. Reputable booksellers may, as a matter of custom, have acknowledged that authors had legitimate claims but there is no evidence that copyright was ever recognized as a common-law right of an author in the sixteenth or seventeenth centuries. The case of *Ponder v. Braddill* (1679) suggests how marginal the author's legal position was in England immediately preceding the passage of the Statute of Anne. Normally a bookseller with a complaint against another bookseller would seek recourse through the Stationers' Company Court of Assistants, the guild's internal board of adjudication. In this case, however, Nathaniel Ponder, the publisher of John Bunyan's *Pilgrim's Progress*, took legal action in the

Court of Common Pleas against Thomas Bradill, who had brought out a competing edition of the book. Because of a temporary lapse in the Licensing Act, Ponder lost the statutory basis for his complaint and eventually the case was aborted. What is significant for us, however, is how little the issue had to do with Bunyan as author; indeed, Ponder does not appear even to have called on Bunyan to give evidence in court. Having failed in court, Ponder published an edition of *Pilgrim's Progress* containing an "Advertisement from the Bookseller" in which he warned potential purchasers about the pirated edition of "his" book and accused Braddill's printings of having "abominably and basely falsified the true Copie" so that "they have abused the Author in the sence, and the Propriator of his right" (qtd. in Harrison 269). Evidently, so far as Ponder was concerned, though the author should have his "sence" fairly represented, the "book" belonged to the printer.

Ponder v. Braddill is an unusual case for the seventeenth century. Nearly all the English literary-property cases of this period concern printing patents and constitute tests of the royal prerogative. In several of these cases, however, the issue of authors' interests at least tangentially arises. *Stationers' Company v. Seymour* (1667) concerned the patent for printing *Gadbury's Almanac,* which was held by the Stationers' Company. Seymour did not argue that he had a positive right to print the almanac, but merely that the king had no power to grant a privilege for such a work and that the company's patent was invalid. The court ruled for the company on the grounds that an almanac had no particular author and so the king held the property in the copy and might grant it to anyone. Perhaps in this decision we can detect some feeling for the author's interest in controlling the publication of his texts, for presumably it would follow that if a text did have an author it would not be in the king's power to grant a patent. Such a corollary would directly parallel the finding in the Muret case in France in which the author's will was found to take precedence over the royal prerogative. But what the English court actually decided—and this decision was made in a period of high royal prerogative—was simply that the king did have the power to grant the company a privilege for *Gadbury's Almanac* (*ER* 86:865–866).

In fact in the two cases in seventeenth-century England in which the author's claim is directly urged against royal prerogative, the prerogative wins. In the first, *The Stationers v. The Patentees* (1666), also known as

Atkins' Case, a group of booksellers and printers challenged Richard Atkins' claim to an exclusive right to publish lawbooks based on a patent of James I issued to his father-in-law, John Moore. The occasion for the case was the attempt of two printers, Francis Tyton and Abel Roper, to publish a lawbook, Serjeant Rolls's *Abridgment,* the copy of which they had purchased and entered in the usual way in the Stationers' Register. But while the book was in press Atkins, the patentee, secured an injunction in Chancery forbidding Tyton and Roper or any other member of the Stationers' Company from printing Rolls's *Abridgment.* The stationers challenged the validity of Atkins' claim to the exclusive right to print lawbooks, bringing the issue to the House of Lords where they argued that the patent was a monopoly and illegal. On the other hand, they claimed, Tyton and Roper's right to publish the *Abridgment* was based on the "absolute property" that an author has in his "copy" and his right to transfer that property to anyone else.

This is an important moment, for it is the first time that the claim that an author has a property right in his work is asserted in an English court. "It is humbly conceived," write the appellants:

> First, That the Author of every *Manuscript* or *Copy* hath (in all reason) as good right thereunto, as any Man hath to the Estate wherein he has the most absolute property; and consequently the taking from him the one (without his own consent) will be equivalent to the bereaving him of the other, contrary to his Will.
>
> Secondly, Those who purchased such Copies for valuable considerations, having the Authors right thereby transferred to them (and a due Licence and Entrance according to Law) 'twill be as prejudicial to deprive them of the benefit of their Purchase, as to Disseise them of their Freehold. (*Case of the Booksellers and Printers Stated*)

The author has a property right that is conveyed to a bookseller and it, like any other property right, exists forever: this will be the argument used by booksellers in the eighteenth century to assert the perpetuity of copyright, but in 1666 such an argument was premature. What was the response? No basis for the decision is given, but the Lords ruled that the royal patent was valid and that it took precedence over any other claims the stationers might have (*ER* 124:842–844).

Two years later in a second case involving the law patent, *Streater v. Roper* (1668), the House of Lords again asserted the superiority of the royal patent to copyright claims based on purchase from the author, this time by overturning a King's Bench decision. The facts in the case were these. Abel Roper had purchased the third part of Justice Crook's *Reports* from his executors. But John Streater held a patent from the king and, despite Roper's purchase of the copy, Streater proceeded to print the work. Roper brought an action against Streater in King's Bench where Streater pleaded his right under the king's grant and Roper denied the validity of the grant. The court found for Roper, but Streater appealed to the House of Lords, which ruled in his favor, determining that the patent was valid (*ER* 22:849).[7]

In the seventeenth century, then, there may have been some feeling that authors should have the right to control the first publication of their writings. But in England at any rate no clearly defined set of authorial rights existed, and English authors had no obvious form of redress if books were published without their permission. Indeed, the very concept of "author" was still incompletely developed. Not only was the modern notion of the author as an autonomous creator, the producer and first proprietor of original works, not yet formed, but even the Renaissance notion of the author as an individuated authority was often problematic.

The most conspicuous instance of this is William Shakespeare. As a member of the King's Men and a shareholder in the Globe Theatre, Shakespeare participated in a collaborative and traditional enterprise of cultural production. Almost none of Shakespeare's stories were original with him—they came from classical and modern history and from tales popular in the late Middle Ages and Renaissance—and he did not

7. As one might expect, the Lords' decision in *Streater v. Roper*, which clearly subordinated the author's right to the grant of a patent to a nonauthor, proved a problem in the following century when the antithetical principle of literary property based on the liberty of the subject and the natural right of the author was being established. Howard Abrams remarks that later proponents of authors' rights "rationalized this case on the grounds that the King paid the judges' salaries and that the Crown had a special interest in the reporting of law" (1148). Throughout the eighteenth century the prerogative was of course on the wane. Significantly, the final delimitation of the prerogative powers over printing came just after *Donaldson v. Becket* and the settlement of the literary-property question when in 1775 the Court of Common Pleas decided in *Stationers v. Carnan* that the crown did not have the authority to grant the Stationers' Company the exclusive right to print almanacs. For discussion of this case, see Blagden, "Thomas Carnan and the Almanack Monopoly."

publish his plays. It would not be wholly inappropriate, I think, to characterize Shakespeare the playwright, though not Shakespeare the author of the sonnets and poems, in a quasi-medieval manner as a reteller of tales. In any case, in the two instances in which Shakespeare's plays use the word "author" in reference to the playwright himself, they do so in a way that presents him as a modest storyteller. Thus in the epilogue to 2 *Henry IV* we hear that, if the audience is "not too much cloyed with fat meat, our humble author will continue the story, with Sir John in it." And the epilogue to *Henry V* begins: "Thus far, with rough and all-unable pen, / Our bending author hath pursued the story, / In little room confining mighty men." Normally Shakespeare's plays use "author" in the general sense of "source" or "originator."

Ben Jonson, only eight years younger than Shakespeare, presented himself as a playwright quite differently from Shakespeare, and Jonson's 1616 folio, in which he proposed himself as a modern embodiment of classical *auctoritas*, marks a significant moment in the development of authorship. The very title of the folio, *The Workes of Benjamin Jonson*, accomplishes, Joseph Loewenstein notes, a complex act of translation and imitation that evokes classic works such as those of Horace or Virgil.[8] Furthermore, Jonson's monumental volume, which he supervised, was the model for the Shakespeare folio of 1623 adorned both with the Droeshaut engraving on the title page—opening the book one is immediately confronted with this emphatic representation of Shakespeare as author—and with Jonson's poetic eulogy, "To the memory of my beloved, The Author Mr. William Shakespeare: And what he hath left us," proclaiming Shakespeare's immortality:

> Triumph, my *Britaine*, thou hast one to showe,
>   To whom all Scenes of *Europe* homage owe.
> He was not of an age, but for all time! (Hinman 10)

Thus was begun, under Jonson's influence, the process in which Shakespeare was retrospectively refashioned into the quintessential author of the modern world.

Loewenstein points out the way that Jonson, through the printer

8. On Jonson's self-presentation as an author, see also Helgerson 101–184. Murray analyzes the Jonson folio suggestively (64–93). Stallybrass and White discuss Jonson's quest for authorial authority in their excellent chapter, "The Fair, the Pig, Authorship," suggesting that Jonson sought "to stabilize and dignify an emergent place for authorship at a distance both from the aristocracy and the plebeians" (74).

William Stansby, recovered authority over his play texts from the acting companies and revised them for the folio, and he suggests that Jonson can be understood as groping toward authorial property rights. This observation is illuminating. Still it is important to note that the authority Jonson recovered had to do principally with the integrity of his texts and with the manner of their presentation. It is also important to remember that Jonson was a court poet deeply enmeshed in the royal patronage structures of the Stuart court. By no means can he be mistaken for the modern figure of the author as a private individual whose worth is calculable in terms of the property he or she has created. But the crucial point, of course, is to recognize the inchoateness at this time of the notions of "authorial rights" and "literary property."

A good example of the vague status of authorial rights and literary property is provided by the contract that John Milton signed with Samuel Simmons for the first publication of *Paradise Lost* in 1667. According to this contract, John Milton, "in consideration of five pounds to him now paid by the said Samuel Symons and other considerations hereunder mentioned" (French 429), granted to Simmons and his executors and assigns "All that Booke Copy or Manuscript of a Poem entitled Paradise lost, or by whatsoever other title or name the same is or shalbe called or distinguished." Furthermore, Milton agreed that Simmons was to "have hold and enjoy the same and all Impressions thereof accordingly without the lett or hinderance of him the said John Milton," and that he, Milton, promised not to "print or cause to be printed or sell dispose or publish the said Booke or Manuscript or any other Booke or Manuscript of the same tenor or subject without the consent of the said Samuel Symons" (French 430). The catchall phrases of this contract—"Booke Copy or Manuscript" and "Booke or Manuscript"—imply the conveyance of more than the physical manuscript, but what in this context could that be? As Lyman Ray Patterson points out, the author at this time could not convey copyright in anything like the modern sense; only the Stationers' Company could grant copyright. Nor could the author convey a clear right to publish the work, since the book was still subject to licensing. According to Patterson's analysis, the operative clause in the contract is the author's promise not to let or hinder the publisher (*Copyright* 73–77), but this clause too is problematic: what legal standing would an author have to object to publication, even if he wanted to? The one thing that Milton clearly could promise was to refrain from assisting any bookseller other than Simmons in bringing out a competitive edition.

The vagueness of the *Paradise Lost* contract is evidence of the unformed concept of authorial literary property; still, so long as the market was the arena for booksellers rather than authors and so long as the regulation of the trade was under the aegis of the guild, the vagueness of the concepts involved in literary property does not seem to have been important. Possibly it was not even noticed. Even if Milton's contract with Simmons does not represent the conveyance of a literary property, however, simply the fact of a contract between author and publisher anticipates an emergent regime of property. And indeed Milton himself, as Peter Lindenbaum argues, anticipates the emergent figure of the proprietary author. Ben Jonson may have made a point of recovering from the players his authority over his texts, but Jonson was still a servant of the Stuart court. The figure of the proprietary author depends on a conception of the individual as essentially independent and creative, a notion incompatible with the ideology of the absolutist state. It was in direct opposition to the absolutist court as celebrated by Jonson that a new form of political subject, the autonomous private man, came into being; and it is in Milton's *Areopagitica* (1644), published in angry response to the reinstitution of licensing by Parliament, that the figure of the autonomous author, the man whose authority is based not on public office or sanction but on personal experience, study, and deliberation, is defined.

In its title *Areopagitica* invokes the Greek Isocrates, "him who from his private house wrote that discourse to the parliament of Athens that persuaded them to change the form of democraty which was then established" (Hughes 719). In this way Milton presents himself as a private man and author protesting an act of state that is insulting to the dignity of authors. Is the mature author to be subject to the state licenser, one "perhaps much his younger, perhaps far his inferior in judgment, perhaps one who never knew the labor of book-writing"? Must the author "appear in print like a puny with his guardian, and his censor's hand on the back of his title to be his bail and surety that he is not idiot or seducer; it cannot be but a dishonor and derogation to the author, to the book, to the privilege and dignity of learning" (Hughes 735). Thus, as Abbe Blum's analysis shows, in a complex dialectic that incorporates the public/private opposition, authorial autonomy is asserted.

Throughout *Areopagitica* it is the individual author who is portrayed as the source of authority and value. Texts are the distillation of authors. Thus Milton speaks of "a good book" as "the precious lifeblood of a master spirit, embalmed and treasured up on purpose to a life beyond life." And he continues by portraying the burning of books by censors as a kind of murder:

> We should be wary, therefore, what persecution we raise against the living labors of public men, how we spill that seasoned life of man preserved and stored up in books; since we see a kind of homicide may be thus committed, sometimes a martyrdom; and if it extend to the whole impression, a kind of massacre. (Hughes 720)

Milton's image of book burning as murder may recall the inquisition in the library in *Don Quixote* where books are treated as living creatures, but in Cervantes it is mostly the romance heroes who are condemned, not the authors. And this contrast highlights the degree to which Milton's presentation of the idea that books are the preserved essences of authors anticipates the Lockean discourse in which literary property is connected to the author's personality.

Milton is concerned with authorial dignity rather than authorial property. Yet he uses commercial metaphors, which anticipate the commodification of writing, as when he insists, "Truth and understanding are not such wares as to be monopolized and traded in by tickets and statutes and standards. We must not think to make a staple commodity of all the knowledge in the land, to mark and license it like our broadcloth and our woolpacks"; or when he remarks, "More than if some enemy at sea should stop up all our havens and ports and creeks, [licensing] hinders and retards the importation of our richest merchandise, truth" (Hughes 736–737, 741). As the last passage suggests, what Milton objects to is not the marketplace as such, not the notion of commerce in ideas, but restraint of trade, monopoly. Why did Parliament restore licensing? "If we may believe those men whose profession gives them cause to inquire most," Milton says,

> it may be doubted there was in it the fraud of some old patentees and monopolizers in the trade of bookselling; who under pretense of the

poor in their Company not to be defrauded, and the just retaining of each man his several copy (which God forbid should be gainsaid) brought divers glosing colors to the House, which were indeed but colors, and serving to no end except it be to exercise a superiority over their neighbors. (Hughes 749)

Milton's dictum on "the just retaining of each man his several copy" plainly refers to the publisher's copyright of the Stationers' Company, not to any authorial right. In *Eikonoklastes* (1649), however, Milton issues a different kind of dictum when he speaks of the "human right, which commands that every author should have the property of his own work reserved to him after death, as well as living." The context of this statement is Milton's denunciation of King Charles's appropriation of Pamela's prayer from Sidney's *Arcadia* as his personal meditation on the eve of his execution. Milton's first objection is religious: it was not appropriate for a Christian in time of trouble to use a pagan prayer taken from a "vain amatorious poem." "But leaving aside what might be justly offensive to God," he continues,

> it was a trespass also more than usual against human right, which commands that every author should have the property of his own work reserved to him after death, as well as living. Many princes have been rigorous in laying taxes on their subjects by the head, but of any king heretofore that made a levy upon their art and seized it as his own legitimate, I have not whom beside to instance. (Hughes 794)

Milton is concerned with propriety rather than property. He is defending Sidney's personal right to be acknowledged as author of his own work. Yet metaphorically, through the taxation conceit, Charles is represented as seizing Sidney's property. In this conceit we can perhaps glimpse an early moment in the process of discursive development through which the notion of the author as an individual whose honor and reputation are implicated in his work would evolve into the representation of the author as proprietor. In Milton this has not quite happened. Both *Areopagitica* and *Eikonoklastes* are concerned with propriety. And yet the taxation conceit in *Eikonoklastes* looks ahead to the future.

3

⌒⌒⌒

Making Copyright

The principal topic of controversy in relation to the book trade at the end of the seventeenth century was the question of licensing. The Licensing Act of 1662, which made it illegal to publish anything without first securing a license from the appropriate authority, was the lineal descendant of the various printing ordinances and decrees dating back to press regulation under Henry VIII. According to the preamble, the purpose of the act—officially titled "An Act for preventing the frequent Abuses in printing seditious treasonable and unlicensed Bookes and Pamphlets and for regulating of Printing and Printing Presses"—was the regulation of printers in order to prevent the printing and sale of "heretical schismatical blasphemous seditious and treasonable Bookes Pamphlets and Papers" (*Statutes of the Realm* 5:428). In addition to providing for censorship, the act limited the number of master printers and presses, restricted the importation of books from abroad, and confirmed the Stationers' Company's near monopoly on the British book trade and its powers of search and seizure for illegal presses and books. It was, in other words, not just a licensing statute but a comprehensive act for publishing control that emerged from the traditional hierarchical social order that I have called the regime of regulation.

Despite periodic objections to censorship and despite the many difficulties in enforcing the licensing provisions, the act was relatively uncontroversial before the 1690s when licensing, as Thomas Babington Macaulay describes in his classic Whig history, became caught up in the factional struggles in Parliament—the dangers of having a partisan licenser in control of the press were becoming evident—and when concerted opposition developed to the printing monopolies created by the act (3:528–39). The act was due for renewal in 1693 but, probably as a result of the opposition, it was renewed for only a short period. In the House of Lords a group of eleven peers dissented from the decision to renew the act at all. Sounding very much like Milton in *Areopagitica*,[1] this group protested that the act in its present form "subjects all Learning and true Information to the arbitrary Will and Pleasure of a mercenary, and perhaps ignorant, Licenser; destroys the Properties of Authors in their Copies; and sets up many Monopolies" (*LJ* 15:280). It is impossible to say whether in speaking of the "properties of authors" the lords were thinking more in terms of propriety—the author's control over the form and content of his writings—or in terms of property in an economic sense. In any case, that the lords mentioned authorial property at all is significant as an index of the developing concern with authorial rights.

John Locke was an important figure in the agitation to end licensing. According to Raymond Astbury, after the limited renewal of the act in 1693, Locke went on a campaign against any further renewal, and about a year later he developed his objections to licensing in a *Memorandum* transmitted to his friend Edward Clarke in order to provide him and other members of Parliament with arguments against licensing. Like Milton, whose *Areopagitica* he knew, Locke objected to prepublication censorship: "I know not why a man should not have liberty to print whatever he would speak" (*Memorandum* 203). Also like Milton, Locke stopped short of demanding a wholly free press, maintaining that it was sufficient that authors and printers of offending works might be held accountable after publication. Locke's major objection to the Licensing Act, however, had to do with monopolies rather than censorship. In particular he was offended that "ignorant and lazy stationers"—as he called the London booksellers in a letter to Edward Clarke

1. It is likely that the Miltonic style of the lords' statement derives from Charles Blount's recently published *Reasons Humbly Offered for the Liberty of Unlicens'd Printing*, which extracts large portions of *Areopagitica* without acknowledgment. Macaulay calls Blount "one of the most unscrupulous plagiaries that ever lived" because of his use of Milton (3:533). But what Blount's appropriation of *Areopagitica* suggests is not so much that he was a shameless plagiarist as that he thought about the process of putting together an anonymous polemical pamphlet according to principles quite different from those that had become the norm a century and a half later, when Macaulay was writing.

dated 2 January 1683 (*Correspondence* 366)—should be able to restrict the printing or importing of new editions of ancient authors:

> That any person or company should have patents for the sole printing of ancient authors is very unreasonable and injurious to learning; and for those who purchase copies from authors that now live and write, it may be reasonable to limit their property to a certain number of years after the death of the author, or the first printing of the book, as, suppose, fifty or seventy years. This I am sure, it is very absurd and ridiculous that any one now living should pretend to have a propriety in, or a power to dispose of the propriety of any copy or writings of authors who lived before printing was known or used in Europe. (*Memorandum* 208–209)

The matter of booksellers claiming rights in ancient authors was a personal one for Locke, who had been frustrated by the stationers when he sought to publish an edition of Aesop. Perhaps it was his strenuous objection on this point that led him to propose that stationers' properties in current authors, who would after all eventually become ancient, be limited in term. Elsewhere Locke also proposed that any new licensing act should include a clause specifying either that printers must obtain the author's permission to use his name or that the author retain the right to reprint, which implies that Locke was concerned in some fashion with authorial rights (Astbury 313). But the *Memorandum* seems to suggest that Locke thought of literary property as a bookseller's affair.

The attempt to renew the Licensing Act in 1695 failed, and on 3 May 1695 the act expired. It is worth noting that the government attempted to push through a bill that would have continued censorship while doing away with the statutory basis for the Stationers' Company's monopolies; but it was found, as a correspondent of Locke's reported, "wanting as to the Security of Property" (Astbury 312). Macaulay noted that the principal issue for the House of Commons in 1695 was not free speech but commerce. In allowing the censorship laws to lapse, Macaulay said, the legislators "knew not what they were doing, what a revolution they were making, what a power they were calling into existence" (4:122). Perhaps so on the matter of free speech—but on the conflict between the traditional ideology of hierarchy and regulation and the emergent ideology of the market, Commons appears to have understood very well what it was doing. In the name of free trade it was seeking to end a monopolistic system of privilege and control with roots in an archaic concept of royal prerogative. Of course there were many who opposed monopoly but supported property. How to protect printers' and booksellers' property claims without establishing monopolies? The lapse of the Licensing Act left this question hanging.

In the decade that followed the lapse of the Licensing Act, the stationers, who were concerned about their properties, collaborated with those who favored censorship on ideological grounds in repeated attempts to restore the old system of press regulation (Feather, "Book Trade in Politics"). It was in the context of one such attempt pressed by the zealous High Church party in 1704 that Daniel Defoe, newly released from pillorying and imprisonment for his satiric *Shortest Way with the Dissenters,* published his *Essay on the Regulation of the Press.* In this moderate pamphlet Defoe acknowledged that the licentiousness of the press was a problem and that some form of regulation was necessary. But he opposed reinstituting licensing because it subjected the press to the interests of whichever party had the power to name the licenser— after his imprisonment by the High Churchmen Defoe must have felt this with particular force—and it subjected the whole body of learning to the arbitrary power of mercenary officials.

> The People of *England* do not believe the Parliament will make a Law to abridge them of that Liberty they should protect, for tho' it were more true than it is, that the Exorbitances of the Press ought to be restrain'd, yet I cannot see how the supervising, and passing all the Works of the Learned part of the World by one or a few Men, and giving them an absolute Negative on the Press, can possibly be reconcil'd to the liberty of the *English Nation.* (6–7)

Like Milton and Locke, Defoe maintained that it was sufficient to prosecute offending authors after publication—"I know no Nation in the World, whose Government is not perfectly Despotick, that ever makes preventive Laws, 'tis enough to make Laws to punish Crimes when they are committed" (7–8)—and, also like them, he favored a law against anonymous publication so that the authors of offending books might be known and punished.

In his treatment of licensing Defoe followed a well-established line of thought, but he went beyond this established line by raising the issue of authorial property. Insisting on the author's name being published would not only act as a restraint on the licentiousness of the press, Defoe said, but would also put an end to piracy:

> The Law we are upon, effectively suppresses this most villainous Practice, for every Author being oblig'd to set his Name to the Book he writes, has, by this Law, an undoubted exclusive Right to the Property of it. The Clause in the Law is a Patent to the Author, and settles the Propriety of the Work wholly in himself, or in such to whom he shall assign it; and 'tis reasonable it should be so: For if an Author has not the right of a Book, after he has made it, and the benefit be not his own, and the Law will not protect him in that Benefit, 'twould be very hard the Law should pretend to punish him for it.
>
> 'Twould be unaccountably severe, to make a Man answerable for the Miscarriages of a thing which he shall not reap the benefit of if well perform'd; there is no Law so much wanting in the Nation, relating to Trade and Civil Property, as this, nor is there a greater Abuse in any Civil Employment, than the printing of other Mens Copies, every jot as unjust as lying with their Wives, and breaking-up their Houses.
> (27–28)

Defoe thus called for a parliamentary law that would protect authorial property rights—this may be the earliest such advocacy in English history—and he continued to argue for authors during the next year with articles in his journal, the *Review*. In one issue he protested against printers who published authors' works without permission: these justified their practice, he said, by claiming that an author had no property in his copy because he was not a member of the Stationer's Company (*Little Review* 20 June 1705). And in another he called again for an act of Parliament "so Property of Copies may be secur'd to Laborious Students, to the Encouragement of Letters and all useful Studies" (*Review* 8 Nov. 1705).

Defoe's agitation on behalf of authorial rights seems to have influenced the London stationers, who perhaps saw in his call for a law to protect authorial literary property a new strategy for pursuing their own interests. In any case, in 1707 the stationers submitted a new petition to Parliament for a bill to secure property in books. Making for the first time no reference to the revival of licensing, the stationers' petition emphasized the negative effect that the disorder in the trade was having on authors:

> many learned Men have spent much Time, and been at great Charges, in composing Books, who used to dispose of their Copies upon valuable Considerations, to be printed by the Purchasers . . . but of late Years such Properties have been much invaded, by other Persons printing the same Books . . . to the great Discouragement of Persons from writing Matters, that might be of great Use to the Publick, and to the great Damage of the Proprietors. (*CJ* 15:313)

In 1695, we recall, an attempt was made to introduce a licensing bill that would provide for censorship without securing literary property; now a bill was being presented that would provide for literary property without licensing. The 1695 bill failed because of objections from those concerned primarily with property; John Feather speculates that the 1707 bill may have failed because the advocates of censorship managed to get licensing clauses tacked on in committee ("Book Trade in Politics" 42n59).

In autumn 1709 there was a second attempt to produce a copyright, as distinct from a licensing, act. This time the attempt was successful, resulting in the Statute of Anne, which was passed in spring 1710. In late 1709 in anticipation of a new bill, Defoe wrote two articles on press regulation in the *Review* (3 and 26 Nov. 1709) where he repeated the position on licensing and the excesses of the press he had developed in the *Essay on the Regulation of the Press* and called on Parliament to pass a law "to secure to the Authors of Books their Right of Property."

A few days after the second of Defoe's articles appeared, another, more elegant journalistic voice joined in the call for an author's bill. Joseph Addison took up the issue of literary property in *The Tatler* calling it a scandalous injustice that authors should be defenseless against piratical printers:

> All Mechanick Artizans are allowed to reap the Fruit of their Invention and Ingenuity without Invasion; but he that has separated himself from the rest of Mankind, and studied the Wonders of the Creation, the Government of his Passions, and the Revolutions of the World, and has an Ambition to communicate the Effect of half his Life spent in such noble Enquiries, has no Property in what he is willing to

produce, but is exposed to Robbery and Want, with this melancholy and just Reflection, That he is the only Man who is not protected by his Country, at the same Time that he best deserves it. (*Tatler* 101, 1 Dec. 1709)

Immediately Defoe pressed home his similar concerns in two more articles in the *Review*. In one, dated 3 December 1709, he argued once more against reviving licensing, calling it "a visible Bondage upon Property":

Every Man who writes *what is no Breach of the Laws of God or Man* to publish; His Work is his Property, and he cannot be divested of that Property at the Will and Pleasure of any Man; no, not his Prince; to suppress his Labour, is to divest him of his Property.

In the other, dated 6 December 1709, he called again for a parliamentary act to protect authors:

Why have we Laws against House-breakers, High-way Robbers, Pick-Pockets, Ravishers of Women, and all Kinds of open Violence [and yet no protection for the author]? When in this Case a Man has his Goods stollen, his Pocket pick'd, his Estate ruin'd, his Prospect of Advantage ravish'd from him, after infinite Labour, Study, and Expence.

And while the bill itself was pending in the House of Commons, he kept the pressure on with a new *Review* article on the subject every few days (2, 11, 18, 21 Feb. 1710).

In attempting to understand Defoe's and Addison's interest in authors' property rights, we should note not only their own positions as writers—and the fact that in this period there appears to have been an increase in the bargaining power of a few major writers[2]—but also the general emphasis on liberty and property in public discourse after the 1688 revolution. In any event, it is important to stress that in the first decade of the eighteenth century the conception of the author as proprietor was still in an early phase of development. The heart of

2. In 1667, we recall, Milton received an initial £5 for *Paradise Lost* with a promise of £5 more if the edition sold out and further payments of £5 each for second and third editions. Twenty-seven years later, Dryden's far more sophisticated contract with Jacob Tonson for his translation of Virgil specified that the author was to be paid £200 in four £50 installments while the work was under way, and it spelled out complex arrangements for two different types of subscription copies. See Bernard; Winn 474–477. The Dryden-Tonson contract for the *Virgil* is printed in *The Works of John Dryden* 6:1179–83.

Defoe's argument in the *Essay* is an appeal to the complementarity of punishment and reward rather than to labor. If an author can be punished for libelous or seditious writing, then it is only just that he be rewarded for useful writing: "'Twould be unaccountably severe, to make a Man answerable for the Miscarriages of a thing which he shall not reap the benefit of if well perform'd" (28). Despite his concern for property and authorial rights, Defoe here presents the issue of authorial property from within the framework of traditional society, where punishment and reward are transmitted from above. In the *Review* pieces, however, the conception of the author's property seems more Lockean, as does that in *The Tatler:* authors are represented as separating themselves from the rest of mankind in order to pursue their laborious studies. But even in *The Tatler* the issue is still presented in terms of the reward that such noble inquiries should receive from the state, rather than in terms of a natural right prior to the social contract.

The metaphors in which these earliest discussions of authorial property are couched reveal something about the sources of a new discourse of authorship. In the sixteenth and seventeenth centuries, various figures were employed to represent the author's relation to his writing, including the author as singing shepherd, tiller of the soil, vessel of divine inspiration, magician, and monarch. But the most common figure in the early modern period is paternity: the author as begetter and the book as child.[3] Philip Sidney, for instance, in his dedicatory epistle to the Countess of Pembroke, speaks of his *Arcadia* as "this child which I am loath to father," yet hoping that, despite its deformities, it will be pardoned "for the father's sake" (3). Similarly, Cervantes apologizes that *Don Quixote* is not "the handsomest, the liveliest, and the wisest" child that could be conceived: "But I could not violate Nature's ordinance whereby like engenders like. And so, what could my sterile and uncouth genius beget but the tale of a dry, shriveled, whimsical

3. The trope is particularly common in dedicatory epistles; see Foster. Gilbert and Gubar observe that "the patriarchal notion that the writer 'fathers' his text just as God fathered the world is and has been all-pervasive in Western literary civilization" (4). Thus political, theological, and literary themes are intertwined in this crucial image. Gallagher, discussing George Eliot and authorship, notes that from ancient times an alternative feminine metaphor was available: the writer as whore. This metaphor was related to anxieties about writing as the "unnatural" proliferation of signs rather than the "natural" generation of real things. My understanding of some of the gender issues involved in the paternity trope has been influenced by Swartz, "Paternity, Patrimony, and the Figuration of Authorship in the Eighteenth-Century Literary Property Debates."

offspring, full of odd fancies such as never entered another's brain" (41). Cervantes with characteristic irony goes on to remark that he is really only Quixote's stepfather, since he is merely transmitting the famous knight's true history to the reader. Whether the child is Don Quixote the character or *Don Quixote* the book is, of course, ambiguous.

Inscribed with the notion of likeness more than of property, the paternity metaphor is consonant with the emergence of the individuated author in the patriarchal patronage society concerned with blood, lineage, and the dynastic principle that like engenders like. But an interesting awkwardness is generated when the figure of paternity is adapted to the discourse of proprietary authorship. Defoe, employing the ancient metaphor embedded in the word "plagiary" (derived from the Latin for kidnapping), speaks of literary theft as a form of child stealing:

> A Book is the Author's Property, 'tis the Child of his Inventions, the Brat of his Brain; if he sells his Property, it then becomes the Right of the Purchaser; if not, 'tis as much his own, as his Wife and Children are his own—But behold in this Christian Nation, these Children of our Heads are seiz'd, captivated, spirited away, and carry'd into Captivity, and there is none to redeem them. (*Review* 2 Feb. 1710)

We can note here the continuation of the patriarchal discourse of traditional society: the author is the master and owner of his wife and children as well as of the children of his inventions. But a sudden disruption of the idyll of patriarchal domesticity occurs as the narrative veers in the direction of romantic adventure, with biblical and religious overtones: "But behold in this Christian Nation, these Children of our Heads are seiz'd, captivated, spirited away, and carry'd into Captivity, and there is none to redeem them." Are these un-Christian child stealers Turks, Moors, or perhaps American savages? In any event, the colorful description of the raid perhaps distracts the reader's attention from the undesirable implications of the less violent form of alienation that has been glanced at. Defoe has just indicated that the author may sell his literary property, which then becomes the right of the purchaser. But if literary pirates are un-Christian child stealers, what are men who sell their children for profit? The slippage in the passage is located in the instability of the key word "own." One's children are one's own, and thus may be regarded as property, but to assert—as Jonathan Swift would ironically do in his *Modest Proposal* (1729)—that they may be freely sold in the marketplace is scandalous.

Defoe receives the paternity trope from the courtly culture of the Renaissance, but his usage evokes a distinctly middle-class patriarchal domesticity. Indeed, Defoe characteristically associates literary property with family, house, and home, as in the *Essay on the Regulation of the Press* when he speaks of the invasion of authors' properties as "every jot as unjust as lying with their Wives, and breaking-up their Houses" (28). Literary property, Defoe says, "both is and ought to be the Due, not of the Author only, but of his Family and Children." The literary pirate "burns his House, and beggars his Children" (*Review* 6 Dec. 1709). So too the London booksellers and printers had regularly couched their pleas and petitions to Parliament in pathetic domestic terms, complaining that they, their wives, and their children were being utterly ruined by piracy. Their copies were their legacies, dowries, and estates.[4] What Defoe has done, then, is to appropriate the rhetoric that the stationers regularly used and apply it to authorial property.

Addison also invokes a discourse of property that may be related to the booksellers' rhetoric and also to the figure of the author as tiller of a field, a trope that goes back to the Bible. In the *Tatler* he describes an author of his acquaintance who showed "good Husbandry in the Management of his Learning" by adapting his literary efforts to the season of the year and the current state of the war with France and Spain:

His Brain, which was his Estate, had as regular and different Produce as other Men's Land. From the Beginning of *November* till the Opening of the Campagne, he writ Pamphlets and Letters to Members of Parliament, or Friends in the Country: But sometimes he would relieve his ordinary Readers with a Murder, and lived comfortably a Week or Two upon *strange and lamentable Accidents*. A little before the Armies took the Field, his Way was to open your Attention with

4. See, for example, *The Humble Remonstrance of the Company of Stationers* (1643), in which the stationers petition the Long Parliament to remedy the disorder in the trade created by the abolition of Star Chamber: "Many Families have now their Lively-hoods by Assignments of Copies, some Orphans and Widows haue no other Legacies and Dowries to depend upon: and there is no reason apparent why the production of the Brain should not be as assignable . . . as the right of any Goods or Chattells whatsoever" (Arber 1:587–588). Defoe directly invokes the sentimental language of the booksellers' petitions when he satirically composes a piratical booksellers' petition against the pending literary-property bill in 1710 (*Review* 21 Feb. 1710).

a Prodigy; and a Monster well writ, was two Guinea's the lowest Price. This prepared his Readers for *Great and Bloody News* from *Flanders* in *June* and *July.* Poor *Tom!* He is gone—But I observed, he always looked well after a Battle, and was apparently fatter in a fighting Year. (*Tatler* 101, 1 Dec. 1709)

The style of this essay is of course more jocular and genteel than Defoe's, and Addison's conceit—amusingly incongruous for the description of what is evidently a Grub Street hack—is of a gentleman farmer rather than an urban householder. But his representation of the author, like Defoe's, is as a propertied man engaged in the working of his holdings.[5]

To conclude, what we are observing in both Defoe's and Addison's writings in the period just before the passage of the Statute of Anne is an early moment in the formation of the discourse of proprietary authorship. How could one think about an author's relationship to his writings? The most familiar metaphor was paternity, but to invoke the representation of a text as a child in order to bolster the author's right to sell his works in the marketplace presented rhetorical difficulties. An alternative metaphor, literary property as a landed estate, had long been available in the rhetoric of the stationers' pleas and claims, and in the *Tatler* essay we can see Addison experimenting with this trope. During the course of the next fifty years, the figuration of the literary work as a form of estate would be reiterated and elaborated, and it contributed to a new way of thinking about literature.[6]

⋄⋄⋄

5. Two years later Addison uses a similar metaphor in the essay in which he distinguishes between natural and cultivated forms of genius: "The Genius in both these Classes of Authors may be equally great, but shews itself after a different Manner. In the first it is like a rich Soil in a happy Climate, that produces a whole Wilderness of noble Plants rising in a thousand beautiful landskips without any certain Order or Regularity. In the other it is the same rich Soil under the same happy Climate, that has been laid out in Walks and Parterres, and cut into Shape and Beauty by the Skill of the Gardener" (*Spectator* 160, 3 Sept. 1711).

6. In "Of Paternal Power," chapter 6 of the second *Treatise of Government,* Locke is careful to distinguish paternal authority from property rights. Locke's project in the *Two Treatises* was to refute Sir Robert Filmer's doctrine of absolute monarchy as presented in his *Patriarcha* (1680), where the absolutist doctrine was derived from the identification of royal with paternal power. In Locke's political theory, of course, the state was derived from the need to protect property. The movement from Filmer's absolutist to Locke's liberal political theory thus incorporates a movement from paternity to property that parallels the shift in the figuration of the author's relation to the text.

The parliamentary records related to the passage of the Statute of Anne begin on 12 December 1709, when a group of major London booksellers and printers petitioned for leave to bring in a bill "for securing to them the Property of Books, bought and obtained by them" (*CJ* 16:240). Despite the agitation in the *Review* and *The Tatler* for a bill to secure authors' property rights, so far as the trade was concerned this was to be a booksellers' bill. The petition mentioned the present "Discouragement of all Writers in any useful Part of Learning" (*CJ* 16:240), but what it emphasized was simply parliamentary confirmation of traditional guild practices. Leave to bring in a bill was granted, and a committee of three was appointed to draft it.[7] A month later on 11 January 1710 Edward Wortley, a close friend of Joseph Addison's, presented the draft to the House under the title "A Bill for the Encouragement of Learning and for securing the Property of Copies of Books to the rightful Owners thereof" (*CJ* 16:260). The priority given to the encouragement of learning plainly reflected the issues that Addison and Defoe had been discussing in their journals, and the preamble expressed concern that piracy was "a great discouragement to learning in general which in all Civilized Nations ought to receive the greatest Countenance and Encouragement." Furthermore, the preamble explicitly addressed the matter of authors' rights, protesting that works were being printed "without the Consent of the Authors thereof, in whom the undoubted property of Such Books and Writings as the product of their learning and labour remains." Booksellers were represented as "such persons to whom Such Authors for good Considerations have lawfully transferred their Right and title" ("A Bill," MS Rawl. D.922, f.380).

Wortley's bill was not a licensing act, but it revealed its lineal relationship to the old Licensing Act of 1662 in its provision of monetary penalties for the reprinting or importing of any book without the consent of the proprietor, in its provision that all books protected under the act were to be entered in the Stationers' Register in the usual manner, and in its provision that deposit copies were to be sent to

7. The members were Spencer Compton, Craven Peyton, and Edward Wortley, who is listed first and who also presented the draft to the House on 11 January 1710, although Compton served as chair in February when the House discussed amendments. I refer to the draft presented on 11 January as Wortley's bill largely for convenience, but it seems plausible to suppose that he was indeed the principal draftsman. The history of the legislation has been traced by Ransom, *The First Copyright Statute* and, more recently, by Feather, "Book Trade in Politics," who discusses the surviving manuscript draft of the bill (Bodleian MS Rawl. D.922, ff. 380–386).

Oxford, Cambridge, and the King's Library. It also provided a mechanism for complaint if any book were issued at an unreasonably high price, and, perhaps showing the influence of Locke's *Memorandum,* it exempted the importation of Greek and Latin classics or other books originally printed abroad. Finally, it made certain technical provisions in the case of suits brought under the act. It said nothing about limiting the term of protection for literary property.[8]

Shortly after Wortley presented his bill, the London booksellers issued a broadside, *The Booksellers Humble Address to the Honourable House of Commons, In Behalf of the Bill for Encouraging Learning,* in which they urged Commons to pass the bill, saying that it merely confirmed "a Right which has been Enjoyed by Common Law above 150 Years."[9] The allusion to the 1557 charter of the Stationers' Company ("above 150 Years") suggests that the booksellers had in mind their own properties rather than any independent author's common-law right. Probably they were referring to the traditional practices mentioned in the original petition of 12 December 1709, the "constant Usage" whereby writers of books sold their copies to stationers "to the end they might hold those Copies as their Property." They went on to warn, in the now familiar rhetoric of pathetic domesticity, that if Parliament failed to confirm literary property, thousands of mechanics and shopkeepers would be deprived of their livelihoods, and "Widows and Children who at present Subsist wholly by the Maintainance of this Property" would be reduced to extreme poverty. Also they reminded Parliament that the bill was not a licensing act and that the liberty of the press would not be restrained.

On 9 February the bill received its second reading. The process of amendment began in a committee of the whole House on 21 February (*CJ* 16:332) with further amendments made when the bill was reported back to the House on 25 February (*CJ* 16:339). The changes introduced

8. The manuscript of Wortley's bill includes a reference to a limited term as an insertion in a hand other than the principal one and in a space left blank for another purpose, which would indicate that it is an amendment. The insertion speaks of "the times granted and limited by this act as aforesaid" (MS Rawl. D 922, f. 381), but no specific limits are mentioned elsewhere. The bill's original title says nothing about a term of protection: the phrase "during the Times therein mentioned," is first reported as part of the title on 14 March, when the bill is read for the third time and passed (*CJ* 16:369).

9. Given the title and the content, this broadside appears to have been issued sometime between the presentation of the bill on 11 January and the start of debate and amendment in late February. On 2 February a separate petition of journeyman printers and bookbinders was presented to the House in support of the bill (*CJ* 16:291).

at this point can be inferred by comparing Wortley's bill with the final statute and subtracting the changes made in the House of Lords, which were reported when the bill was returned to Commons on 5 April (*CJ* 16:394). Some of the changes made in Commons were minor—for example, provision was made for further deposit copies to go to Sion College, London, and to the Faculty of Advocates, Edinburgh—but some were significant. Most important, the traditional character of the stationers' copyright was radically altered by the introduction of a limited term.

The idea of limiting the term of copyright appealed to those who were concerned about monopolies and restraint of trade. Such an idea had been in the air at least since Locke's *Memorandum,* and it seems likely that the question of limiting copyright was debated immediately after the bill's second reading. It seems likely too that the booksellers were now led to issue their second broadside, *More Reasons Humbly Offer'd to the Honourable House of Commons.* It repeats the assertion that they were only seeking to have their common-law rights confirmed and then addresses the question of the limited term:

> But it is said, That it is sufficient for us to enjoy a Term of Years in our Sole Right of Printing. To this we Answer, That if we have a Right for Ten Years, we have a Right for Ever. A Man's having possess'd a Property for Ten or Twenty Years, is in no other Instance allow'd, a Reason for another to take it from him; and we hope it will not be in Ours.

And probably soon after this they published a third broadside, *The Case of the Booksellers Right to their Copies,* insisting once again that the whole issue was one of common-law property rights: the author was the "absolute Master of his own Writings," and it was the practice of authors to sell their copies to booksellers; booksellers had always regarded copies as properties; they had given great sums of money for them; they had used them as marriage settlements; they had willed them to their children. "And we conceive, this Property is the same with that of Houses and other Estates." Given the vehemence of these broadsides, it is plausible to suppose that the decision to amend Wortley's bill to limit the term of copyright was not uncontested.

Locke had somewhat arbitrarily proposed a term of fifty or seventy years for copyright, but naturally the legislators would have preferred to ground the specifics of their statute in precedent, and a suitable precedent for the copyright term existed in the old Statute of Monopolies, which controlled the law of patents for mechanical innovations. According to that statute, new inventions could be patented for fourteen years; existing patents were to be reduced to a twenty-one-year term. Also, the bill as it emerged from Commons set the term of protection for new books at fourteen years; books already in print were to be protected for twenty-one years. As we have seen, when printing privileges first appeared, printing patents and grants for mechanical inventions were not different in kind. Now, a hundred and fifty years later, traces of this original undifferentiation were inscribed in the statute. The analogy with patents implied that literary property was not truly property at all, but a privilege granted by the state. In order to argue that they had property in the copies they had bought, the booksellers would have to demonstrate why authors should be treated differently from inventors. Was a literary invention different from a mechanical invention? This was to become one of the heated questions in the debate.

A second interesting amendment concerned the language in which authors' rights were described. Even as a term was set for copyright, the emphatic statement about authors possessing "undoubted property" in their "Books and Writings as the product of their learning and labour" was eliminated from the preamble. Why? When the issue of limiting the term of protection arose, the booksellers objected that, if they had a property in their copies, they had it forever. This assertion rested on the claim that theirs was a common-law right based on ancient trade practice. Thus the question of whether a limited term was compatible with a common-law right was introduced. Given the decision to limit the term of copyright, perhaps some of the legislators became uneasy about including a statement that might be taken to imply that authors had a common-law right.[10] That this may indeed have been the case is suggested by changes in the bill's title. The original

10. John Feather sees the hand of the book trade at work in the amendments that weakened the statements about the author's right. The original bill included language that raised the possibility of the author's not selling his copy to a bookseller or printer but reserving it to himself. This was "anathema to the trade for it struck at the root of its prosperity: investments in copyrights" ("Book Trade in Politics" 36). Feather may be right that the prospect of an author's being able to reserve his copy distressed the booksellers, but in fact the final act incorporated much the same principle, although perhaps not so conspicuously, when it spoke of books that the author "hath not transferred to any other." The substitution of the negative

title was "A Bill for the Encouragement of Learning and for Securing the Property of Copies of Books to the Rightful Owners thereof." The amended title became "A Bill for the Encouragement of Learning by Vesting the Copies of Printed Books in the Authors, or Purchasers, of such Copies, during the Times therein Mentioned" (*CJ* 16:369). Here authors were mentioned for the first time, but the key word "securing," descended from the booksellers' December 1709 petition to bring in a bill "for securing to them the Property of Books," was changed to "vesting." Whereas "securing" implied that an extant right was confirmed, "vesting" implied that a new right was conferred.[11] And the limited term of copyright was made prominent.

Other amendments included a clause providing for an alternate method of registration in case the clerk of the Stationers' Company refused to place an entry in the Register. This made it impossible for the company to reestablish its monopoly on copyrights by refusing to register books for anyone who was not a member. Also included was a clause specifying how an action under the statute was to be taken in Scotland. An important saving clause for the universities and holders of printing patents was introduced as well, specifying that nothing in the act was intended "either to prejudice or confirm" printing rights that the universities or any persons might have. Finally, a limiting clause was added, specifying that actions had to be brought within three months of the commission of any offenses under the act (*CJ* 16:394–395).

Thus amended, the bill was passed and carried to the House of Lords, where between 16 March and 4 April 1710 it went through a parallel process of consideration (*LJ* 19:109, 123, 134, 138–139, 140–141). Further amendments were made, including the removal of the provision against exorbitant prices and the addition of the four Scottish universities to the list of deposit libraries. Most significantly, however, the Lords added a provision according to which, after the expiration of the fourteen-year

---

"not transferred" for the positive "reserved to himself" occurred when the bill reached the House of Lords (*CJ* 16:394).

11. The act, however, is inconsistent: although "vesting" is used in the title, "securing" is employed in the preamble to the second section, where the act defines its intent to ensure that property in books "be secured to the Proprietor or Proprietors thereof." This phrasing was unchanged from the original draft of the bill. Later in the century the proponents of perpetual copyright would seize on this inconsistency and argue that the use of "securing" in the body of the act had more force than the use of "vesting" in the title.

term of protection, copyright would return to the author, if living, for a second fourteen-year term. Most likely the Lords felt that the single fourteen-year term was too short—John Locke, after all, had recommended fifty to seventy years—and yet they were reluctant in the light of the Jacobean Statute of Monopolies' provision against any monopoly terms longer than fourteen years simply to declare a longer term. Perhaps too they recollected Locke's suggestion that, after first publication, the right to reprint should revert to authors. The House of Commons accepted all the Lords' amendments except the removal of the provision against exorbitant prices, but the Lords agreed not to insist on this, and on 5 April the bill received the royal assent and became law (*LJ* 19:143–144; *CJ* 16:394–396). On 10 April 1710 the act went into effect.

What the legislative history of the statute shows, then, is the way the final act was the result of Parliament's resistance to the full force of the booksellers' claims that literary property was the same as that of houses and other estates. The booksellers were pressing for an act that would, as far as possible, restore the control of the trade they had enjoyed in the days of licensing. Parliament, however, was concerned about stationers' monopolies, and so the statutory copyright was limited in term.

But what of the inclusion of the author in the act? In addition to being concerned about individual stationers' monopolies, Parliament was also concerned with the near monopoly that the Stationers' Company itself had held on the book trade by virtue of its charter. Patterson suggests that the inclusion of the author was essentially a device to break the company's control:

Emphasis on the author in the Statute of Anne implying that the statutory copyright was an author's copyright was more a matter of form than of substance. The monopolies at which the statute was aimed were too long established to be attacked without some basis for change. The most logical and natural basis for the changes was the author. Although the author had never held copyright, his interest was always promoted by the stationers as a means to their end. Their arguments had been, essentially, that without order in the trade provided by copyright, publishers would not publish books, and therefore would not pay authors for their manuscripts. The draftsmen of the Statute of Anne put these arguments to use, and the author was used primarily as a weapon against monopoly. (*Copyright* 147)

Patterson is surely correct about the use to which Parliament was putting the author, but, as we have seen, a number of influential writers had raised the issue of authorial rights. Yet even if the bill's drafters were sympathetic, the legislature drew back from making any statement about authors having an "undoubted property" in their writings.

Was Parliament resisting a clear theory of authorial rights put forward in the previous decade? Had Locke, Defoe, and Addison supposed that the author possessed a common-law right of property, or were they asking Parliament to grant authors something they had not possessed before? It is hard to say. Some of the early calls for legislative action on behalf of authors seem to be requests for Parliament to vest a new kind of right in authors, but others—for example, Defoe's claim in the *Review* that not even the prince can divest the author of his property— do sound like assertions of a common-law right. Probably the truth is that the exact status of authorial property was not something to which anyone had given a great deal of thought prior to the parliamentary consideration of a literary property bill—and it is unlikely that the matter was examined in any great detail during the deliberations over the statute. But it was considered—and with great thoroughness—later in the century, for on the determination of the precise status of the author's right hung the crucial commercial issues involved in the long struggle over literary property.

The Statute of Anne, then, did not settle the theoretical questions behind the notion of literary property. Still it did represent a significant moment in a process of cultural transformation. In the sixteenth and seventeenth centuries, a general feeling for the author's personal interests had developed in England and elsewhere. Based more on ideas of honor and reputation than on property in the economic sense, this notion of authors' interests had emerged in the context of a traditional patronage society. Matters relating to printing were dealt with under the rubric of regulation, and so censorship and copyright were deeply intertwined. The passage of the statute marked the divorce of copyright from censorship and the reestablishment of copyright under the rubric of property rather than regulation.

4

⁓⊙⁓⊙⁓⊙⁓

The Author in Court

After the passage of the Statute of Anne, the booksellers had an instrument with which to pursue pirates, but in this respect the statute was not a radical departure from the past. Until the lapse of the Licensing Act in 1695, London booksellers had always, at least in principle, been able to take action against pirates. What was novel about the statute was that it constituted the author as well as the bookseller as a person with legal standing. After 1710 an author could, in his own capacity as author, go to court in pursuit of his rights as the proprietor of his works; and, indeed, the first case to arise under the statute, *Burnet v. Chetwood* (1720), was an author's case.

Burnet involved the work of Dr. Thomas Burnet (1635?–1715), best remembered today as the author of *Telluris Theoria Sacra*, a proto-geological study that proposed a theory of how the earth was physically altered at the time of the Deluge. After completing this study, Burnet wrote, another book in Latin, *Archaeologia Philosophica*, in which he attempted to reconcile his theory of the earth with Genesis. Published in the Netherlands in 1692, the *Archaeologia Philosophica* included a facetious conversation between Eve and the serpent, which became widely known and caused Burnet considerable embarrassment when excerpts were published in English without his permission. Burnet took measures to prevent any future translations or reprintings of his book. Shortly after Burnet's death in 1715, however, William Chetwood and a group of other booksellers arranged to have this still notorious book printed in English, whereupon George Burnet, asserting his rights under the statute as the author's executor, sought an injunction against Chetwood in Chancery.

According to the terms of the statute, the *Archaeologia Philosophica*, as a book published before 1710, would be protected until 1731, and therefore the author's—and his executor's—rights might be supposed to be clear. But the defendants maintained that a translation was not within the intent of the act

> which being intended to encourage learning by giving the advantage of the book to the author, could be intended only to restrain the mechanical art of printing . . . but not to hinder a translation of the book into another language, which in some respects may be called a different book, and the translator may be said to be the author . . . and therefore should rather seem to be within the encouragement than the prohibition of the act. (*ER* 35:1008–9)

Lord Chancellor Macclesfield, who ruled for Burnet, based his opinion not on the issue of whether a translation was an independent work but on his sense that, given the nature of its contents, the *Archaeologia Philosophica* should not be circulated in English:

> *Lord Chancellor* said, that though a translation might not be the same with the reprinting the original, on account that the translator has bestowed his care and pains upon it, and so not within the prohibition of the act, yet this being a book which to his knowledge (having read it in his study), contained strange notions, intended by the author to be concealed from the vulgar in the Latin language, in which language it could not do much hurt, the learned being better able to judge of it, he thought it proper to grant an injunction to the printing and publishing it in English; that he lookt upon it, that this Court had a superintendency over all books, and might in a summary way restrain the printing or publishing any that contained reflections on religion or morality. (*ER* 35:1009)

Benjamin Kaplan, who remarks on the strangeness of *Burnet*, observes that the case "went off on an erratic ground" (10). This is true, of course; the lord chancellor's assertion of the court's moral superintendency over books is beside the point. But what is striking here is precisely the persistence of the concern with regulation; evidently to Macclesfield a book was not just another piece of property like a house or a barn. It is interesting too that Burnet's motives in suing were not economic; his concerns were, rather, with matters of what I have called "propriety." In this respect too we can observe the continuing play of issues from the earlier period. But something novel had arisen in *Burnet*. Was a translation a new work and was a translator, therefore, an author? Macclesfield's opinion implied that he was inclined to think that a translator was indeed an author, and a number of years later in *Gyles v. Wilcox* (1740) a similar issue arose. Was an abridgment of an existing book a new work, and was an abridger an author? Lord Chancellor Hardwicke's decision was that an abridgment—a genuine abridgment and not merely a nominal one put together to evade the statute—was indeed a new work and that an abridger, whose efforts required invention, learning, and judgment, was an author (*ER* 26:489– 491, 957). What was an author? What was a protectable work? When disputes between stationers arose under the old regime of guild regu- lation, they were generally settled in the guild court, which sought to arrange compromises rather than to lay down principles. But now, with a statute on the books, the need for interpretation and for the articu- lation of principles had to arise.

Burnet v. Chetwood was unusual: most of the early cases that arose under the statute involved major London booksellers seeking injunc- tions in Chancery against other booksellers. Interestingly, in the 1720s and 1730s the London booksellers were successful in securing injunc- tions even in cases over books for which the statutory term had expired. In *Eyre v. Walker* (1735), for instance, Sir Joseph Jekyll—as master of the rolls, Jekyll sat as an assistant judge in Chancery—issued an injunction against the notorious pirate Jeffrey Walker for reprinting Richard Alles- tree's *The Whole Duty of Man*, a book originally published in 1657 and clearly not protected by the statute. In *Walthoe v. Walker* (1736) Jekyll again granted an injunction against Walker, this time for publishing Robert Nelson's *Companion for the Festivals and Fasts of the Church of England*, which first appeared in 1704. And in *Tonson v. Walker* (1739) Lord Chancellor Hardwicke also granted an injunction against Walker, who this time had taken on the redoubtable Jacob Tonson by seeking to reprint *Paradise Lost*, first published in 1667. Why were these injunc- tions granted? In *Burnet* Macclesfield may have been thinking in regu- latory rather than proprietary terms, but by and large the Chancery judges tended to treat literary property like any other form of property. The crucial point for the judges, as John Feather remarks, was the establishing of a proper title: "Once that point was proved, the copy was as much the property of the owner as if he had bought a piece of land" ("Publishers and the Pirates" 7). In the early years of the statute, then, the limitation of term was simply ignored.

Still the London booksellers were dissatisfied with the statutory term, and on 3 March 1735 they petitioned Parliament for a bill to make the 1710 act "more effectual" (*CJ* 22:400). Their stated goal was to secure greater protection against the illegal importation of books from abroad, particularly from Ireland where it was common practice to print cheap editions of new English books. But they also sought to change the term of copyright for all books, old and new, to a single term of twenty-one years, instead of the current provision for two fourteen-year terms. The most significant effect of this change would be to extend the statutory copyright on old books such as Shakespeare and Milton until 1756. The booksellers were having great success defending their properties in Chancery—why did they bother with Parliament? Probably they were inspired by the fact that Parliament was at the time deliberating a related issue, a proposal for a bill to protect copyright in engravings, and that it seemed well disposed toward granting protection. This bill was the result of a concerted effort by a group of artists, including William Hogarth, who sought to gain rights similar to those granted to authors by the Statute of Anne.[1] The success of these artists in securing the sympathy of Parliament also seems to have influenced the approach that the booksellers adopted. Whereas in 1710 they had emphasized their rights, the booksellers now presented themselves as acting "on behalf as well of the Authors and Compilers of such Books, as of themselves":

> the Expence of printing and publishing learned and useful Books, frequently obliges the Authors thereof to transfer their Property therein; and that the Property of the Authors of such Books, and their Assignees, hath, of late Years, been, and still continues to be, injured by surreptitious Editions and Impressions. (*CJ* 22:400)

1. Sometimes known as Hogarth's Act, the statute is usually referred to as the Engraving Copyright Act. On the making of this statute, see Hunter, "Copyright Protection for Engravings and Maps in Eighteenth-Century Britain," who corrects the impression that Hogarth single-handedly moved Parliament to pass the Engraving Act. On Hogarth's concerns see Paulson 1:8–9.

In a significant departure, the booksellers were representing literary property as essentially an author's affair and themselves as merely the author's agents and assigns.

The booksellers' petition was referred to committee for hearings and a recommendation, and the booksellers naturally arranged to have several authors appear as witnesses. They brought forward the compiler of a Latin-English dictionary, who testified that his work had taken twenty years to produce, and they produced the author of a learned book on Philo Judaeus, who testified that he had spent nearly £400 in procuring materials for his study. In order to make their point about foreign piracies, they prepared an exhibit of surreptitious editions printed abroad of twenty-nine individual "Authors of great Repute" (*CJ* 22:411–412). Moreover, they reprinted Addison's *Tatler* essay on literary property and published several new pamphlets, among them *The Case of Authors and Proprietors of Books*, which stressed the difficulties that authors faced, in particular "the great Expence of a Liberal Education" (2) and the money, labor, and time required to produce a useful book. It opened with a militant assertion of the author's property right:

> Authors have ever had a Property in their Works, founded upon the same fundamental Maxims by which Property was originally settled, and hath been since maintained.
>
> The Invention of Printing did not destroy this Property of Authors, nor alter it in any Respect, but by rendering it more easy to be invaded.

This pamphlet maintained throughout that the purpose of the proposed bill was to improve the author's position and to foster learning and knowledge.

The bill for improving the Statute of Anne was introduced at the end of March. Shortly thereafter an anonymous *Letter to a Member of Parliament*, probably written by a printer or someone else who would have reason to resent the great booksellers' control of the most valuable copies, was delivered to the door of the House of Commons. The writer spoke of the "many deceitful Arts, and false Insinuations," including the artifice of reprinting the *Tatler* essay, which the booksellers had employed to lead the House of Commons to believe that the bill would encourage learning and aid authors in securing their properties, when its real effect would be to hinder learning, raise the price of books to the public, and "increase the Profits of those, who have neither Colour of Title, nor Pretence of Merit"—to wit, the booksellers. Prior to the Statute of Anne, this writer argued,

> there was no Law which vested in any one the sole Copy-Right of any Books which were published to the World; but when once a Treatise was made publick, every one was at Liberty to make free with it. This, to be sure, was a great Discouragement to Authors, who were by this means in great measure deprived of the Profit of their Works; and this was the Grievance which gave Occasion to the making of that Act. *(Letter to a Member of Parliament)*

It was for authors, then, that the act was made. The limited term of protection was designed to provide for the encouragement of authors without establishing perpetual monopolies, and it appeared that the authors were satisfied with the term because it was not they but the booksellers who were seeking an extension. If an extension were once granted, the writer argued, it would have to be granted again and again each time the old term expired, and thus a perpetual monopoly would be established.

The booksellers retorted with *A Letter from an Author to a Member of Parliament.*[2] This questioned how the writer of the earlier *Letter* could pretend to be the friend of authors if he denied them a property in their own work. The earlier writer had claimed that there was no copyright before the statute. The writer of the *Letter from an Author* replied that the foundation of literary property was not the statute but the common law:

> By that Common Law, is warranted the Property of Authors, and their Assigns, in their printed Works, which they have constantly devised by Will, or conveyed by Assignment, as regularly, and as indisputably,

2. This is dated 17 April 1735. It contains a reference that allows us to date the *Letter to a Member of Parliament* as earlier in April. *A Letter from an Author* was followed shortly by *A Second Letter from an Author* dated 23 April 1735 with a second issue dated 28 April 1735. This series of letters appeared between the introduction of the bill in the House of Commons on 26 March 1735 and the meeting of the House as a Committee of the Whole to consider amendments on 29 April 1735. Whoever wrote them, the two letters from an "author" are closely affiliated with other documents in the booksellers' campaign for the 1735 bill, which indicates that they are in effect official statements by proponents of the bill. The first, for example, makes use of *A Short State of the Publick Encouragement;* the second makes extensive use of *The Case of Authors and Proprietors of Books.* The British Library copy of *Letter from an Author,* reprinted in the Garland *English Publishing* series, is defective. A good copy is included in Bodleian MS Carte 207 (ff. 67–68), a useful collection of manuscript and printed documents mostly related to the agitation for an improved copyright statute in the 1730s.

as any other Part of their Estate . . . And if . . . the reasonable Customs of this Nation are Part of the Law of *England,* so constant, uninterrupted, unquestioned, and inviolated a Practice; inviolated, though it had no Aid from any Statute, or any Privilege of the Crown, from the very Original of Printing, 'till of late; must certainly be founded in Law; especially if the Law of Reason and Nature . . . is Part of the Law of *England.* For if there be such a Thing as Property upon Earth, an Author has it in his Work. A Father cannot more justly call his Child, than an Author can his Work, his own. Every Reason, for which Property was at first introduced, and has been since maintained in other Cases, holds equally in this. (1)

The *Letter from an Author* continued with an assertion that literary property had always been carefully respected "'till about 40 Years ago, when Pyrating of Books first began to be practised." To protect themselves authors first had recourse to royal privileges, but, these proving ineffective, the Statute of Anne was passed "in hopes that Pyrates would pay more Regard to a Parliamentary Privilege, than they had done to a Royal one" (2). Both the royal privileges and the statutory copyright were merely instruments to protect the property rights that authors had always possessed.

The historical narrative that the first letter told was one of radical discontinuity: literary property did not exist before the statute, which was passed to assist authors. Technically it was of course true, as the writer claimed, that there was no copyright law prior to 1710, but it was disingenuous to imply that literary property had never been protected before the Statute of Anne. Moreover, as we have seen, the statute was by no means simply an authors' law, but an act that provided considerable continuity with the old guild system. The competing historical narrative that the second writer provided was one of essential continuity: authors had always had property in their works and this was always the basis of the bookselling trade. Why had the statute been necessary? Because about forty years before—the event alluded to is the lapse of the Licensing Act, though this is never specifically mentioned—piracy first began to be practiced. Thus in order to explain the statute within his representation of continuity, the second writer was constrained to resort to a story of abrupt and unexplained moral decline. The second writer's narrative of essential continuity was no less directed to an immediate polemical purpose, and it was also, finally, no closer to the truth. The first writer was seeking to influence Parliament against the 1735 bill, the second was seeking to persuade Parliament to support the bill. The two narratives are diametrically opposed, but they have this in common: both place the author at the center of the story as the protagonist of the narrative of literary property.

Unlike the engravers' bill, which became law on 15 May, the booksellers' bill died in the House of Lords, which was in no way inclined to grant an extension of the term of protection.[3] But even if no bill was passed, a significant evolution had occurred in which the focus of the literary-property question shifted from the bookseller to the author. We should also note that in recasting the literary-property issue as a matter of the author's rights, the booksellers had made use of the discourse of proprietary authorship developed by Defoe and Addison a quarter of a century earlier. Thus the booksellers' invocation of "the great Expence of a Liberal Education" echoes Addison's observation that a liberal education "consumes a moderate Fortune" and his complaint that such an education should be "the only one which a polite Nation makes unprofitable" (*Tatler* 101, 1 Dec. 1709). Furthermore, the slippage we noted in Defoe's use of the paternity trope recurs in the assertion, "A Father cannot more justly call his Child, than an Author can his Work, his own." More generally, the booksellers' pamphlets appropriate and recirculate assertions about the nature of the author's labors and expenses and about the absoluteness of the author's claims.

Most interesting, perhaps, is the way the *Letter from an Author* elaborates the trope of literary property as real estate in a narrative about the origin of property. Property was first established, the writer explains, when the world grew populous and it became necessary to secure more effective cultivation of the land: whoever took first possession became the owner of an estate. Like every other property owner's claim, the author's ultimately rests on possession, and the author has the same right to his property as anyone else. But in fact, the writer argues, the author's claim is often stronger than that of the usual proprietor, "for, in some Cases, he may be said rather to create,

3. As discussed later, Alexander Pope contributed to the defeat of this bill. A second attempt to extend the term of copyright, one even more explicitly centered on the author rather than the bookseller, was made in 1737, but it too was defeated in the House of Lords. In 1738 a bill that dealt with the issue of the importation of surreptitious copies but made no mention of the extension of the term was also rejected by the Lords. Reintroduced in 1739, however, the importation bill was finally passed, though not without some struggle.

than to discover or plant his Land," and in any case "it cannot be said, that an Author's Work was ever common, as the Earth originally was to all the World" (1). Thus no one is dispossessed by literary property:

> The Field of Knowledge is large enough for all the World to find Ground in it to plant and improve. Let every Body do it; let them be encouraged and protected in so doing; let them write and print on the same Subject: But let them not lazily borrow that individual Work, which is the Produce of another's Labours, to make a Gain to themselves, to a deserving Author's Detriment or Ruin. (2)

Let us note that while on the one hand the writer has asserted that the author's property was never common, on the other he has spoken of authorship as if it were a matter of appropriating ground from the common field of knowledge. But the general narrative about possession as the foundation of property was conventional, and probably neither the writer nor his readers noticed this contradiction. The writer goes on to argue that "laying all Copies open" would have disastrous consequences:

> There must be a fixed Property in this, as well as in other Cases, otherwise Learning will soon be lost, the Land of Knowledge will be left desolate; and the laying all Copies open, will have as terrible Effects in Point of Learning, as the not introducing of Property would have had upon Land, by discouraging Industry and Improvement, and laying Grounds for endless Disputes, Disorders, and Confusion.

The writer uses the real-estate metaphor to represent the author's claim. If a cottager has a right of common on the unimproved land of a manor and builds on it, the improvements will belong to the landlord because the ground is his. Likewise, the writer remarks, the author's work "is so absolutely his own, that no Body else can pretend the least Right of Common in it" (2).

In seeking to establish the author's property in his work, the booksellers were of course equally seeking to establish their own claims. In form this argument went back at least as far as the stationers' unsuccessful attempt to argue to the House of Lords in *The Stationers v. The Patentees* (1666) that the bookseller's claim, derived from the author's claim, took precedence over patent claims derived from the royal prerogative. But although the argument had been available for some seventy years, it had never before been so fully elaborated. This important moment in the development of the discourse of literary property was marked as well by the appearance in general circulation of the new term "copyright."[4] The traditional stationers' term, "copy," retained some feeling for copy as a material object, the manuscript on which the printed edition was based. "Copyright" suggests an attenuation of this feeling for the manuscript as the material basis of the property: an abstract right was being formulated, a legal claim based on a general idea of the author's creative labor. When the literary-property issue was looked at from the point of view of the laboring author, his right was readily warranted by the familiar paternity trope: "A Father cannot more justly call his Child, than an Author can his Work, his own." But when the issue was looked at from the point of view of the work as a commodity, the right of the proprietor, who might or might not be the author, was warranted by the metaphor of land. The real-estate metaphor provided a comforting sense of weight and tangibility; however, at the same time that the discourse of literary property was acquiring metaphorical mass, it was moving away from its old foundation in the materiality of the manuscript as an object.

Despite the shift in focus from the bookseller to the author and the elaboration of the discourse of proprietary authorship in the campaign of 1735, literary property in the 1730s was still in practice a bookseller's rather than an author's concern. Polite authors were reluctant to see themselves as deeply involved in commerce, and in any case most

4. The earliest use of "copyright" I know occurs in the Stationers' Register for 31 May 1701, where Timothy Childe records in connection with his entry as proprietor of *A New Ecclesiastical History*: "Mr Awnsham Churchill is and shall bee intituled to one moiety of this book & copy right" (Eyre 3:494). See also the entry for the second volume of the same book on 6 August 1703. The next usage I know occurs in an agreement between Pope and the bookseller Benjamin Motte dated 29 March 1727; see Foxon 243. In 1732 Pope wrote to John Gay that Motte together with some other "idle fellow" had written to Swift "to get him to give them some Copyright"; see Swift 4:64–65. The term occurs in Tonson's advertisement for his 1734 edition of *The Merry Wives of Windsor* in which he speaks of the damages of piracy of Shakespeare's plays to "the Proprietors of the Copy-Right of the said Plays" (Dawson 30). And it is used in the preamble to the 1735 booksellers' bill, which complains about the publishing activities of "Persons who have paid no Considerations for the Copy-right of such Books," in *The Case of Authors and Proprietors of Books,* and in *A Letter to a Member of Parliament.* The earliest use of "copyright" that the second edition of the OED records is the preamble to the 1735 bill.

authors continued to sell their works outright. Alexander Pope was an exception. He represented himself as a gentleman and scholar rather than as a professional writer:

> Why did I write? what sin to me unknown
> Dipt me in Ink, my Parents', or my own?
> As yet a Child, nor yet a Fool to Fame,
> I lisp'd in Numbers, for the Numbers came.
> I left no Calling for this idle trade,
> No Duty broke, no Father dis-obey'd.
> The Muse but serv'd to ease some Friend, not Wife,
> To help me thro' this long Disease, my Life. (*Poems* 4:104–105)

Despite this representation of himself as a natural poet writing to amuse himself and his friends, Pope was passionately concerned with all aspects of the book trade, including his copyrights.

Pope was not the first English author to go to court. In 1729 his friend John Gay, perhaps in part under Pope's influence, secured an injunction against a series of booksellers in connection with piracies of his *Polly*, the sequel to *The Beggar's Opera*.[5] But Pope was the first author to make regular and repeated use of the statute. He did so in consultation with his good friend William Murray, later Lord Mansfield, who as chief justice of King's Bench was to become one of the major figures in the copyright struggle later in the century. Pope was directly and indirectly involved in a number of cases, but by far the most important was his 1741 suit against Edmund Curll over the publication of his letters.[6] *Pope v. Curll*, in which the rule was established that copyright in a letter

5. See Sutherland, "'Polly' Among the Pirates," for an account of *Gay v. Read* (1729). I am aware of only two other authors' cases between *Burnet v. Chetwood* (1720) and *Pope v. Curll* (1741). In *Webb v. Rose* (1732) the son of a well-known conveyancer secured an injunction to prevent the publication of his father's draft conveyances; in *Forrester v. Waller* (1741) Alexander Forrester, a barrister of some eminence and a court reporter, secured an injunction to prevent publication of surreptitiously obtained legal notes.

6. The first case in which Pope was involved was *Gulliver v. Watson* (1729) in which, acting through the bookseller Lawton Gilliver as a surrogate, he attempted to use the statute to suppress a pirated edition of *The Dunciad*. In *Dodsley v. Watson* (1737) Pope was briefly a coplaintiff with the bookseller Robert Dodsley in another action against James Watson, this one having to do with his *Letters*, but ultimately his name was removed from the complaint. After *Pope v. Curll* (1741), the first case in which he was the plaintiff of record, Pope brought suit against Jacob Ilive and Henry Lintot in two 1743 actions related to *The Dunciad*. And in *Pope v. Bickham* (1744) he brought suit against George Bickham who had produced an unauthorized engraved edition of the *Essay on Man*. On Pope's law cases in general, see McLaverty, "Pope and Copyright." On the three cases involving *The Dunciad*, see also

belongs to the writer, remains a foundational case in English and American copyright law. It also records, I shall suggest, a transitional moment in the conception of authorship and a pivotal moment in the production of the concept of intellectual property. Who owns a letter, the writer or the receiver? In the court's response to this question, the notion of the essentially immaterial nature of the object of copyright was born.

At issue in *Pope* was a volume of letters that Curll had published, *Dean Swift's Literary Correspondence*, which contained letters to and from Pope and Jonathan Swift along with others. Pope had just published an authorized edition of these letters as part of his collected works. "That Rascal Curl has pyrated the Letters, which would have ruin'd half my Edition, but we have got an Injunction from my Lord Chancellor to prohibit his selling them for the future, tho doubtless he'l do it clandestinly" (*Correspondence* 4:350). So Pope wrote to Ralph Allen after his victory in the case. As the comment suggests, commercial considerations no doubt figured. But the background to the case suggests that Pope may have been as much concerned with matters of propriety as with the effect of Curll's edition on the sales of his own.

In 1735, as is well known, Pope tricked Curll into publishing his correspondence. For a gentleman to publish his own letters would have seemed inexcusably vain, but a prior unauthorized publication by Curll would open the way for Pope to publish his own edition as a way of setting the record straight. Despite this ruse, however, Pope was genuinely distressed by the practice of rogue booksellers surreptitiously printing personal letters, and he wished to see Parliament take action on the matter. It was at just this moment that the London booksellers, flying the banner of authors' rights, were pressing for an extension of the copyright term. Pope does not seem to have cared about extending the term, but he saw an opportunity to make Curll serve as an example of an irresponsible bookseller in order to dramatize the bill's limitations. So, as James McLaverty suggests in "The First Printing and Publication of Pope's Letters," he contrived to have the surreptitious edition of his letters appear while the bill was pending in the House of Lords. Just before the bill was taken up for its second reading, Curll's

---

Sutherland, "*The Dunciad* of 1729"; Vincent; McLaverty, "Lawton Gilliver" esp. 104–105; and Feather, "Publishers and the Pirates" 14–16. On the 1744 action against Bickham, see Hunter, "*Pope v. Bickham.*"

advertisement for the volume, which made it sound as if the book included letters from various peers, was read aloud to the House. Unauthorized publication of a peer's words was a breach of privilege, and the lords ordered the books to be seized and Curll summoned. As it turned out, no peers' letters had actually been printed, but this was not established until after the second reading had been postponed beyond the end of the term (*LJ* 24:550). Writing shortly after this affair, in a pamphlet explaining how the unauthorized edition of his letters came to appear, Pope credited the peers' indignation with the defeat of the "booksellers' bill," as he called it. If the bill were brought in again, Pope said, he hoped that

> the Legislature will be pleas'd not to *extend* the *Privileges,* without at the same Time *restraining the Licence, of Booksellers.* Since in a Case so *notorious* as the printing a Gentleman's Private Letters, most Eminent, both *Printers* and *Booksellers,* conspired to assist the Pyracy both in printing and in vending the same. (*Narrative of the Method* 345)

In the same year as the affair in the House of Lords, Pope published the *Epistle to Dr. Arbuthnot* (1735), in which he portrayed himself as a private gentleman outrageously besieged by the world. Interestingly, in the Advertisement prefixed to this poem Pope invokes a legal metaphor and speaks of the epistle as "a Sort of Bill of Complaint" (*Poems* 4:95).

Pope's concern with what he considered an outrage against decency continued beyond the events of 1735. Two years later in the preface to his own edition of his correspondence, he speaks of the illicit publication of letters as a form of "betraying Conversation":

> To open Letters is esteem'd the greatest breach of honour; even to look into them already open'd or accidentally dropt, is held ungenerous, if not an immoral act. What then can be thought of the procuring them merely by Fraud, and printing them merely for Lucre? We cannot but conclude every honest man will wish, that if the Laws have as yet provided no adequate remedy, one at least may be found, to prevent so great and growing an evil. (*Correspondence* 1:xl)

In the suit against Curll in 1741 the legal conceit in the *Epistle to Dr. Arbuthnot* would prove to have been prophetic. Pope may have had economic motives for seeking an injunction against Curll's edition of the letters, but through this action he was trying to answer his own call to find an adequate remedy for what he considered a "great and growing" evil by establishing that private letters fell under the statute. In *Pope*, then, as in *Burnet v. Chetwood* two decades earlier, a commercial regulatory statute was being employed to pursue matters that had as much to do with propriety as with commerce.

Pope's preface to the 1737 edition of his letters is dominated by the genteel discourse in which he displays his indignation as a man of honor against booksellers' violation of his privacy. But what we can call the "discourse of property" makes itself felt as well in the preface, as when Pope complains that the booksellers' practice of soliciting copies of authors' letters leads to petty thievery: "Any domestick or servant, who can snatch a letter from your pocket or cabinet, is encouraged to that vile practise." Moreover, if the quantity of material procured falls short, the bookseller will fill out the volume with anything he pleases, so that the poor author has "not only Theft to fear, but Forgery." And the greater the writer's reputation, the greater will be the demand for the books and so the greater the injury to the author: "your Fame and your Property suffer alike; you are at once expos'd and plunder'd" (*Correspondence* 1:xl). The blending of the discourse of propriety (marked by such terms as "honor," "generosity," "fame") with that of property (marked by such terms as "theft," "snatch," "plunder") produces a certain instability in the preface that is evidence of the way it inscribes a transitional point in cultural history. Pope's suit against Curll is equally a mingled affair, an action that takes place between two worlds, the traditional world of the author as a gentleman and scholar and the emergent world of the author as a professional.

Drafted by Murray, Pope's *Bill of Complaint* (see Appendix A) begins by invoking the Statute of Anne and its provision for authors. Pope specifies by date twenty-nine of his letters to Swift that Curll published contrary to his right as author. As for twenty-nine other letters written to him by Swift, Pope does not quite claim property by virtue of possession but he comes close, saying that he hoped none of them would ever have been published without his consent. He waives the penalties allowed by the statute, asking instead for an injunction against any further sales of the book and for an accounting of Curll's activities and profits. His aim in this was evidently to acquire full compensation through seeking a remedy in equity, but there is no evidence that the case proceeded to an accounting. As Justice Edward Willes remarked some twenty-five years later in the context of *Millar v. Taylor*, once an injunction had been obtained and the sale of an edition stopped, it was seldom worth the plaintiff's while to go further (*ER* 98:213).

Curll's *Answer* (Appendix A) makes three points in his defense. First, he argues, that since

> all the letters mentioned in the complainant's said bill of complaint were, as this defendant verily believes, actually sent and delivered by and to the several persons by whom and to whom they severally purport to have been written and addressed . . . the complainant is not to be considered as the author and proprietor of all or any of the said letters.[7]

Second, he raises the question of whether familiar letters fall under the terms of the statute, since he has been advised "that the said letters are not a work of that nature and sole right of printing whereof was intended to be preserved by the said statute to the author." Third, he says he reprinted the letters in question from the Dublin edition printed by George Faulkner, and it is his understanding that any book first published in Ireland may be lawfully reprinted in England.[8]

The decision in the case was rendered by Lord Chancellor Hardwicke, who rejected out of hand the claim that any book first printed in Ireland became "lawful prize" to English booksellers. If that were so, all it would take to evade the statute would be to send a book to Ireland to be printed and then claim only to be reprinting the Irish edition. But did familiar letters come within the intention of the statute, which was after all an act for the encouragement of learning? Hardwicke declared that it would be "extremely mischievous" to distinguish between a book of letters and "any other learned work." Would not the same objection hold against a book of sermons? Moreover, it was no valid objection to point out that these were only familiar letters:

> It is certain that no works have done more service to mankind, than those which have appeared in this shape, upon familiar subjects, and

7. The phrase "author and proprietor" is, I take it, to be understood in the conjunctive: Curll is certainly not denying that Pope actually wrote the letters he sent to Swift but only that he can claim property in them.

8. In fact Curll used Pope's London edition as copytext. As Pat Rogers observes, it might have been effective to demonstrate in court that Curll was reprinting the London and not the Dublin edition, but Pope probably did not realize that this was so (329). The Dublin edition was one that Pope had arranged in order to have an excuse to bring out the London edition (Mack 665–671).

which perhaps were never intended to be published; and it is this makes them so valuable; for I must confess for my own part, that letters which are very elaborately written, and originally intended for the press, are generally the most insignificant, and very little worth any person's reading. (*ER* 26:608)

The case had led to a circumstance in which a legal question—were letters on familiar subjects protected under the act?—involved a judge in making a literary-critical proclamation from the bench. If there was to be a statute protecting learned writings, judges would perforce find themselves making pronouncements on generic matters and on literary value. Hardwicke's judgment is rendered in the somewhat pompous language of refinement, but the issue is also one of commercial value. Under the aegis of the statute, literary and legal questions were converging in such a way that significant sums of money might depend on whether a particular kind of text was deemed worth protecting and admitted to the privileged category. Two senses of value, the literary and the commercial, were becoming entangled.

But another question remained. Who owns a letter? Pope claimed protection both for the letters he had written and, more tentatively, for those addressed to him. Curll denied that Pope owned even the letters he himself had written, arguing that a letter is a gift to the receiver. Hardwicke's decision on this matter depended on a distinction between the physical letter and the copyright:

> I am of opinion that it is only a special property in the receiver, possibly the property of the paper may belong to him; but this does not give a licence to any person whatsoever to publish them to the world, for at most the receiver has only a joint property with the writer. (*ER* 26:608)

Thus he ruled that Pope's injunction against Curll was valid but that it held only for those letters written by Pope, not for those written to him.

Hardwicke's decision involved an important abstraction of the notion of literary property from its physical basis in ink and paper. The Statute of Anne, let us recall, prescribed specific and concrete penalties for the invasion of literary property: offending books were to be forfeited to the rightful proprietors to be destroyed, and offenders were to forfeit one penny for each illegally printed sheet found. Precisely what kind of property, material or immaterial, Parliament supposed it was protecting in the statute is unclear, for in all likelihood such metaphysical questions about the nature of literary property never occurred to the legislators. As Benjamin Kaplan remarks, the draftsman of the statute was "thinking as a printer would—of a book as a physical entity; of rights in it and offenses against it as related to 'printing and reprinting' the thing itself" (9). So too Curll's reply represented a letter as a physical entity, an object that once actually sent and delivered passed wholly to the recipient. But, as we have seen, in the years preceding *Pope v. Curll* the new term "copyright" had appeared, implying that the discourse of literary property was moving away from its old foundation in the materiality of the author's manuscript. In Hardwicke's decision, the author's words have in effect flown free from the page on which they are written. Not ink and paper but pure signs, separated from any material support, have become the protected property.

We should observe, however, that Hardwicke's decision is couched in cautious language: "possibly the property of the paper" may belong to the receiver, who "at most" has "only a joint property with the writer." This tentativeness is to be attributed, no doubt, to the fact that the notion of copyright as intangible property was still novel, and the theory of a property that inheres in words alone had not yet been worked out. But, despite the novelty of the doctrine, the potential for its production was latent in the provision of the Statute of Anne which made authors as well as booksellers into possible owners of literary property, for booksellers are concerned with material objects—books— whereas authors are concerned with compositions, with texts. If the author was to be a proprietor and an agent in the literary marketplace, if the author was to appear in court in his own person to protect his interests, then inevitably the conception of the property owned would be affected.

Hardwicke's decision also affected the representation of authorship, for in severing the immaterial from the material aspect of literary property, as Irene Tucker has noted, he severed the act of writing a letter from that of sending or receiving it. In this way Hardwicke separated writing from social exchange, constructing it as a solitary and self-sufficient act of creation. We recall Addison's Poor Tom, who worked his brain like an estate and brought varied produce to market according to the season. Hardwicke's decision also implied an author who created in privacy a work he might either bring to market or not as he chose. And this representation of writing implied a reciprocal representation of reading as a private act of consumption, which was what reading had become by the middle of the eighteenth century.

5

⚬⚬⚬

Battle of the Booksellers

In the first thirty years after the passage of the Statute of Anne, the question of literary property came to center on the author; in the next thirty years, from the 1740s to the early 1770s, the crucial issue became the exact nature of the author's right. Did the Statute of Anne confer a limited privilege on authors, a patent for a specific term of protection such as that which the Statute of Monopolies provided for inventors? Or did it provide an additional protection to supplement an underlying common-law right to a property that was in principle no different from any other kind of property and therefore unlimited? In the course of litigation, the question of the nature of the author's right came to turn on questions about the nature of the supposed property. What exactly was literary property? How could one have a property in ideas, whose existence was purely in the mind? How could a literary composition be seen as different from any other kind of useful invention?

The series of cases in which these questions were litigated starts with *Millar v. Kinkaid*, initiated in the Scottish Court of Session in 1743, where the question of the author's common-law right was formally raised for the first time since the passage of the statute. Some years later in *Tonson v. Collins* the common-law issue was argued at length in King's Bench, but no decision on the question was reached until 1769, when the same court ruled in *Millar v. Taylor* in favor of the common-law right. Four years later, however, the Scottish Court of Session took exactly the opposite position in *Hinton v. Donaldson;* whatever might be the law in England, the court ruled, in Scotland copyright was a privilege, not a property. The conflict between the English and the Scottish courts was resolved in the great case of *Donaldson v. Becket*, to be discussed in the next chapter.

To some extent, the period from *Millar v. Kinkaid* to *Donaldson v. Becket* was dominated by the commercial struggle between the patriotic Scots, who were proud of their growing printing and publishing trade, and the booksellers of London, who wanted to maintain their centralized control of all publishing in Britain. The intellectual style and the legal substance of the struggle were to a remarkable degree shaped by one man, William Murray, Lord Mansfield, who is generally considered the single most influential English jurist of the eighteenth century. Throughout this period one encounters Murray, either as counselor or as judge. By his own account he was counsel in most of the important Chancery cases concerning literary property, including *Pope v. Curll*. When the London booksellers appealed *Millar v. Kinkaid* to the House of Lords, it was he who argued their case. And as chief justice of the Court of King's Bench after 1756, he presided over both *Tonson v. Collins* and *Millar v. Taylor*.

Mansfield's legal intelligence and powers of persuasion were regarded with awe by most of his contemporaries, and from his position on King's Bench he launched one of the great campaigns of legal reform in English history, seeking to make the law responsive to the needs of a commercial nation. As his biographer C. H. S. Fifoot points out, Mansfield was committed to the integration of England's peculiar double system of courts of equity and courts of law into a single harmonious system of jurisprudence, and to the subjection of both to the overarching authority of principle. Reason, fitness, and the common consent of mankind as to the law of nature and nations: these rather than accumulated precedents were the true sources of legal authority. As Mansfield remarked in *Jones v. Randall* (1774):

> The law of England would be a strange science indeed, if it were decided upon precedents only. Precedents only serve to illustrate principles and to give them a fixed authority. But the law of England, which is exclusive of positive law enacted by statute, depends upon principles; and these principles run through all the cases, according as the particular circumstances of each have been found to fall within the one or other of them. (qtd Fifoot 221)

It was this devotion to principle that empowered Mansfield as a reformer. Moreover, his fidelity to principle contributed to his sense of the superiority of the common law to statute law, which was subject to the pressure of interests and often marred by careless drafting (Lieberman 124–126).

Mansfield's strong support of an author's common-law right was probably shaped by his experience as a counselor in literary-property cases in Chancery in the 1730s and 1740s, in particular by his admiration for Alexander Pope. The common-law issue probably would have been seized on by whomever was representing the London booksellers' interests in court in the middle years of the century. Still, it can be claimed that Murray, more than any other person, was responsible for founding the booksellers' claims to perpetual copyright on the principle of the author's natural right to the fruits of his labor. This was the argument he employed in his appeal of *Millar v. Kinkaid,* and it was the argument he used again in *Tonson v. Walker* in Chancery. Moreover, Murray later carried his convictions to the bench, where he did everything possible to see that the common-law right became established as law. Ultimately, of course, he failed when the House of Lords in *Donaldson v. Becket* overturned his ruling. Nevertheless, by 1774 the discourse of literary property was indelibly marked with his stamp.

Scottish booksellers retailed books they purchased from the booksellers of London. In the 1730s and 1740s, however, some Scottish booksellers, frustrated by the control that London exercised over the trade, began printing their own editions of both classical and English authors (*Considerations* 14). In 1743 a group of London booksellers responded with a suit in the Court of Session—the court specified in the Statute of Anne as having jurisdiction for literary-property actions in Scotland—against a group of booksellers from Edinburgh and Glasgow.

The plaintiffs identified a miscellaneous collection of English books that they claimed were illegally printed by the Scots. As had been done in English Chancery cases, they provisionally waived the statutory penalties and asked instead for damages based on an accounting of profits. This raised what became the central issue in the case, for damages were not mentioned in the statute. But, the plaintiffs argued, the statute declared a property to belong to the author, and so authors and their assigns had a right to any kind of relief the common law provided. The defendants replied that the statute did not create a property in the true sense since there was no material basis for it:

> When a man composes a book, the manuscript is his property, and the whole edition is his property after it is printed. But let us suppose that this whole edition is sold off, where is then his property? As property by all lawyers, ancient and modern, is defined to be *jus in re*, there can be no property without a subject. The books that remain upon hand, are, no doubt, the property of the author and his assigns: but after the whole edition is disposed of, the author's property is at an end: there is no subject nor *corpus* of which he can be said to be the proprietor. (Home 157)

Therefore, the defendants argued, authors could only sue according to the limited provisions of the statute, and in 1748, after years of hearings and preliminary decisions in which the judges more than once reversed themselves, the court ruled in favor of the Scots.

The London booksellers, counseled by Murray, appealed to the House of Lords. In the Court of Session, the plaintiffs cautiously avoided a direct claim that they had a common-law right, perhaps because the books in question had been printed and published in London and therefore might be considered not subject to Scottish common law (*ER* 98:210). In the appeal, however, Murray argued the author's common-law right. Instead of meeting this challenge, though, the respondents' lawyers pointed to technical flaws in the appellants' case and succeeded in having the case dismissed.[1] The decision in the House of Lords was made without prejudice to the ultimate determination of any of the substantive points at issue, and the English booksellers had the option of starting their action over again in the Court of Session. They decided—probably wisely, given the unsympathetic attitude of the Scottish court—that it was not in their interests to press the matter further (*Considerations* 27).

1. Their major assertion was that the appellants had never finally waived the statutory penalties and that it was inconsistent to press a case both for penalties and for damages; that is, to press a case simultaneously on statutory and on common-law grounds. They also argued that the action was improper since a single accusation was brought against separate traders without charging them to be joint offenders. See Craigie 1:488–492.

The motion to dismiss the case on technical grounds was made by Lord Chancellor Hardwicke, who seems also to have been inclined against the common-law right.[2] Hardwicke emphasized, however, that there was much still to be said on this subject and that he did not want to give an opinion that might bind him. Murray had great respect for Hardwicke, and the following year he had an opportunity to try to change the lord chancellor's mind when he argued the author's common-law right before him in the second case of *Tonson v. Walker* (1752), which like the one of 1739 concerned *Paradise Lost*. One of the arguments Murray made on this occasion had to do with the seventeenth-century cases testing the royal prerogative and the king's right to issue printing patents. If the king could hold a property in books and grant it to a printer by royal patent, then so could a private person. Evidently this argument swayed the lord chancellor, who now was reported to favor the property.[3] Yet Hardwicke was a cautious judge and, given the doubts that *Millar v. Kinkaid* had raised, refused to make a general determination in Chancery, which was after all a court of equity, not law. Hardwicke issued a provisional injunction but remarked that, if the case came to a hearing, he would send the question of the author's right to the common-law judges so that the point of law might finally be settled. Thus the common-law issue came into focus.

In 1747, while *Millar v. Kinkaid* was pending in the Court of Session, William Warburton published *A Letter from an Author to a Member of Parliament Concerning Literary Property*, a pamphlet that discussed the author's common-law right and provided the first theoretical treatment of literary property. Warburton, who had trained as a lawyer in his youth, may have developed strong feelings on the subject of literary property in the course of his friendship with Pope. Besides being an

2. Hardwicke's comments were reported to the Scottish booksellers in a letter from their solicitor, which is printed in *Considerations* 25–27. The letter does not directly report Hardwicke's sentiments, but a phrase in it—Hardwicke, the letter reports, "observed on the Precedents cited by Mr. Solicitor-General, in Support of the contrary Opinion, that they were made on Motion, and hearing of one Side only, therefore of little Weight" (26)—suggests that they were contrary to those of Murray, the solicitor general.

3. See Mansfield's comments in *Tonson v. Collins* (ER 96:173, 189–190). This argument, which finally came down to a conviction about the primacy of property in civil society, remained important to Mansfield. He spoke about it again at length in *Millar v. Taylor* (ER 98:253–256).

author himself, Warburton was Pope's literary executor and the heir of all Pope's properties in his works in print. Thus he had a direct interest in the protection of literary property that was in some respects not unlike that of a bookseller. Although *Millar v. Kinkaid* is nowhere explicitly mentioned, this case seems to have been the immediate occasion for the *Letter*, which was published, it is worth noting, by John Knapton, one of the London booksellers engaged in the suit. In any event, Warburton's *Letter* directly considers the key issue of the immateriality of literary property that the Scottish booksellers raised in their defense. Taken as a whole, it is a brief for the English plaintiffs.

Warburton begins by remarking that it seemed odd that so little regard had been paid to authors' property rights: "surely if there be *Degrees of Right*, that of *Authors* seemeth to have the Advantage over most others; their Property being, in the truest Sense, their *own*, as acquired by a long and painful Exercize of that very Faculty which denominateth us Men" (2). The reason authors had not pressed their claims earlier was because they could depend on patronage. The settlement of the literary-property issue had been neglected until it became a question whether authors had any property at all. Property, Warburton says, can be divided into two classes, movables and immovables. Movable properties can in turn be either natural or artificial. And artificially produced movables can be still further divided into products of the hand and products of the mind, for example, a utensil and a book:

> For that the Product of the *Mind* is as well capable of becoming Property, as that of the *Hand*, is evident from hence, that it hath in it those two essential Conditions, which, by the allowance of all Writers of Laws, make Things susceptible of Property; namely common *Utility*, and a Capacity of having its Possession *ascertained*. (7)

Note that Warburton never actually demonstrates that literary property has "a Capacity of having its Possession *ascertained*," but this point might be lost in the smooth development of his analysis, which, moving by progressive division into familiar binary oppositions (movable/immovable, natural/artificial, mind/body), makes the notion of intellectual property seem natural and inevitable.

What was the nature of the author's right? According to Warburton, property produced by the hand was "confined to the individual Thing made." Like the instrument of its creation, the property was wholly material. "But, in the other Case of Property in the Product of the Mind, as in a *Book* composed, it is not confined to the Original MS. but extends to the *Doctrine* contained in it: Which is, indeed, the true and peculiar Property in a Book" (8). The essence of the author's property was thus immaterial, consisting solely of the "doctrine" or ideas that were the product of his mental labor. Six years earlier in *Pope v. Curll* Lord Chancellor Hardwicke had tentatively distinguished between the receiver's property right in the possession of a letter and the author's property right in the words. Now, in Warburton's *Letter,* the notion of a property in pure signs abstracted from any material support was being systematically developed.

The clincher in Warburton's argument was his treatment of the relation between literary property and patents. He was arguing that since copyrights were property rights and not mere privileges, literary properties were perpetual. But why should an author's rights be treated any differently from the rights that an inventor might have in a new and useful machine? Warburton's approach was to demonstrate that inventions were of a mixed nature, being both manual and mental products. Insofar as a machine was a kind of utensil, it was appropriate that the maker's property be located in the individual material object. Nevertheless, because the operation of the mind was so intimately concerned in inventions, it was appropriate to extend to inventors a patent, a grant that reached beyond the individual material object, but only for a term of years. Thus patent protection, which by long-established principle was limited to a specific term, was a special category of limited rights designed to accommodate the mixed nature of mechanical inventions, as opposed to the purely intellectual nature of literary compositions. Rhetorically, then, the introduction of this third, mixed, category of property situated between products of the hand and products of the mind helped to confirm the idea of literary property as wholly immaterial.

We should observe that Warburton's division of labor into mental and manual activities, when fused with the traditional coding of spirit as superior to matter, produced a hierarchical ordering. His classification of moveable properties into three ranks—the purely material in which property was limited to the object itself, the mixed form in which in addition to a property in the object there was also a patent for a limited term, and the purely mental in which the property was neither confined nor limited—reproduced a discourse of social stratification. Being all spirit and no dross, literary property was plainly the most noble of the three classes, and it would follow that the makers of this form of property, authors, were the aristocrats of productive society. What we have here is an early moment in the formation of the professional writer as a mystified figure of special authority. As the recipients of divine inspiration, writers had long been mystified, but Warburton's representation departed from this traditional conception: his author was above all a commodity producer.

❧❧❧

After deciding not to press further against the Scots in *Millar v. Kinkaid*, the London booksellers for a time simply ignored the Scottish reprints. In 1759, however, they became active again in seeking to suppress the reprint trade. In April a general meeting was held in London, a committee was chosen, and money was subscribed for a campaign chest. Next they circulated letters—later printed by Alexander Donaldson in *Some Thoughts on the State of Literary Property* (11–20)—to all booksellers in England, offering to take off their hands any Scottish or other pirated editions of English books at the price they had actually cost and to provide the same value in genuine English editions. After 1 May, they threatened, anyone found selling pirated editions would be prosecuted.

In threatening legal action, it seems likely that the booksellers were taking into account William Murray's recent elevation to King's Bench and his reputation as a champion of the author's common-law right. Also encouraging to them perhaps was the first decision in a literary-property matter handed down by Lord Mansfield's court, *Baskett v. University of Cambridge* (1758), in which the court considered that the crown held a perpetual prerogative copyright on certain works that, like any other copyright, could be assigned. In any event, shortly after the April 1759 meeting, a test case on the common-law question was initiated in Mansfield's court against Benjamin Collins, a respected bookseller from Salisbury, for selling Scottish copies of *The Spectator* in April and May 1759. The plaintiffs were Jacob and Richard Tonson— Jacob Tonson was the leading member of the booksellers' committee and the largest single contributor to the common fund—whose title to *The Spectator* was clear by virtue of the first Jacob Tonson's purchase of the copyright from Addison and Steele. Equally clear was the fact that the statutory copyright on *The Spectator* had long expired. The sole question, then, was whether the Tonsons still owned *The Spectator* even though the statutory term had expired, and this depended on a determination of whether authors did have a common-law right. Possibly Addison's reputation as a champion of authorial rights was a factor in selecting *The Spectator* as the property in dispute.

Whatever might be said about the relationship of the case to the London booksellers' scheme to intimidate the country booksellers and drive the Scottish reprints out of the English market, or about the collusive relationship between plaintiff and defendant—it appears that the Tonsons were in agreement with Collins that there would be no appeal if the decision went against him—there is no question that *Tonson v. Collins* was fairly and seriously argued. Alexander Wedderburn, an ambitious young Scot who was later to become a lord chancellor but who at this time may have been recommended because of his Scottish background, made the first argument for the plaintiff. Edward Thurlow, a young lawyer who also later became a lord chancellor, argued for the defendant. The second argument for the plaintiff was made by William Blackstone, who was at this point Vinerian professor at Oxford and who also reported the case. Joseph Yates, who was soon to sit on the Court of King's Bench, argued for the defendant.

> I have been informed, from the best authority, that so far as the Court had formed an opinion, they all inclined to the plaintiff. But as they suspected that the action was brought by collusion; and a nominal defendant set up, in order to obtain a judgment, which might be a precedent against third persons; and that therefore a judgment in favour of the plaintiff would certainly have been acquiesced in; upon this suspicion, and because the Court inclined to the plaintiff, it was ordered to be heard before all the Judges. (*ER* 98:214)

So said Justice Edward Willes several years later, reporting Mansfield's representation of the case to him. Mansfield's somewhat unusual decision to have the case heard by all twelve common-law judges—the judges of King's Bench, Common Pleas, and Exchequer assembled *en banc*—was evidently intended to give the decision the widest possible authority so that, even if no appeal were filed, the court's determination would stand. When positive evidence of collusion was found, however, the judges refused to proceed because they thought that the precedent of a collusive judgment would set a dangerous example. Even so, the pleadings were important: this was the first time that the common-law question was fully argued.

Wedderburn opened for the plaintiff by defining the issue in the form that the booksellers now wanted it to be understood: the case concerned the rights of authors in general, not the rights of any particular bookseller. The author, he argued, had a natural right to the profits of his industry. Through the author's efforts, a property grounded in invention was created; learning would be adversely affected if this property were not recognized. Moreover, English law had always recognized this property. To demonstrate, he ran through the history of literary property from the start of printing. Nothing in the early printing privileges, the crown copyrights and patents, or the various laws relating to the Stationers' Company, he said, contradicted the idea of a prior right of property, and there was much to support it. The Statute of Anne was not intended to take away the author's property right but merely to provide additional remedies; indeed the statute included a saving clause for all antecedent rights. Finally, the Chancery cases where injunctions were issued even for works on which the statutory terms had expired confirmed the existence of common-law property.

Wedderburn's argument for the common-law right descended from Mansfield's a decade earlier in *Tonson v. Walker* (1752). Thurlow probably modeled his argument for the defense on that of the Scottish booksellers in *Millar v. Kinkaid* in the Court of Session. A literary composition—or, more precisely, "the idea of the composition, as it lies in the author's mind, before it is substantiated by reducing it into writing"—was not a possible subject of property: it had not "one idea of property annexed to it" (*ER* 96:171). And if such a property were recognized for books, how would it be possible not to extend it to other inventions? Thurlow, who had a reputation for sarcasm, dismissed Warburton's *Letter from an Author* as "miserable stuff" (*ER* 96:172); in fact, he said, the right of property in books and machines was the same, and both depended on acts of the state rather than natural right. He too went through the history of literary property, arguing that both the printing privileges and the Stationers' Company's monopoly on printing derived from the crown, that the term "property" in the statute arose from the stationers' assertions and was not to be taken literally, and that the Chancery injunctions were not definitive.

The second hearing took place in the following term. Blackstone opened for the plaintiff with a response to Thurlow's rejection of the notion that ideas could be property. Echoing Warburton, he asserted that property was established as much by mental as by bodily labor. Indeed, he said, even the idea for a composition had all the essential requisites to make it the subject of property. The chief requisite for property was that it must be a thing of value. Where was the value in a literary property? Not in the writing and not in the words: "Characters are but the signs of words, and words are the vehicle of sentiments. The sentiment therefore is the thing of value, from which the profit must arise" (*ER* 98:181). Next he turned to the historical record, discussing the Chancery precedents with particular attention to those cases about unpublished manuscripts or those about works whose statutory term had clearly expired.

Yates, speaking for the defendant, acknowledged that property might be established by mental labor, and acknowledged the author's right to his composition before it was published, but he maintained that the act of publication necessarily made the work common:

> I allow, that the author has a property in his sentiments till he publishes them. He may keep them in his closet; he may give them away; if stolen from him, he has a remedy; he may sell them to a bookseller, and give him a title to publish them. But from the moment of publication, they are thrown into a state of universal communion. (*ER* 98:185)

What were the plaintiffs claiming? The defendants had never taken the original manuscript of the work; the paper and print from which the books had been made belonged to the defendants. The plaintiffs could not then claim that the printed books were theirs.

> All the plaintiffs can claim is, the ideas which the books communicate. These, when published, the world is as fully in possession of as the author was before. From the moment of publication, the author could never confine them to his own enjoyment . . . The act of publication has thrown down all distinction, and made the work common to every body; like land thrown into the highway, it is become a gift to the public. (*ER* 98:185)

Yates went on to examine the precedents, discussing, as the other lawyers had done, the practices of the Stationers' Company (company by-laws were private regulations), the privileges (given to printers rather than authors and limited in term), the statute (the specification for fourteen years and no longer was sufficient to determine the issue), and the Chancery injunctions (not final rulings and not necessarily grounds for a case at common law).

The arguments in *Tonson v. Collins* reveal much about how the copyright issue was approached by the eighteenth-century lawyers in Mansfield's court. Considerable effort was expended in the examination of precedents. Whatever Mansfield's devotion to principle, precedents were still the traditional source of the common law. But the precedents were confusing and inconclusive. Could the old practices of the sixteenth and seventeenth centuries provide precedents for the mid-eighteenth century? Moreover, the statute itself was in some respects ambiguous: despite the obvious intent to establish a limited term of protection, its text was a palimpsest inscribed with traces of the entire history of press regulation as well as an earlier version of precisely the same struggle it was now being asked to resolve. The heart of the struggle became the argument from principle. Drawing on reason and natural law, the pleaders attempted to demonstrate that in the very nature of things there either was or was not a common-law right of literary property.

In *Tonson v. Collins* the basic shape of the literary-property debate was realized. The struggle came to a head in *Millar v. Taylor* (1769) in which Mansfield's court, ruling on an issue that involved James Thomson's poem *The Seasons*, upheld the author's common-law right and the perpetuity of literary property. Many of the same actors reappear. William Blackstone—joined by John Dunning, who had a great reputation as a pleader—again argued for the right; Edward Thurlow—joined by Arthur Murphy, well known as an author as well as a lawyer—argued against it. Joseph Yates, who dissented from the majority, delivered his opinion from the bench.

The divided decision in *Millar v. Taylor*—three to one in favor of the common-law right—was unusual. Indeed, as Mansfield pointed out, *Millar* was the first instance of a final difference of opinion in his court since he became chief justice thirteen years earlier in 1756 (*ER* 98:250). That unanimity was a tribute to Mansfield's powers of administration and persuasion, but on the literary-property question neither Mansfield nor his brethren could move Yates from the anti-common-law position he had taken before the bar in *Tonson v. Collins*.[4] Yates gracefully apologized for the "singularity" of his opinion and expressed his regret at his "misfortune" in finding himself alone in it, but he refused to yield. "I can safely say," he added, "that, be it ever so erroneous, it is my sincere Opinion" (*ER* 98:248). Yates's conviction is striking. So too is the conviction expressed by the three judges in the majority. To Justice Edward Willes, the principle at stake was straightforward: "It is certainly not agreeable to natural justice, that a stranger should reap the beneficial pecuniary produce of another man's work" (*ER* 98:218). Justice Richard Aston concurred:

> The invasion of this sort of property is as much against every man's sense of it, as it is against natural reason and moral rectitude. It is against the conviction of every man's own breast, who attempts it. He knows it not to be his own; he knows, he injures another: And he does not do it for the sake of the public, but malâ fide et animo lucrandi. (*ER* 98:222)

And Lord Mansfield said he was in complete agreement with Willes and Aston (*ER* 98:251).

Mansfield's own opinion in *Millar v. Taylor* was founded on an author's prepublication right. It had "all along been expressly admitted," he said, "that, by the common law, an author is intitled to the copy of his own work until it has been once printed and published by his authority" (*ER* 98:251). There were Chancery cases that had been cited in support of this right, and Mansfield explicitly recalled two, *Pope v. Curll* (1741) and *Duke of Queensberry v. Shebbeare* (1758), in which the court remarked that possession of a manuscript of a book did not necessarily mean that one had the right to print it. But the source of the prepublication right could be found neither in the Chancery cases, which were recent and few in number, nor in immemorial custom

---

4. Yates dissented again the following year in *Perrin v. Blake* and shortly after this arranged to be transferred to Common Pleas. It was said that his decision to leave King's Bench was caused by Mansfield's resentment, but he might also have been distressed by feeling that he was the only judge to disturb the unanimity of the court. See Holdsworth, *History* 12:482–483.

because the introduction of printing was itself within memory. From what source, then, was the author's prepublication right drawn?

> From this argument—Because it is just, that an author should reap the pecuniary profits of his own ingenuity and labour. It is just, that another should not use his name, without his consent. It is fit, that he should judge when to publish, or whether he ever will publish. It is fit he should not only choose the time, but the manner of publication; how many; what volume; what print. It is fit, he should choose to whose care he will trust the accuracy and correctness of the impression; in whose honesty he will confide, not to foist in additions: with other reasonings of the same effect. (*ER* 98:252)

The whole question in the case, accordingly, was whether the author's right continued after publication. If the continuance of his right were denied, the author would "not only be deprived of any profit, but lose the expence he has been at." There would be other consequences as well:

> He is no more master of the use of his own name. He has no control over the correctness of his own work. He can not prevent additions. He can not retract errors. He can not amend; or cancel a faulty edition. Any one may print, pirate, and perpetuate the imperfections, to the disgrace and against the will of the author; may propagate sentiments under his name, which he disapproves, repents and is ashamed of. He can exercise no discretion as to the manner in which, or the persons by whom his work shall be published.

"For these and many more reasons," Mansfield concluded, "it seems to me just and fit, to protect the copy after publication."

The opponents of the common-law right had questioned whether property could be immaterial. Mansfield observed that any general arguments against literary property made on the basis of the kind of property could be dismissed because they would also work against the prepublication right, which was admitted by both sides. The only objection made to the property specifically after publication was the argument that the copyright was necessarily made common by the act of publication. But why should the transfer of the paper of a printed book be regarded as a transfer of the copyright any more than the transfer of the paper of a manuscript? The objection that the copyright had to be common was based on circular reasoning: "The copy is made common, because the law does not protect it: And the law can not protect it, because it is made common" (*ER* 98:253). The question of the continuance of the author's right was not in fact one of possibility—copyright would be protected if the law protected it—but of choice: *ought* the law to recognize copyright as property? Was it "agreeable to natural principles, moral justice and fitness" to provide for the author's right after publication as well as before? Mansfield had already answered this question on the basis of principle. Now he added that the "general consent of this kingdom, for ages, is on the affirmative side" and proceeded to invoke Milton's authority,[5] the authority of the Chancery injunctions, the general agreement of the court in *Tonson v. Collins*, and the established principle of perpetual crown copyright. The most plausible objection to the continuation of the right, Mansfield said, would be an argument that the statute abolished the common-law right. But had there been any intention on the part of the legislators to take away the common-law right, it would have been expressly enacted.

In pointing out the circularity of Yates's objection that publication rendered the author's property common, Mansfield reached deep into the idea of property. Copyright would be protected if the law chose to protect it—that is to say, at least by implication, property was whatever the law said it was. (But this was not to say that property was wholly arbitrary, for the law after all was based either on common usage or on natural justice.) In basing his argument on the author's prepublication right, Mansfield also reached deep into history. As we have seen, the sense that the author properly controlled the publication of his texts developed toward the end of the middle ages. This early concept of authorial control was based on honor and reputation rather than on specifically economic interests; yet, in practice, any inchoate right to control first publication could imply a specific right to license publication for a sum. Thus matters of propriety became entangled with matters of property. The Statute of Anne was of course essentially a trade-regulation act concerned with economic interests. But the very first case under the statute, *Burnet v. Chetwood*, in which Thomas Burnet's heir sought to prevent the publication of an English translation

5. "The single Opinion of such a Man as *Milton*, speaking, after much Consideration, upon the very Point, is stronger than any Inferences from gathering Acorns and seizing a vacant Piece of Ground" (*ER* 98:253). Mansfield was probably thinking of Milton's much-cited dictum in *Areopagitica* about "the just retaining of each man his several copy" (Hughes 749).

of a work that had caused Burnet embarrassment, was more concerned with propriety. Likewise, *Pope v. Curll* was a mingled affair in which matters having to do with propriety found a means of legal expression through the statute.

Mansfield's opinion in *Millar v. Taylor* continued this mingling of propriety and property. In fact, Mansfield founded his notion of copyright precisely on the aporia between the two—significantly, in the eighteenth century "propriety" was still interchangeable with "property"—that had been present from the earliest days of printing. The prepublication right, he argued, was based both on the justness of the author's receiving the profits of his labors and on the fitness that he should control the use of his name and the release of his work. If the postpublication right were denied, the author would be deprived of his profit and would not be master of his name and his text. In his presentation, the claims of propriety and property reinforced and validated each other: the personal interests moralized the economic claim, while the property claim gave legal weight to the personal interests. This was a compelling representation of the total authorial interest in a work.[6] Implicitly, this was also a representation of the work itself as a commodity. The crucial point was that the work was an integral product of the author's will. Its value therefore depended on its correctness and accuracy in propagating the author's sentiments, and the testament to its correctness was the mark of the author's name.

Mansfield concluded his opinion in *Millar v. Taylor* with a reminder that he personally had "traveled" in the literary-property question for many years, starting with the early Chancery cases in which he was counsel. He recounted in detail his long association with the issue, declared that the elaborate arguments both in *Tonson v. Collins* and in the present case confirmed him in the opinion he had always held: the Court of Chancery had done right in giving relief to authors independent of the statute; so far as he was concerned, the subject of literary property at large was "exhausted."

---

6. Patterson, who regards the mingling of personal and economic rights as a key weakness in Anglo-American copyright law, remarks that in *Millar v. Taylor* Mansfield "skillfully conflated the rights of the author and bookseller and invested copyright with the author's moral rights. The end result was to foreclose the future development of the author's rights in his work independent of copyright because copyright preempted the field" ("Free Speech, Copyright, and Fair Use" 30).

Shortly after *Millar v. Taylor* was decided, a partisan account of the case entitled *Speeches or Arguments of the Judges of the Court of King's Bench in the Cause of Millar against Taylor* was published in Scotland, with explanatory notes that derided the majority views and praised Yates's dissent. In an appended essay, the editor of the volume discussed the general state of literary property and assured Scottish printers and booksellers that in Scotland there was no right of literary property apart from the statute. Within two years, this point was confirmed by the Court of Session in *Hinton v. Donaldson* (1773).

This case, which concerned a popular compilation of biblical materials made by an English vicar, Thomas Stackhouse, in effect provided a resolution for Scotland of issues that had first been evoked in the same court some thirty years earlier in *Millar v. Kinkaid*. Was there an author's common-law right? In declaring that there was not, the Scottish judges were conscious of dissenting from Lord Mansfield's judgment: "I have had much difficulty, from the weight of the sentiments of a learned judge, who presides in the Court of King's Bench; for whose opinion, as well as for his person, I entertain the highest esteem, and whom I have ever considered as one of the brightest ornaments of the law" (Boswell, *Decision* 33). So spoke the presiding judge as he prepared to deliver his opinion against the common-law right. Lord Gardenston also pointedly alluded to Mansfield when he remarked, "The splendid error of one great man may mislead many" (22). But no matter how respectful of Mansfield they might be, the Scottish judges were not inclined to defer to the King's Bench decision.

A patriotic note runs through their opinions. Lord Kennet, the first to speak, began by announcing that English law was beside the point. "I will not meddle with the law of England," Kennet said, "in the first place, because I do not profess to understand that law; and, secondly, because I think it ought to have no influence in determining upon the law of Scotland" (1). Likewise, Lord Kames remarked, "What may be the law of England, with respect to the question at present under deliberation I pretend not to know. Nor is it necessary that I should know; because an alleged trespass committed in Scotland against the pursuer, and prosecuted for damages in the Court of Session, must be determined by the law of Scotland" (18). And Scottish law did indeed differ from English law in several important respects, one being that the Scots had received Roman law, which never recognized the concept of immaterial property, as part of their common law, whereas the English had not. Political and national considerations aside, this in itself would probably have been sufficient to determine the Court of Sessions' decision.

In King's Bench the authorial right had been affirmed on grounds of principle. As Mansfield had said, it was "just and fitting" that the author should have dominion over the products of his intellectual labor, and he could find no evidence that the Statute of Anne was intended to limit or take away such a property. As for the practical consequences of establishing the common-law right—would an author's right give the London booksellers a perpetual monopoly and a stranglehold on the book trade in Britain?—Mansfield had said nothing. So far as he was concerned, evidently, the justness of the fundamental principle rendered all other considerations secondary. The Scottish judges, on the other hand, were concerned with consequences, and Lord Coalston pointed out that the economic consequences of affirming the common-law right would be considerable. Coalston remarked that although the issue was framed in terms of authors' rights, the court's decision would in fact make little difference in the price that authors were paid for their works. "But though the question is of no great importance to authors," he continued,

> yet it is a question in which the booksellers of London, on the one side, and the whole subjects of this country in general, and more particularly all the other booksellers in Britain, on the other side, are deeply concerned: for if the pursuer shall prevail in this question, the plain consequence will be, to establish a perpetual monopoly in favour of the booksellers of London, not only over most of the valuable books which have been hitherto published in this kingdom, but also over all books which may be published in time coming. (27)

Thus Coalston identified how establishment of the common-law right would assure the London booksellers an eternal monopoly.

By an overwhelming vote of eleven to one, the judges of the Court of Session determined that whatever might be the law in England, in Scotland the author did not have a common-law right. After *Hinton v. Donaldson*, then, there were two directly contradictory precedents on the literary-property question: in England literary property was perpetual; in Scotland it was limited in term.

"Labour gives a man a natural right of property in that which he produces: literary compositions are the effect of labour; authors have therefore a natural right of property in their works" (Enfield 21). This was the essence of the argument for the author's right as it was made in the law courts and in the controversial pamphlets associated with the literary-property debate. This argument was compelling precisely because it so perfectly incorporated the classical liberal discourse with its assumptions about the priority of the individual and the sanctity of property. Liberty and property: the freedom of the individual to employ his efforts to create property and the freedom to dispose of that property as he saw fit. These were the principles inscribed by reason in the very order of nature. How could they be denied in the case of the author?

The classical discourse of possessive individualism did not exhaust the possibilities for political thought in eighteenth-century England. J. G. A. Pocock, among others, has explored the power of the discourse of republican virtue—"civic humanism," as Pocock terms it in *The Machiavellian Moment*—and one might well imagine a counterargument from the opponents of perpetual copyright framed in terms of the claims of the public and its need to ensure free circulation of ideas. Samuel Johnson touched on such a counterargument in 1773 when, according to Boswell, he "descanted on the subject of Literary Property" at dinner:

> There seems, (said he,) to be in authours a stronger right of property than that by occupancy; a metaphysical right, a right, as it were, of creation, which should from its nature be perpetual; but the consent of nations is against it, and indeed reason and the interests of learning are against it; for were it to be perpetual, no book, however useful, could be universally diffused amongst mankind, should the proprietor take it into his head to restrain its circulation . . . For the general good of the world, therefore, whatever valuable work has once been created by an authour, and issued out by him, should be understood as no longer in his power, but as belonging to the publick; at the same time

the authour is entitled to an adequate reward. This he should have by an exclusive right to his work for a considerable number of years. (Boswell, *Life* 2:259)

And in the debate over *Donaldson v. Becket* on the floor of the House of Lords the following year, Lord Effingham said that perpetual copyright constituted a danger to the liberty of the press and the constitutional rights of the people.

But in English law courts, the usual mode of argument was, as David Lieberman has reminded us, associated most closely with scholastic legal traditions and the discourse of individualism (9–10).[7] Then what principle could the opponents of perpetual copyright invoke in order to counter the claims of property? Was perpetual copyright a monopoly? Not at all, the proponents responded; the author's exclusive right to his work did not deprive the public of anything that had existed before the composition was created. Was publication a gift to the public?[8] No, responded the proponents, only an explicit transfer could take a property away. The strategy, finally, of the opponents was not to counter the author's property claims directly, but to shift the grounds of the debate so as to raise questions about the definition of property. "That every man is intitled to the fruits of his own labour, I readily admit," Yates said in *Millar V. Taylor*. "But he can only be intitled to this, according to the fixed constitution of things; and subject to the general rights of mankind, and the general rules of property" (*ER* 98:231). An object of property must be capable of distinct and separate possession.

> But the property here claimed is all ideal; a set of ideas which have no bounds or marks whatever, nothing that is capable of a visible

7. In republican France and early nineteenth-century America, however, the discourse of civic virtue did figure in copyright matters. In "Enlightenment Epistemology and the Laws of Authorship in Revolutionary France, 1777–1793," Carla Hesse points out that the French authors' rights laws of 1791 and 1793 represented the author not as a property-owning private individual but as a public servant who received limited rights in his work as recompense for service to the state. Likewise, in the great American copyright case of *Wheaton v. Peters* (1835), which raised the question of whether U.S. Supreme Court reports were private property, the classical liberal claims were, as Meredith McGill observes, effectively countered by the argument that the free circulation of texts is an essential guarantor of liberty.

8. In arguing that publication constituted a gift to the public, Yates came close to the characteristic republican concern with the commonweal. But the foundation of his contention was a scholastic argument from the nature of property rather than an argument from civic duty. Even if he wished to do so, Yates maintained in *Tonson v. Collins,* there was no way that an author could confine his published ideas to his own enjoyment (*ER* 96:185).

possession, nothing that can sustain any one of the qualities or incidents of property. Their whole existence is in the mind alone; incapable of any other modes of acquisition or enjoyment, than by mental possession or apprehension; safe and invulnerable, from their own immateriality: no trespass can reach them; no tort affect them; no fraud or violence diminish or damage them. Yet these are the phantoms which the Author would grasp and confine to himself: and these are what the defendant is charged with having robbed the plaintiff of. (*ER* 98:233)

The same ideas might very well occur independently to different people. Would this mean that each would be a separate proprietor of the same idea? Could Newton claim exclusive property in the laws of the universe?

The crux of this argument was the premise that a literary composition was essentially a collection of ideas. This was plausible at a time when the category of "literature" had not yet been specialized toward imaginative writing, and Bacon, Newton, and Locke were regarded equally with Shakespeare and Milton as classics of literature. Moreover, the dominant conception of composition at this time was derived, as M. H. Abrams emphasizes (159–167), from empirical psychology with its notion of the mind as a mechanism producing a train of associated images and ideas. Such ideas were the materials from which the writer, like an intelligent artisan or architect, assembled his composition according to a plan. But if a literary composition was essentially a collection of ideas, why should copyrights be treated differently from patents? This was the question raised in *A Letter to a Member of Parliament* in 1735, when the booksellers were seeking an extension of the copyright term, and it was the point made by both Thurlow and Yates in *Tonson v. Collins*. Indeed it was, as the author of a pamphlet published shortly after *Tonson v. Collins* remarked, "the strongest hold, wherein the opponents of literary property have entrenched themselves."[9] As Baron James Eyre put it in his opinion in *Donaldson v.*

9. *A Vindication of the Exclusive Right of Authors* 9. This was one of two pamphlets that carried on the arguments from *Tonson v. Collins* in the public press while the case was still pending. *A Vindication* was a response to *An Enquiry into the Nature and Origin of Literary Property*, which gave further arguments for why ideas could not be property and for why literary and mechanical invention were to be seen as similar. The anonymous author of *An Enquiry* says that at first he supported the author's right, but upon examining "the Principles on which it was founded, they proved so unsubstantial, so void of Reality, that they eluded

Becket, the "Exactitude . . . of the Resemblance between a Book and any other mechanical Invention" was plain:

> There is the same Identity of intellectual Substance; the same spiritual Unity. In a mechanic Invention the Corporeation of Parts, the Junction of Powers, tend to produce some one End. A literary Composition is an Assemblage of Ideas so judiciously arranged, as to enforce some one Truth, lay open some one Discovery, or exhibit some one Species of mental Improvement. A mechanic Invention, and a literary Composition, exactly agree in Point of Similarity; the one therefore is no more entitled to be the Object of Common Law Property than the other. (*Cases of the Appellants and Respondents* 34)

Furthermore, it was plain that the Statute of Anne treated copyrights on the model of patents.

The proponents of perpetual copyright focused on the author's common-law right. Those who argued against it focused on the work. Thus the two sides established their positions by approaching the issue from opposite directions. Yet, however approached, the question centered on the same pair of terms, the author and the work, a person and a thing. The complex social process of literary production—relations between writers and patrons, writers and booksellers, booksellers and readers—became peripheral. Abstracting the author and the work from the social fabric in this way contributed to a tendency already implicit in printing technology to reify the literary composition, to treat the text as a thing. In the early modern period, as I mentioned earlier, the dominant conception of literature was rhetorical. A text was conceived less as an object than as an intentional act, a way of doing something, of teaching and delighting. Also the old copyrights of the Stationers' Company were not so much property rights in the sense of rights of possession of an object as personal rights to do something, namely to multiply copies of a particular title. Now, however, in the course of the literary-property struggle, copyright was coming to be thought of as, to use Blackstone's phrase in the *Commentaries,* a claim to "sole and despotic dominion . . . in total exclusion of the right of any other individual in the universe" (2:2). Indeed Blackstone himself, a jurist who

---

my Search" (2). Part of the pamphlet is a refutation of Warburton's *Letter of an Author.* Collins attributes *An Enquiry* to Warburton himself, who would thus have experienced an extraordinary change of mind (85). But I can find no supporting evidence for this attribution.

consistently supported the author's common-law right, was an identifiable figure in the process of this transformation.

The opponents of perpetual copyright spoke of literary property as "ideal." Blackstone at first seemed to accept this characterization when he maintained in *Tonson v. Collins* that the "one essential requisite of every subject of property" was "that it must be a thing of value," and that the value of a literary property lay wholly in the "sentiment" (*ER* 96:180, 181). But then, under pressure from Yates who was insisting that no distinction could be made between copyrights and patents, he elaborated his discussion of the subject of property. Invoking Warburton on the difference between literary and mechanical invention, Blackstone observed that whereas two engines might resemble each other, they could never be identical because materials and workmanship must differ. But every duplicate of a literary text was the same text, because its essence was immaterial. Warburton had characterized this essence as the book's "doctrine," a term equivalent to Blackstone's own earlier "sentiment." Now, though, Blackstone, subtly shifted the characterization of the essence of a book to a fusion of idea and language:

> Style and sentiment are the essentials of a literary composition. These alone constitute its identity. The paper and print are merely accidents, which serve as vehicles to convey that style and sentiment to a distance. Every duplicate therefore of a work, whether ten or ten thousand, if it conveys the same style and sentiment, is the same identical work, which was produced by the author's invention and labour. (*ER* 96:189)

And a few years later, he restated this new formula in authoritative form in the second volume of his *Commentaries:*

> When a man by the exertion of his rational powers has produced an original work, he has clearly a right to dispose of that identical work as he pleases, and any attempt to take it from him, or vary the disposition he has made of it, is an invasion of his right of property. Now the identity of a literary composition consists intirely in the *sentiment* and the *language;* the same conceptions, cloathed in the same words, must necessarily be the same composition: and whatever method be taken of conveying that composition to the ear or the eye of another, by recital, by writing, or by printing, in any number of copies or at any period of time, it is always the identical work of the

author which is so conveyed; and no other man can have a right to convey or transfer it without his consent, either tacitly or expressly given. (2:405–406)

"The same conceptions, cloathed in the same words"—dressed in language, the author's sentiments have assumed an aura of corporeality.

The writer of the 1735 *Letter of an Author to a Member of Parliament* had identified first possession as the ground for the author's property. Likewise, Blackstone in the *Commentaries* identified "occupation"—the Roman doctrine whereby one might establish an estate by taking possession of unclaimed land—as the ground for the author's right, and it was in the section devoted to "Title to Things Personal by Occupancy" that he took up the topic of literary property. Occupancy, he explained at the start of this section, was once the only way to acquire property, but in civil society it had been restrained and for the most part things found without owners belonged to the king. In a few instances, however, "the original and natural right of occupancy is still permitted to subsist" (2:401). Blackstone listed seven instances, each directly related to the material world, after which he turned to literary property. Thus even as he defined literary property as essentially incorporeal—"the identity of a literary composition consists intirely in the *sentiment* and the *language*"—Blackstone presented it in the *Commentaries* as only another in a list of material goods that included, for example, items seized from an enemy or items found in the sea.[10]

The reifying metaphor of literary property as a landed estate was, as we have seen, well established by the middle of the eighteenth century. This trope does not appear directly in the *Commentaries*, but it is implicit in Blackstone's use of "occupancy." The estate metaphor did, however, emerge in *Tonson v. Collins.* Yates, we recall, had spoken of a published work as abandoned "like land thrown into the highway." Blackstone replied that, on the contrary, publishing a book was like providing a number of keys to a private estate. By attaching his name

10. Duncan Kennedy discusses the way Blackstone's *Commentaries* transforms social relations into property relations through a process of abstraction and reification. Blackstone's characteristic strategy is to divorce a personal right such as an advowson—the right of choosing a parson for a church—from its corporeal basis and then to treat the abstracted right as a kind of thing. In this process a right of a person assumes the appearance of an absolute property right (see Kennedy 334–350). This is exactly how Blackstone treats literary property. In the case of literary property, however, the process of abstraction had started well before Blackstone in Hardwicke's decision in *Pope v. Curll.*

and other proprietary signs, an author indicated that he did not abandon his work: "it is more like making a way through a man's own private grounds, which he may stop at pleasure; he may give out a number of keys, by publishing a number of copies; but no man, who receives a key, has thereby a right to forge others, and sell them to other people" (*ER* 96:188). Thus Blackstone treated copyright as if it were indeed a kind of estate. Dressed in language, the writer's ideas became a property that could be conveyed from owner to owner in perpetuity according to the same principles as a house or a field.

To summarize the logic of the arguments in *Tonson v. Collins* and the succeeding cases, then, we might say that there were three principal exchanges between the parties. First, the proponents of perpetual copyright asserted the author's natural right to own his creation. Second, their opponents replied that ideas could not be treated as property and that copyright could only be regarded as a limited privilege of the same sort as a patent. Third, the proponents responded that the property claimed was neither the physical book nor the ideas communicated by it but something else, an entity consisting of style and sentiment combined. What we observe here is the simultaneous emergence in legal discourse of the proprietary author and the literary work. The two concepts are bound to each other. To assert one is to imply the other, and together, like the twin suns of a binary star locked in orbit, they define the center of the modern literary system.

6

⌒⌒⌒

Literary Property Determined

At one level, the literary-property question was a legal struggle about the nature of property and how the law might adapt itself to the changed circumstances of an economy based on trade. At another, it was a contest about how far the ideology of possessive individualism should be extended into the realm of cultural production. At still another, it was a commercial encounter, played out in the form of a national contest between England and Scotland, in which a deeply entrenched business establishment was challenged by outsiders. The complex layering of the literary-property struggle generated a number of intriguing contradictions, among them that it was in the name of the liberal value of "property"—and authorial property no less—that the London booksellers were defending a monopolistic system with roots in the medieval guild culture. Their principal challenger was a scrappy and determined Scottish businessman, "who saw a new and lucrative opening in the bookselling trade, and availed himself of it" (Gray 182).

Alexander Donaldson's career as a bookseller began in 1750 in Edinburgh shortly after the determination of *Millar v. Kinkaid* in the Court of Session. After this decision was announced, Donaldson, according to his own account, took counsel from both Scottish and English lawyers who confirmed him in his opinion that copyright was limited to the statutory term. Thereupon he went into the bookselling business in a large way, specializing in inexpensive reprints of standard works whose copyright term had expired, including according to the *Eighteenth-Century Short Title Catalogue* works by Defoe, Fielding, Gay, Locke, Milton,

Pope, Shakespeare, Swift, Thomson, and Young. Donaldson prospered, and his house and shop became something of a center for literary Scotsmen, among them the young James Boswell who, together with his friend Andrew Erskine, published an anthology of contemporary Scottish poems with Donaldson. Eventually Donaldson started a journal, the biweekly *Edinburgh Advertiser,* which also did very well.

For many years after their unsuccessful appeal of *Millar v. Kinkaid,* the great London booksellers ignored Donaldson and the other Scots. But then in the late 1750s and early 1760s they took up their campaign to establish the common-law copyright and to drive the Scottish reprint business out of England. In 1763 Donaldson responded by boldly opening his own shop in London, where he sold his books at 30–50 percent under the usual London prices. Samuel Johnson, for one, was incensed. Boswell reports that Johnson, who held the London booksellers in high regard, "was loud and violent against Mr. Donaldson," saying that it had always been understood by the trade that "he, who buys the copy-right of a book from the authour, obtains a perpetual property" (*Life* 1:438, 439). A barrage of harassing Chancery lawsuits followed the opening of the shop. Donaldson retaliated by publishing *Some Thoughts on the State of Literary Property Humbly Submitted to the Consideration of the Public* in which he threatened to sue for damages caused by "unlawful combination, whereby the *London* booksellers have conspired to beat down all opposition, and to suppress the sale of every book reprinted in the other part of the united kingdom" (10).

Despite having to contend with what he later, in his petition against the Bookseller's Relief Bill of 1774, termed "the united force of almost all the eminent booksellers of London and Westminster" (*Petitions and Papers* 10), Donaldson was determined to keep his reprint business—from which he was making a fortune, despite his legal expenses. In 1765, after the aborted decision in *Tonson v. Collins,* Donaldson succeeded in getting dissolved two injunctions against him for publication of James Thomson's poems. Sounding much like his predecessor Lord Hardwicke in *Tonson v. Walker* a dozen years earlier, Lord Chancellor Northington, who heard the arguments in *Osborne v. Donaldson* (1765) and *Millar v. Donaldson* (1765), remarked that the issue of the common-law right was "a point of so much difficulty and consequence, that he should not determine it at the hearing, but should send it to law for the opinion of the judges." Northington said that "he desired to be understood as giving no opinion on the subject." He added, however, that he thought it might be "dangerous to determine that the author has a perpetual property in his books, for such a property would give him not only a right to publish, but to suppress too" (*ER* 28:924). Probably Donaldson would have welcomed taking the question further, as Northington invited—it was, he said, "his fixed purpose that the law should be finally settled in the Supreme Court of the kingdom" (*Petitions and Papers* 10)—but neither Osborne nor Millar wished to pursue the issue. Instead, Millar took action against Robert Taylor of Berwick upon Tweed, again in connection with Thomson's *The Seasons*, and thus began the landmark case of *Millar v. Taylor.*[1]

Why Taylor and not Donaldson? The London booksellers probably wanted to avoid another appeal to the House of Lords; the peers, after all, had a history of being unsympathetic to their claims, going back at least as far as their resistance in 1735 to the booksellers' attempt to extend the copyright term. Very likely the desire to avoid an appeal was one of the motives that led to collusion in *Tonson v. Collins*. So the booksellers selected Taylor, whom they were able to persuade to acquiesce in the judgment against him (*Speeches and Arguments* 121–122), as the target for their next big case. Donaldson would not have been so easily persuaded. Relegated for the moment to the legal sidelines, Donaldson used his press to continue his campaign. In 1767, shortly after Millar initiated his suit against Taylor, Donaldson brought out a carefully argued pamphlet against perpetual copyright, *Considerations on the Nature and Origin of Literary Property*, and in 1768 he provocatively issued three new Thomson publications: another edition of *The Seasons*, a two-volume edition of Thomson's *Dramatic Works*, and a four-volume complete *Works*. The following year, within weeks of the King's Bench determination, he published an angry comment on the case, *A Letter from a Gentleman in Edinburgh to his Friend in London Concerning Literary Property.*[2]

1. Millar did not charge Taylor with printing the books, only with publishing, exposing them to sale, and selling them in England, and indeed the *Eighteenth-Century Short Title Catalogue* lists no editions of *The Seasons* with Taylor's imprint. Possibly the books involved were printed by Donaldson, who had issued *The Seasons* in 1761 shortly after the statutory copyright expired, and a two-volume set of Thomson's complete *Poetical Works* in 1763.

2. This pamphlet is dated 8 May 1769—the *Millar* decision was announced on 20 April—and signed "A Reader of Books." It bears no imprint, but the typography suggests that the pamphlet was printed for Donaldson (see Ransom, "From a Gentleman in Edinburgh"). The *Letter* repeats passages and phrases verbatim from the earlier Donaldson

Andrew Millar died in June 1768 while *Millar v. Taylor* was pending. A year later, after the momentous King's Bench decision, Millar's copyrights were put up for sale by his estate, and Thomas Becket and a group of other London printers and stationers purchased the rights in *The Seasons* and a number of other Thomson poems for £505. In January 1771 the new proprietors of Thomson, armed with the King's Bench decision, filed a bill in Chancery against Donaldson and his brother John, with whom he was associated in connection with the 1768 edition of *The Seasons*. An injunction was granted, and in November 1772 it was made perpetual in a hearing before Lord Chancellor Apsley who, as he explained later at the time of Donaldson's appeal, was merely affirming the decree as a matter of course, pursuant to the decision in *Millar v. Taylor*. Simultaneously, John Hinton's case against Donaldson over *Stackhouse's Bible*, initiated in the Court of Session just before the start of Becket's action in Chancery, was making its way to a decision. On 27 July 1773 the Court of Session rendered its decision in favor of Donaldson, and with this precedent in hand to offset *Millar v. Taylor*, Donaldson appealed the Chancery injunction to the House of Lords. It was time to achieve his "fixed purpose" of seeing the law of literary property settled by Britain's highest court.

Donaldson v. Becket, then, represented both an appeal of *Millar v. Taylor*, to which Donaldson was not a party, and an attempt to secure a confirmation of the Court of Session's decision in *Hinton v. Donaldson*. Sir James Burrow's report of *Millar v. Taylor*, entitled *The Question Concerning Literary Property Determined by the Court of King's Bench*, had been brought out the previous spring while the Scottish case was pending.[3] In order to make available a comparable account of *Hinton v. Donaldson*, Donaldson's old friend James Boswell, who was one of the junior counselors in the case, "worked up his notes" and persuaded

---

pamphlet, *Considerations,* which is attributed by the *Eighteenth-Century Short Title Catalogue* to John Maclaurin, later Lord Dreghorn, the Scottish lawyer who later served as Donaldson's senior counsel in *Hinton v. Donaldson* (1773).

3. In the preface to *The Question Concerning Literary Property* Burrow notes that the Scottish account of *Millar v. Taylor*—*Speeches or Arguments of the Judges of the Court of King's Bench in the Cause of Millar against Taylor*—was both "full of Faults" and "in Every Body's Hands" and that therefore "Some whom I have long known, and whose Friendship I am proud of" urged him to prepare his own report as a separate publication. Burrow's "Preface," dated 5 April 1773, suggests that his book was published in time for the Court of Session to read before ruling on *Hinton v. Donaldson* in July. In any event, the book was available and widely advertised the following winter at the time of the appeal to the House of Lords.

"several of the judges to revise their opinions freely for the benefit of peers and posterity" (Brady 88). Boswell's *Decision of the Court of Session upon the Question of Literary Property,* published by Donaldson in an elegant edition, appeared according to an advertisement in the *Morning Chronicle* on 1 February 1774, just in time for the opening of the appeal three days later.

Throughout the proceedings in the House of Lords, public interest was intense. On the first day of argument, according to a letter from London in Donaldson's *Edinburgh Advertiser,* several hundred people had to be turned away for lack of space (8 Feb. 1774), and the *Morning Chronicle* reported that the "House below the Bar was . . . exceedingly crowded" and that "Mr. Edmund Burke, Dr. Goldsmith, David Garrick, Esq; and other literary characters, were among the hearers" (5 Feb. 1774). Dr. Johnson was probably not in attendance—at least during the first days of proceedings—but he was, as one would expect, interested. Johnson's thoughts on the literary-property question seem to have developed since 1763, when he had declaimed against Donaldson. Although he insisted on the strength of the author's right, he still held that, for "the general good of the world," copyright should be limited (Boswell, *Life* 2:259). On 7 February he wrote to Boswell, noting that the issue was before the Lords and affirming that he "would not have the right perpetual" (Boswell, *Life* 2:272–273). Meanwhile the London newspapers devoted multiple columns to the proceedings, reporting the arguments of the lawyers and judges in great detail, and they printed dozens of letters to the editor from lawyers, booksellers, and others commenting, often very colorfully, on the case. The general interest even spawned at least one rather feeble joke. Having been reprimanded for stealing an old woman's gingerbread cakes baked in the form of letters, a cheeky schoolboy was supposed to have defended himself by explaining that "the supreme Judicature of *Great Britain* had lately determined that *lettered* Property was common" (preface, *The Cases of the Appellants*).

"No private cause has so much engrossed the attention of the public, and none has been tried before the House of Lords, in the decision of which so many individuals were interested." So reported the *Edinburgh Advertiser* after the decision was rendered (1 March 1774), and though Donaldson's paper can hardly be regarded as a neutral source, there is no reason to doubt its assertion about the perceived significance of the case at the time. "There hardly exists a person connected in the most distant manner with the press, who will not, in some degree, be affected by the event of this appeal," wrote William Woodfall in the *Morning Chronicle* as he acknowledged his own warm interest in the matter (5 Feb. 1774). On 22 February the peers voted to overturn the Chancery injunction, and in Scotland the reaction was tumultuous: "Great rejoicing in Edinburgh upon victory over literary property: bonfires and illuminations" (Ross 143). In England, at least among those connected with the London book trade, the reaction was also intense. A paragraph that appeared in the *Morning Chronicle* and in a number of other places after the decision claimed that a vast amount of property had been annihilated:

> By the above decision of the important question respecting copy-right in books, near 200,000 l. worth of what was honestly purchased at public sale, and which was yesterday thought property is now reduced to nothing. The Booksellers of London and Westminster, many of whom sold estates and houses to purchase Copy-right, are in a manner ruined, and those who after many years industry thought they had acquired a competency to provide for their families now find themselves without a shilling to devise to their successors. (*Morning Chronicle* 23 Feb. 1774)

Whether the London booksellers' panic was justified is doubtful—they were by no means ruined by the decision—but the note of desperation that marks their utterances is probably sincere enough. The works of Shakespeare, Bacon, Milton, Bunyan, and others, all the great properties of the trade that the booksellers had been accustomed to treat as private landed estates, were suddenly declared open commons.

In 1774 the House of Lords decided cases by a general vote of the peers, lawyers and laymen alike. Great weight was usually given to the opinions of the lawyers, but the practice of lay peers not being recognized when the House of Lords sat as a court had not yet been instituted. In important cases such as *Donaldson v. Becket*, however, the twelve common-law judges of the realm—the judges of King's Bench, Common Pleas, and the Exchequer—would be summoned to the House to hear the arguments of counsel and to give their advice on matters of law, after which the peers would debate the issue and vote.

The arguments in *Donaldson* were made by lawyers who had been involved in the literary-property question for years. Alexander Wedderburn and John Dunning made the arguments in favor of the common-law right, as they had earlier in *Tonson v. Collins* and *Millar v. Taylor* respectively. (William Blackstone, who had also argued in *Tonson* and *Millar*, was now on the bench and would deliver his opinion as a judge.) Edward Thurlow, who had made the opening arguments on the opposite side in both *Tonson* and *Millar*, did so again in this climactic case, joined by Sir John Dalrymple. Arthur Murphy, who had joined Thurlow on the defendant's side in *Millar*, drew up the written brief against the perpetual right (Boswell, *Life* 2:273–274). After the arguments, which added little of substance to what Sir James Burrow called this "old and often-litigated question" (*ER* 98:201), Lord Chancellor Apsley put three questions to the judges. First, did the author have a common-law right to control the first publication of his work? Second, did the author's right, if it existed, survive publication? Third, if the right survived publication, was it taken away by the statute? To these questions Charles Pratt, Lord Camden, who was a former chief justice of Common Pleas, a lord chancellor, and the major opponent of perpetual copyright in the House of Lords, added two more. Did the author or his assigns have the sole right to a composition in perpetuity by the common law? Was this right in any way restrained or taken away by the statute? Insofar as they repeat the substance of the second and third of the original questions, Camden's questions were redundant, but he was trying to remind the judges and peers that the case was not just one of authors' rights but of booksellers', and that the issue was copyright in perpetuity.

The opinions of the judges, delivered one by one over the course of three days, were divided. On the first question, the judges divided 8 to 3 in support of the author's right. On the second, the vote was 7 to 4, again in support of the author's right. There is, however, a puzzle connected with the vote on the third question. According to both the *Journal of the House of Lords* and the standard legal and historical references, the vote on this question was 6 to 5 against the author's right—that is, the majority of the judges were of the opinion that the statute took away the author's right. But contemporary newspaper and other accounts give good reason to believe that the clerk of the House of Lords made an honest error in recording the opinion of one of the judges. Most likely the tally was 6 to 5 in favor of the common-law right surviving the statute (see Appendix B). Note that only eleven judges voted: Lord Mansfield remained silent. James Burrow explained that Mansfield, whose opinion was well known, abstained "from reasons of delicacy" since the case was in effect an appeal from his own court (*ER* 98:262). Had Mansfield voted, the tally would have been a substantial seven to five in favor of the common-law right surviving the statute. But the judges' opinions were only advisory; the final decision would be made by vote of the entire House; and in *Donaldson* the floor debate appears to have been very important.

Any issue thrown into the House of Lords was always in danger of becoming entangled in a network of personal and political rivalries. Lord Mansfield was the acknowledged champion of the common-law right. Lord Camden, who opened the debate with a speech of an hour and a half together with a motion that the Chancery decree against Donaldson be reversed, was Mansfield's "lifelong political opponent" (Holdsworth, *History* 12:306). Camden, a Chathamite Whig, differed from Mansfield on most matters and had clashed with him many times before, most recently and bitterly in December 1770 when the issue was the rights of juries in cases of seditious libel. In that affair Camden directly challenged Mansfield to defend his opinion in a debate in the House of Lords, but Mansfield, to the dismay of some, refused.[4] Before the *Donaldson* appeal came on for debate, Camden had been inactive in the House of Lords for several years, but now he rose to challenge his old antagonist. Given their acrimonious history, it is hard to avoid the suspicion that part of Camden's purpose in leading the attack on the common-law right was a desire to embarrass Mansfield by having the peers repudiate his determination in *Millar v. Taylor*.

Camden differed from Mansfield in matters of jurisprudence even as he did in matters of politics. Whereas Mansfield was willing to ignore

4. This famous episode involved Mansfield's instructions to the jury in *Rex v. Woodfall*, which concerned the Junius letters. Mansfield had instructed the jury only to consider whether Woodfall had printed the letters, not whether the letters themselves were libelous, which he reserved as a point of law. According to one opinion, Mansfield in not responding to Camden's challenge showed an "equal want of courage and of self-possession" (Fifoot 46). But perhaps Mansfield, as Holdsworth suggests, refused to rise to the bait because he was beginning to weary of political strife (*History* 12:475). The episode is recounted in Cobbett 16:1302–22, as well as in Eeles 113–114.

precedents if they conflicted with what he regarded as fitness, Camden as lord chancellor was "always careful to follow precedents, and to give full effect to the statute law" (Holdsworth, *History* 12:308). The substance of Camden's most Whiggish speech against the common-law right—a speech that was reported in great detail in the London press and was referred to for decades—had to do with precedents. All the supposed precedents for the common law right were "founded on Patents, Privileges, Star-chamber Decrees, and the Bye Laws of the Stationers Company; all of them the Effects of the grossest Tyranny and Usurpation; the very last Places in which I should have dreamt of finding the least Trace of the Common Law of this Kingdom" (*Cases of the Appellants* 48). Nor could the Chancery decrees be taken as an authority for the common-law right: indeed he himself, like other lord chancellors before him, had issued such injunctions even though he knew the claim was doubtful. Where, then, was its foundation? It had been said that it would be "contrary to the Ideas of private Justice, moral Fitness and public Convenience" not to adopt the notion of literary property. But the business of the common-law judges was "to tell the Suitor how the Law stands, not how it ought to be." If it were otherwise, if each judge were to have "a distinct Tribunal in his own Breast," the law would become irregular and uncertain.

> That excellent Judge, Lord Chief Justice *Lee*, used always to ask the Council, after his Argument was over, "Have you any Case?" I hope Judges will always copy the Example, and never pretend to decide upon a Claim of Property, without attending to the old black Letter of our Law, without founding their Judgment upon some solid written Authority, preserved in their Books, or in judicial Records. In this Case I know there is none such to be produced. (*Cases of the Appellants* 52–53)

Thus Camden, accusing Mansfield of disregarding precedent and undermining the objectivity of the law, directly challenged Mansfield's premises in the literary-property question and indeed his whole jurisprudence. In effect he charged him, as David Lieberman notes in his discussion of the matter, with legislating from the bench (95–98).

As early as 16 February, after the first group of four judges had read their opinions, the *Public Advertiser* reported that Mansfield would not give his opinion as a judge but would speak later as a peer. On 22

February, after all the judges had spoken, the *Advertiser* repeated that Mansfield would speak as a peer. Camden's speech plainly called for a response, but, contrary to all expectation, Mansfield was silent. "As Lord Mansfield had so warmly taken the Respondents side of the question on the determination in the Court of King's Bench between Miller and Taylor in 1769, it was yesterday much wondered at that his Lordship did not support his opinion in the H. of Peers." So reported the *Morning Chronicle* on 23 February. The London booksellers, who had counted on Mansfield as their strongest bulwark in the House of Lords, felt betrayed and they were furious:

> It was his duty to have given an opinion on one side or other, and the neglecting to do so, was a manifest breach of his duty. Judges are paid by the public, and should render those services attendant on their office; and I should be glad to see a law passed to oblige them to a strict performance of their duty. (*Edinburgh Advertiser* 29 April 1774)

Why was Mansfield silent? The situation was reminiscent of Camden's challenge over jury rights four years earlier. Whatever it was that impelled him to keep his peace then—lack of courage or, more likely, lack of spirit for further bruising conflict—perhaps restrained him again. His opinion on literary property was a matter of public record, and it had been supported by a majority of the judges. If the House of Lords were inclined to overturn the Chancery decree and thereby declare that literary property was not perpetual, probably nothing he could say would materially affect the outcome.

Lord Camden was followed in the debate by Lord Chancellor Apsley, who had issued the original injunction and now delivered the coup de grâce to perpetual copyright by seconding the motion to overturn his own decree. He had made the decree, Apsley said, entirely as a matter of course pursuant to the judgement in *Millar v. Taylor*, and he viewed the action merely as a step toward a final determination of the copyright question in the House of Lords. As for the substance of the matter, he saw no precedents that could support the respondents in their argument. Moreover, he said he had evidence in the form of original letters from Dean Swift showing that the sense of Parliament was against the common-law right at the time of the Statute of Anne.[5] So his opinion was with the appellants. Three other peers spoke—Lord

5. I have not been able to identify any such letters.

Lyttleton, who supported perpetual copyright as an encouragement to authors; the Bishop of Carlisle, who believed that literary property was limited to the statutory term, though the statute was defective and needed revision; and Lord Effingham, who thought perpetual copyright a danger to constitutional rights—and then the question was called. Eighty-four peers were present for the vote, an extraordinary show of interest (*LJ* 34:33).[6] Although Cobbett reports that the vote was 22 to 11 in favor of reversing the Chancery decree (17:1003), neither the *Journal of the House of Lords* nor the contemporary newspapers indicate a formal division of the House, and the *Public Advertiser* explicitly says there was no division (23 Feb. 1774). Most likely the decision was by simple voice vote. As Donaldson's newspaper reported, undoubtedly with some exaggeration about the unanimity of the House, Lord Chancellor Apsley desired "all who were for reversing the judgment, to say Content, and such as were of a different opinion to say, Not: Nothing was heard but the word Content" (*Edinburgh Advertiser* 1 March 1774).

In voting as they did against the perpetual right, the Lords went against the judges, whose vote on the third question was 6 to 5—7 to 5 if Mansfield were counted—in favor of the common-law right surviving the statute. There is no great mystery about why they did so: the House of Lords had long been antipathetic to the London booksellers' monopolies, and the outcome in *Donaldson v. Becket* was consistent with the House's previous treatment of copyright questions. But on what basis did the peers make their determination? What understanding of the nature of copyright did they adopt? Were they persuaded that there never was a common-law right? Or did they believe that there was but that it ended with publication? Or that it was taken away by the statute? Were they persuaded by Lord Camden's argument that common-law determinations had to be founded on solid written authorities, or were they more influenced by the position associated with Joseph Yates that ideas could not in the nature of things be treated as property? Some peers may have voted on the basis of a legal theory, but many others, I suspect, were less concerned with the basis than with

6. For comparison, sixty-eight peers heard the king's speech from the throne on 13 January 1774, the opening day of the session. Fifty-six peers were present on 4 February, the opening day of the arguments of counsel, and approximately the same number for the later days of argument. Seventy-four peers were present on 15 February, the first day that the judges' opinions were heard, and sixty-five on the two later days of opinions, 17 and 21 February.

the result. Thus the peers gave an answer to the literary-property question, but they did not provide a rationale. "It is more satisfactory . . . to convince by reason, than merely to silence by authority," Blackstone had said in the course of arguments in *Tonson v. Collins* (*ER* 96:182). But what the House of Lords did in *Donaldson v. Becket* was finally no more than to declare by authority that copyright henceforth would be limited in term.[7]

The drama was not yet quite over. Within a week of the Lords' decision, the booksellers of London and Westminster had a petition signed by 87 persons before the House of Commons. For years they had relied on the King's Bench determination in their dealings, the petitioners said, but now many thousands of pounds of property had suddenly been declared to have no existence; they hoped that the House, taking their hardship into consideration, would grant them whatever relief seemed appropriate (*Petitions and Papers* 3–4). A committee was appointed, and acrimonious hearings were held in which many of the lawyers who had taken part in the appeal, including Dalrymple, Murphy, Thurlow, and Wedderburn, participated (Cobbett 17:1077–1110). Meanwhile a flood of counterpetitions from Scottish booksellers and others were placed on the table, including an individual counterpetition from Alexander Donaldson, describing his struggle and hoping that Commons would not now grant the London booksellers a further term (*Petitions and Papers* 9–12). After many hearings and much debate, a relief bill providing for an additional fourteen years of copyright was passed by Commons at the end of May (*CJ* 34:788). But when it reached the House of Lords, where according to the *Public Advertiser* (3 June 1774) Lord Denbigh said "it was nothing else but encouraging a Monopoly," and where Lord Camden and Lord Chancellor Apsley once again both spoke strongly against it, it was thrown out on the first

7. Howard Abrams suggests that the lords "grounded their decision on the position that copyright had never existed as a right at common law" (1157). This was the position both of Lord Camden, who made the motion to reverse the decree, and of Lord Chancellor Apsley, who seconded it. But Camden's and Apley's speeches, important as they were, cannot be regarded as the equivalent of a modern majority opinion. Many lay peers perhaps deferred to Camden and Apsley on the technical legal issues, though there was always the contrary opinion of Lord Mansfield to give pause to any lay peer who was seeking a legal authority to follow. As Whicher remarked some years ago, the House of Lords overturned the ruling in *Millar v. Taylor*, but "when we ask what doctrine, precisely, the lords preferred to that which they thus cast aside, Clio (that coy muse) simply shrugs" (126).

reading by a vote of 21 to 11 (*LJ* 34:232). "Lord Mansfield," noted the *Public Advertiser* (3 June 1774), "did not attend the House of Peers upon the Occasion."

The literary-property question was a legal and commercial struggle, but it was also a contest between representations of authorship at a time when writings were becoming commodities. The proponents of perpetual copyright spoke of the need to reward authors. John Dalrymple, however, argued to the House of Lords that perpetual copyright would be pernicious to the interests of literature. It would "encourage the Spirit of writing for Money; which is a Disgrace to the Writer, and to his very Age." Honor and reputation should be sufficient inducements for authors "without that mean one of Profit" (*Cases of the Appellants* 24). Lord Camden picked up this theme. There was, he said, speaking to the question of whether copyrights could be distinguished from patents, no real difference between authors and inventors, since both were equally beneficial to society. No common-law claim could be made for inventors, and none should be made for authors. "Science and Learning are in their Nature *publici Juris,* and they ought to be as free and general as Air or Water." Camden went on in the high rhetorical style, speaking of authors and inventors as "those favoured Mortals, those sublime Spirits, who share that Ray of Divinity which we call Genius" and must not keep to themselves "that Instruction which Heaven meant for universal Benefit" (*Cases of the Appellants* 53–54). Note here the collapse of any differentiation between invention and writing under the heading of "instruction" or "science." As the passage continues, however, science becomes equivalent to writing and the point that Camden is making becomes clear: genuine authors do not write for money.

> We know what was the Punishment of him who hid his Talent, and Providence has taken Care that there shall not be wanting the noble Motives and Incentives for Men of Genius to communicate to the World those Truths and Discoveries which are nothing if uncommunicated . . . Glory is the Reward of Science, and those who deserve it, scorn all meaner Views: I speak not of the Scribblers for bread, who teize the Press with their wretched Productions; fourteen Years is too long a Privilege for their perishable Trash. It was not for Gain, that

Bacon, Newton, Milton, Locke, instructed and delighted the World; it would be unworthy such Men to traffic with a dirty Bookseller for so much as a Sheet of Letter-press. When the Bookseller offered *Milton* Five Pounds for his Paradise Lost, he did not reject it, and commit his Poem to the Flames, nor did he accept the miserable Pittance as the Reward of his Labor; he knew that the real price of his Work was Immortality, and that Posterity would pay it. (*Cases of the Appellants* 54)

Camden's strained rhetoric in this much-quoted passage suggests his difficulty in finding an effective representation of authorship to accord with his representation of science as naturally free. By 1774 many respectable writers—most notably Samuel Johnson—were acknowledged authors by profession. The bookselling trade was elaborately developed, representing one of the most significant accumulations of capital in the country. But Camden's need to present the author as uncontaminated by economic transaction drives him into an archaic expression of disgust with dirty booksellers, perishable trash, and scribblers for bread in the anti-Grub Street vein of the earlier part of the century. And this negative evocation of mortality and materiality generates the reciprocally exaggerated representation of genuine authors as sublime spirits infused with "that Ray of Divinity which we call Genius" and driven by noble motives of glory and immortality. The allusion to the parable of the talents betrays the religious springs of this rhetorical dematerialization. But the invocation of Milton is significant as well, for it is Milton in "Lycidas" and *Paradise Lost* who seems to be the immediate source of the image of the divinely inspired poet thirsting for immortality, a topos here drained of all but the traces of Miltonic spiritual urgency.

Lord Camden's mystification of authors as sublime spirits divorced from the marketplace elicited a quick response from the celebrated republican historian Catharine Macaulay, who had followed the case and the reports of Camden's speech in the press and who within weeks of the decision issued *A Modest Plea for the Property of Copyright.*[8] Macaulay accepted Camden's dismissal of the precedents claimed for

8. Macaulay's preface, dated 9 March 1774, just over two weeks after the decision, explains that she wrote the pamphlet in a great hurry and at a distance from London with only the newswriters to depend on for her information about the case. The avowed purpose of the pamphlet was to persuade Camden, whom Macaulay professed to admire and to whose

literary property—the right was founded on equity and moral fitness rather than on precedent, she said—but she was sarcastic about his representation of authors:

> There are some low-minded geniusses, who will be apt to think they may, with as little degradation to character, traffic with a bookseller for the purchase of their mental harvest, as opulent landholders may traffic with monopolizers in grain and cattle for the sale of the more substantial product of their lands. They will be apt to consider, that literary merit will not purchase a shoulder of mutton, or prevail with sordid butchers and bakers to abate one farthing in the pound of the exorbitant price which meat and bread at this time bear. (14–15)

Camden had invoked Shakespeare, Bacon, Newton, Milton, and Locke to show that true geniuses had no view of personal gain in their works. Macaulay discussed each of these writers to show that none was quite so disinterested as he represented. Shakespeare, for example, was plainly more concerned with filling the theater than with instructing mankind, as was evident from "that abundance of low ribaldry to please a barbarous audience, which load and disgrace the most excellent of his dramatic pieces" (20).

But Macaulay had difficulty with another aspect of Camden's speech as well, for she mightily objected to his classifying authors with inventors. Just as writers had been unrealistically elevated—"with the intention of depriving authors of the honest, the dear-bought reward of their literary labours, they have been raised a little higher instead of lower than the angels"—they had been "levelled with the inventors of a very inferior order" (17). The author was engaged in the improvement of the human mind, whereas the inventor was concerned with the production of luxuries or at any rate "conveniencies, which are not absolutely necessary to the ease of common life." Also there was a great

---

influence she attributed the Lords' decision, to support a legislative securing of permanent copyright. But if this was truly her purpose, her sarcastic style was, to say the least, impolitic. The *Public Advertiser* for 25 March 1774 reported the following anecdote: "A noble L—d, who took a great Lead in the Affair of Literary Property, was asked his Opinion of Mrs. M——y's 'Modest Plea for the Property of Copy Right:' I think, replied his L——p, *it is a Copy of the Lady's Countenance.* That is very probable, said a Gentleman who stood by, and I do not wonder since that is the Case, that she should be desirous of converting her *Copy-hold* into *Free-hold.*" For information about Macaulay, whose best-known work was a multivolume history of England under the Stuarts, see Donnelly.

difference in the way the products of inventors and authors were received by the public. "Every common capacity can find out the use of a machine; but it is a length of time before the value of a literary publication is discovered and acknowledged by the vulgar" (18). Camden's resuscitation of the anti-Grub Street rhetoric of dirty booksellers and perishable trash betrays his anxiety about the contamination of authorship by the marketplace. Macaulay accepts the marketplace; yet her deprecatory rhetoric of inferior orders and common capacities betrays her anxiety about its leveling force. She objected to Camden's mystification of authors, his raising of authors "a little higher instead of lower than the angels." But she too was engaged in mystifying authorship. If authors were not higher than angels, they were evidently not greatly lower and plainly were superior to most of humankind.

The opponents of perpetual copyright were unable to produce an effective representation of authorship with which to counter the Lockean representation developed by the defenders of the author's right. Indeed Camden's comments about the proper reward for authors not only prompted Catharine Macaulay's sarcastic remarks about low-minded geniuses and shoulders of mutton, but they became something of a locus classicus for an obsolete view of authorship and a target at which defenders of authors' rights continued to take aim for many decades. Robert Southey, for example, agitating for revision of the copyright law in an essay in the *Quarterly Review* in 1819, cited the passage about glory and asked, "Is it possible that this declamation should impose upon any man?" (211). And Thomas Noon Talfourd in 1837, also citing the glory passage, asked, "Do we reward our heroes so? Did we tell our Marlboroughs, our Nelsons, our Wellingtons, that glory was their reward, that they fought for posterity, and that posterity would pay them?" (9). Thus although the struggle concluded with a rejection of the London booksellers' claim that copyright was perpetual, it by no means concluded with a rejection of the powerful representation of authorship on which that claim was based—and this affected the way in which the Lords' decision came to be understood.

A year before the decision in *Donaldson v. Becket*, Samuel Johnson, we recall, "descanted on the subject of Literary Property" at dinner, coming down on the side of limited copyright. So he was reasonably satisfied with the result in *Donaldson*, though he thought the present copyright term too short. In a letter dated 7 March 1774, probably written at the request of the bookseller William Strahan to use in lobbying for the booksellers' relief bill, Johnson called the Lords' decision "legally and politically right." On the one hand, the author had a natural right to the profits of his work; on the other, it was wrong that a useful book should become "perpetual and exclusive property"; therefore the author must purchase the protection of society by resigning "so much of his claim as shall be deemed injurious or inconvenient to Society." Johnson recommended an extension of the present two fourteen-year terms to a single one of the author's lifetime plus thirty years. This would in most cases yield a total term of about fifty years, which would be "sufficient to reward the writer without any loss to the publick" (*Johnsonian Miscellanies* 2:444–445).

Johnson understood the decision in *Donaldson* as a compromise between the author's claim and the broader needs of society, but the peers themselves had articulated no such theory. As we have seen, they simply resolved the practical question of perpetuity. This was sufficient for the needs of the moment, but in the longer run it was necessary to make some sense of their vote, to reach some understanding as to the theory of copyright behind the limited term. What developed in the years after 1774 was a belief that *Donaldson* represented a compromise along lines similar to those that Johnson articulated, a belief that the decision curtailed the author's right without rejecting it entirely.

This understanding of *Donaldson* was made possible by the way the case was reported by James Burrow, whose excellent law reports were, and still are, regarded as authoritative. At the time of *Donaldson* it was technically a crime to print an account of a case on appeal in the House of Lords. *Donaldson* had of course been widely reported in the press, and in fact shortly after the decision two full reports were published as pamphlets under the titles *The Cases of the Appellants and Respondents in the Cause of Literary Property* and *The Pleadings of the Counsel Before the House of Lords in the Great Cause Concerning Literary Property*. But Burrow held an official position as Master of the Crown Office; so when he gave notice of *Donaldson* as part of his account of *Millar v. Taylor* in his 1776 collection of King's Bench reports, he discreetly limited himself to printing the record as it appeared in the *Minute Book* of the House of Lords. Like the *Minute Book,* Burrow gave the questions and the judges' votes, but no account of their speeches. At the conclusion he added a tally, a comment about Lord Mansfield, and a note about the reversal:

> So that of the eleven Judges, there were eight to three, upon the first question; seven to four, upon the second; and five to six, upon the third.
>
> It was notorious, that Lord Mansfield adhered to his opinion; and therefore concurred with the eight, upon the first question; with the seven, upon the second; and with the five, upon the third. But it being very unusual, (from reasons of delicacy,) for a peer to support his own judgment, upon an appeal to the House of Lords, he did not speak.
>
> And the Lord Chancellor seconding Lord Camden's motion "to reverse; the decree was reversed." (*ER* 98:262)

In presenting the tally for the third question as 5 to 6 against the author's right, Burrow perpetuated the error of the clerk of the House and made it appear as if the reversal followed as a matter of course from the judges' vote. Moreover, his suppression of Lord Camden's and Lord Chancellor Apsley's speeches made it seem as if the author's common-law right was not seriously challenged; on the contrary, he conveyed the impression that the determination in *Donaldson* consisted of a solid affirmation of the author's right, followed by a narrow decision that perpetuity was taken away by the statute.[9] This representation was a distortion in a number of respects. In fact only a single judge, Henry Gould of Common Pleas, had held that there was a common-law right impeached by the statute. (The others had either

9. Josiah Brown's subsequent account in the seventh volume of his *Reports of Cases, Upon Appeals and Writs of Error, in the High Court of Parliament* (1783) would not correct this impression. Brown's report includes a summary of the cases of the appellants and respondents as well as the questions put to the judges, but it does not give the substance of the judges' opinions or say anything about the floor debate. Unlike Burrow, Brown gives only the vote on the question of whether the statute impeached the common-law right. Five of the judges were in favor of the perpetuity or common-law right, he reports, and six were opposed whereupon it was ordered that the decree be reversed (*ER* 1:837–849). The fuller report of the case in the seventeenth volume of *Cobbett's Parliamentary History* was not published until 1813 and was less cited than Burrow and Brown. On the development of the interpretation of *Donaldson v. Becket* see Whicher, esp. 130, and Howard Abrams, esp. 1164–66. Both Whicher and Abrams emphasize the crucial role of Burrow's and Brown's reports.

held that there was no common-law right—or at any rate none that survived publication—or that it was not taken away by the statute.) But even so it had much to recommend it, for it made it possible to suppose that, even if perpetual copyright had been rejected, still an author had a natural right to property in his work. Thus some years later in *Beckford v. Hood* (1798), the King's Bench found that *Donaldson* did not take away a plaintiff's right to sue at common law during the statutory term (*ER* 101:1164–68), and by the early nineteenth century Robert Maugham was able to state bluntly in his important *Treatise on the Laws of Literary Property* (1828) that in *Donaldson* "it was determined by the House of Lords that the common law right was merged in the statute" (27).[10]

In the eighteenth-century debates themselves, the copyright issue had nearly always been framed in terms of absolutes: either authors had a common-law right or they did not. But if copyright was seen as a kind of compromise, then it became possible to reconsider the length of the copyright term, as Johnson had done. In 1814 a revised statute extended the copyright term to twenty-eight years after publication or the author's lifetime, whichever was longer, but this seemed paltry to those such as Robert Southey or William Wordsworth, who objected to any limitation. "The question is simply this," Southey said in his 1819 *Quarterly Review* essay: "upon what principle, with what justice, or under what pretext of public good, are men of letters deprived of a perpetual property in the produce of their own labours, when all other persons enjoy it as their indefeasible right—a right beyond the power of any earthly authority to take away?" (211–212). And in a letter to J. Forbes Mitchell dated 21 April 1819, Wordsworth asked "why the laws should interfere to take away those pecuniary emoluments which are the natural Inheritance of the posterity of Authors" (*Letters* 3:535).

In 1837 Thomas Noon Talfourd, a friend of Wordsworth's and an author as well as a member of Parliament, opened a campaign for revision of the copyright act. Talfourd reminded Parliament that a majority of the judges in *Donaldson* determined that an author had a

10. This tradition of interpretation continues to the present day. In *Copinger and Skone James on Copyright*, the standard modern British treatise, Burrow's report is cited and we are told in terms similar to those in Maugham that it was "held by the majority of the judges that the common law right which an author had to copyright in his works became merged in the statutory right conferred by the Copyright Act" (5).

perpetual common-law right. In principle, he saw "no reason why authors should not be restored to that inheritance which, under the name of protection and encouragement, has been taken from them." Nevertheless, because copyright had long been treated as a matter of compromise between those who denied the author's right altogether and "those who think the property should last as long as the works which contain truth and beauty live," he would "rest satisfied with a fairer adjustment of the difference than the last act of Parliament affords" (8).

The term that Talfourd proposed—the author's lifetime plus sixty years—drew opposition from the book trade, most notably from Thomas Tegg, who specialized in cheap reprints, and this roused Wordsworth to action.[11] The poet addressed some fifty letters to individual members of Parliament urging them to support Talfourd's bill. He declined to present his own petition. "I am loth to think so unfavourably of Parliament as to deem that it requires petitions from authors as a ground for granting them a privilege, the justice of which is so obvious," he wrote to Talfourd on 18 April 1838 in a letter intended as a "public declaration" of his sentiments on the copyright bill and in which he reasserted his conviction that the author's right should be perpetual (*Prose Works* 3:313). But, in fact, personal petitions from authors were necessary to overcome the opposition. In 1839 Wordsworth, Southey, Thomas Carlyle, and Hartley Coleridge as well as other literary figures submitted petitions to Parliament (*CJ* 94:237); finally, under the stewardship of Lord Mahon, Parliament passed the Copyright Act of 1842, which lasted until the twentieth century. This provided a term of the author's lifetime plus seven years or forty-two years from publication, whichever was longer—a resolution not far off from what Johnson had proposed in 1774.

Let us note a striking reversal. In the eighteenth century the proponents of perpetual copyright were the booksellers. By the early nineteenth century, however, the trade had adjusted to the limited copyright term, and many had a vested interest in it; it was authors such as

11. On Wordsworth's involvement in the campaign that led to the copyright act of 1842, see Zall, Moorman 551–555, and the commentary in Owen and Smyser 3:303–306. On Tegg and the resistance to Talfourd's proposal, see Zall 134–135, and Feather, "Publishers and Politicians, Part II" 48–50.

Southey and Wordsworth who were now claiming that their rights should be perpetual.[12] *Donaldson v. Becket* is conventionally regarded as having established the statutory basis of copyright, and of course it did. But given the way *Donaldson* came to be understood, perhaps it should be simultaneously regarded as confirming the notion of the author's common-law right put forward by Mansfield and Blackstone.

12. Moreover by the nineteenth century the notion of the author's right might be internalized by a writer. Susan Eilenberg points out the frugality of Wordsworth's style, his characteristic blurring of the distinction between the verbal and the material, his literary territoriality and resentment of plagiarism, and remarks that Wordsworth's "attitude towards his poems sometimes resembled that of a landowner towards his lands" (357). Part of Wordsworth's concern with copyright was his interest in providing an estate for his family, but the obsessiveness of his concern suggests that psychological factors were also at work. The length of the copyright term was linked to the length of an author's life. Eilenberg argues, then, that Wordsworth's campaign can also be understood as associated with a fear of death and annihilation: to reform copyright was for him "to secure a refuge from oblivion" (369).

7

⤳ ⤳ ⤳

Property / Originality / Personality

As it happened, both *Millar v. Taylor* and *Donaldson v. Becket* were fought over the same property, James Thomson's long, reflective landscape poem, *The Seasons*. This was perhaps not entirely accidental. From the London booksellers' point of view, Thomson's poem—one of the most frequently reprinted works of the century and plainly a valuable property—was an excellent choice for litigation designed to establish the author's common-law right. Despite its popularity, *The Seasons* was not considered a national treasure on the order of Shakespeare's plays or *Paradise Lost*. Moreover, the title to Thomson's poem, purchased directly from the author, was easy to establish. For Alexander Donaldson too *The Seasons* represented an excellent choice for appeal because he was no doubt interested in forming his case in a way that challenged the King's Bench ruling as directly as possible.

But there is something almost uncannily appropriate in *The Seasons* being the text on which the two landmark literary-property cases turned, for in a sense Thomson's poem was the perfect Lockean literary work, the paradigm of the new mode of proprietary authorship. In *The Seasons* a changing landscape of mountains, meadows, forests, rivers, plains, and valleys is portrayed and made the occasion for moral and philosophical meditations. As John More wrote in a critical study published three years after *Donaldson v. Becket*, Thomson's method was to go directly to nature for materials and then to superimpose his original ideas and sentiments, with the result that familiar objects were cast in a new light. Thomson, writes More,

had immediate recourse to nature for all his materials, and she in-
trusted with confidence her secrets to his care. For however in other
respects he should offend against the established dogmas of criticism,
his poetry every where discovers the strongest traits of originality. All
his ideas, sentiments and versification seem peculiarly his own . . .
And what of all others is perhaps the most decisive mark of a poetical
mind, the objects he describes, though frequently common and familiar, strike us some how in a new light. (167–168)

According to Locke, private property is created when the individual
removes materials from the state of nature and mixes his labor with
them, thereby producing an item of personal property. Just so in *The
Seasons* the British landscape is appropriated by the poet and stamped
with the mark of his reflective personality.

"I confess, I do not know, nor can I comprehend any property more
emphatically a man's own, nay, more incapable of being mistaken, than
his literary works," wrote Justice Aston in *Millar v. Taylor* (*ER* 98:224).
What Aston had in mind, clearly, was just this imprinting of the
author's personality on his work. A work of literature belonged to an
individual because it was, finally, an embodiment of that individual.
And the product of this imprinting of the author's personality on the
common stock of the world was a "work of original authorship." The
basis of literary property, in other words, was not just labor but
"personality," and this revealed itself in "originality."

Joseph Addison was, we have seen, one of the first authors to call for
a statute to protect authors' property rights; and he was also one of the
earliest critics to espouse the superiority of original to imitative composition. In *The Spectator* 160 (3 Sept. 1711), published less than two
years after his discussion of literary property in *The Tatler*, Addison
distinguished between natural geniuses and those who submitted their
talents to the discipline of art. The latter kind of writer was by no means
inferior, but was always in danger of cramping his abilities with too
much imitation. "An Imitation of the best Authors, is not to compare
with a good Original," Addison wrote, "and I believe we may observe
that very few Writers make an extraordinary Figure in the World, who
have not something in their Way of thinking or expressing themselves
that is peculiar to them and entirely their own." A half century later

William Blackstone, writing about literary property in the *Commentaries,* also invoked originality: "When a man by the exertion of his rational powers has produced an original work, he has clearly a power to dispose of that identical work as he pleases, and any attempt to take it from him, or vary the disposition he has made of it, is an invasion of his right of property" (2:405–406). As already indicated, the production of the discourse of original genius coincided with that of authorial property. The logical point of connection was the idea of value: both were concerned with the worth of texts.

Henry Fielding was at once a practicing magistrate and a man of letters. Shortly after it was published in 1742, his own *Joseph Andrews* was the object of litigation in *Millar v. Ilive.* It is not surprising, then, to find the legal discourse of property interacting with literary issues in his work, albeit in a form suffused with irony. From January to July 1748 Fielding included a column entitled the "Court of Criticism" in his satirical paper, the *Jacobite's Journal.* Here in the manner of the newspaper court reports, Fielding dealt with literary matters. In number 11 (13 Feb. 1748), for example, he recounted how the "Corporation of *Grubstreet,*" asserting their sole proprietary right to publish "all low, scandalous Invectives, without the least Wit, Humour, Argument, or Fact" brought suit against the "Corporation of *Billingsgate*" over a scurrilous pamphlet. The defendants replied that when scandalous invectives included the use of opprobrious terms and downright name calling, then such works had always been adjudged the property of Billingsgate. The court agreed and the suit was withdrawn. In number 26 (28 May 1748) Fielding reported the suit of a group of booksellers against the author of a current political pamphlet "for having fraudulently taken a vast Quantity of Abuse against the Ministry" from other pamphlets already in print. The court issued a temporary injunction. At the "hearing," however, reported in the next issue (4 June 1748) the author responded that this abuse had all been printed many times over and therefore could not be considered the property of any particular bookseller; the court agreed and dismissed the case.

In the *Jacobite's* columns, the literary litigation in Chancery and elsewhere over the previous two decades provides Fielding with an extended metaphor for satire. In *Tom Jones* too the theme of literary property arises when Fielding discusses his practice of translating passages from ancient authors without acknowledgment: "The Antients may be considered as a rich Common, where every Person who hath the smallest Tenement in *Parnassus* hath a free Right to fatten his Muse"—or rather, since the moderns are so much poorer than the ancients, modern writers may be compared to "the large and venerable Body which, in *English,* we call The Mob" (620). The ancients are "so many wealthy Squires, from whom we, the Poor of *Parnassus,* claim an immemorial Custom of taking whatever we can come at" (621). But just as it is a point of honor among the mob not to rob one another, so it ought to be a point of honor among modern authors not to plagiarize one another, and so he pledges to "preserve strict Honesty towards my poor Brethren, from whom if ever I borrow any of that little of which they are possessed, I shall never fail to put their Mark upon it, that it may be at all times ready to be restored to the right Owner" (621).

Fielding's concern with literary ownership touches on the connection between originality and property: stupidly derivative writing cannot be treated as property, he would seem to be saying in the *Jacobite's Journal.* Samuel Richardson makes the connection clear. In 1753 a group of Irish booksellers surreptitiously procured the text of Richardson's new novel, *The History of Sir Charles Grandison,* and advertised it for sale in Dublin before it had been published in London. Richardson was furious: "Never was Work more the Property of any Man, than *this* is his. The Copy never was in any other Hand: He borrows not from any Author: The Paper, the Printing, entirely at his own Expence" (*Case of Samuel Richardson* 2). Richardson's claim can be related to that made two decades earlier in 1735 when it was asserted that the author's right was founded on an even more powerful argument than "occupation," for the author might be said "rather to create, than to discover or plant his Land" (*Letter to a Member of Parliament* 1). Richardson's was not merely an abstract claim to an author's right, but a specific assertion that in the case of this book the conception, the manuscript, the copyright, and the ink and paper of the printed volumes were all his own. Since the Statute of Anne did not reach to Ireland, however, Richardson had no recourse other than to complain in print—some months later he continued his protests in a second pamphlet, *An Address to the Public*—and to call for an improved law.

As both a substantial printer and an important author, Richardson was a unique figure in eighteenth-century book production. We can take him as a kind of emblem of the link between the book trade, concerned with property, and the discourse of originality, for it was Richardson who suggested to Edward Young that he write a treatise on original and moral composition—the full title, *Conjectures on Original Composition in a Letter to the Author of Sir Charles Grandison,* spells out the book's connection to Richardson—and it was also Richardson who printed it.[1] Between 1756 and 1759 the manuscript of the *Conjectures* went back and forth several times between Young and Richardson, and Richardson made detailed comments on it. Most of these comments had to do with matters of piety—Richardson suggested, for example, that Young insert a warning about setting human genius above revealed truth—but in at least one the connection between originality and property is implicit. "Suppose, sir, when you ask, What does the name of poet mean?" Richardson suggested, "you answer after some such manner as this—'*It means a maker,* and, consequently, *his work is something original, quite his own*'" (Young, *Correspondence* 449). Young himself touched on the connection when he addressed the author's need for independence. Writers must not be intimidated by the great authors of the past but must study and cultivate themselves. From this will come the distinctiveness of their works and their right to call themselves authors:

> Thyself so reverence as to prefer the native growth of thy own mind to the richest import from abroad; such borrowed riches make us poor. The man who thus reverences himself, will soon find the world's reverence to follow his own. His works will stand distinguished; his the sole Property of them; which Property alone can confer the noble title of an *Author.* (*Conjectures* 53–54)

"Property" here has more to do with "ownness" than with "ownership." Yet the word emerges from a metaphorical context that is emphatically mercantile in the contrast it draws between the home-produced goods of the original author and the imported goods of the imitative writer. The term inevitably takes on a commercial aura. But Young quickly

1. See McKillop, who discusses the surviving correspondence between Richardson and Young. On the relationship between Richardson and Young in general, see Eaves and Kimpel 182–187. For the correspondence between Richardson and Young, see Young, *Correspondence* 440–452, 482–492. In a stimulating paper William Warner discusses the association between Richardson and Young, arguing that there are ideological connections between Richardson's fictional projects and the doctrines of authorial property and original genius.

suppresses the word's commercial potential when, drawing on the trope of the literary work as an estate, he invokes the ancient feudal linkage between real estate and aristocracy—it is the literary estate itself that confers the "noble title of an *Author*." Thus "author" becomes analogous to "baron" or "earl," an honorific title grounded in authenticity and originality.

Perhaps if we are aware of the resonances of the real-estate image, we will hear a hint of suppression, too, in Young's characterization of original authors as public benefactors because "they extend the Republic of Letters, and add a new province to its dominion," as well as in his assertion that "The pen of an *Original* Writer, like *Armida*'s wand, out of a barren waste calls a blooming spring" (*Conjectures* 10). In any case, as the passage about the author's property suggests, the sense of the commodity value of writing is often just beneath the surface of eighteenth-century discussions of literary worth.

In the preface to his edition of Shakespeare, Samuel Johnson addressed the issue of worth in terms of longevity, proclaiming Shakespeare a classic on the basis of his having "long outlived his century, the term commonly fixed as the test of literary merit" (*Johnson on Shakespeare* 61). Johnson's claim was most conspicuously supported by the impressive series of annotated editions—Rowe (1709), Pope (1725), Theobald (1733), Warburton (1747)—through which the Tonson firm maintained its proprietorship of Shakespeare. Johnson's own edition, published in 1765, was the fifth and latest in this series, and it may not be unreasonable to suppose that the Tonsons provided Johnson with a full set of the previous editions from which to work. Literary value might thus be tangibly conceived as a row of books on a shelf—or as a record of receipts for regular republication. Shakespeare's universality was demonstrable: his works had proven themselves a perennially vendible commodity.

In both Johnson's preface and Young's *Conjectures* the sense of the commercial is, as it were, the unconscious of the text. What Johnson dwells on is Shakespeare's excellence, and what Young dwells on is the original author's nobility. As Linda Zionkowski has shown, there was considerable anxiety among authors in the middle years of the century about the commodification of writing. It was in the context of this anxiety—in particular a concern about the leveling that commodification involved—that authors such as Johnson, Goldsmith, and Fielding dismissed the mass of writers as "mere Mechanics" (Fielding, *Covent-Garden Journal* 1, 4 Jan. 1752) and developed the notion of the literary profession as a canonical group of "legitimate" authors.[2] Thus Johnson distinguished between the large number of "drudges of the pen, the manufacturers of literature, who have set up for authors" and the few writers who "can be said to produce, or endeavour to produce new ideas" (*Rambler* 145, 6 Aug. 1751). Likewise, Young represents imitative composition as "a sort of *Manufacture*." In a passage frequently cited as an anticipation of romantic organicism, Young contrasts the "vege-table nature" of original composition—"it rises spontaneously from the vital root of Genius"—with the lesser nature of imitative composition, which is "wrought up by those *Mechanics, Art,* and *Labour,* out of preexistent materials not their own" (*Conjectures* 12). The magician "raises his structure by means invisible," whereas the architect merely makes "skilful use of common tools" (*Conjectures* 26–27).

Young's mingled invocation of class and mechanism associates the *Conjectures* with the mid-century literary movement that Zionkowski has identified. Note that similar themes emerged at midcentury in the literary-property debates as well. Here, though, the concern was to differentiate not between higher and lower orders of literary producers but between authors and inventors in order to establish that copyright should be founded on a different basis. We recall, for example, that William Warburton in his *Letter from an Author to a Member of Parliament* (1747) presented literary composition as superior to mechanical invention, which was a mixed form of property, partly material and partly immaterial. William Blackstone, arguing the plaintiff's case in *Tonson v. Collins* (1760), invoked the language of class. "Mechanical inventions tend to the improvement of arts and manufactures, which employ the bulk of the people," Blackstone said. "But as to science, the case is different. That can, and ought to be, only the employment of a few" (*ER* 96:189). And, similarly, Catharine Macaulay in her *Modest Plea for the Property of Copyright* (1774) protested the grouping of authors with inferior inventors.

Both in the literary-property debates and in Young's *Conjectures* the task was to differentiate true authorship from mechanical invention and to mystify and valorize the former. As Terry Eagleton has observed, the

2. John Barrell discusses the eighteenth-century debate over the parallel question of whether painting was to be considered a mechanical or a liberal art (12–18).

representation of the artist as a transcendent genius is born "just when the artist is becoming debased to a petty commodity producer," and this mystification can be understood in part as "spiritual compensation for this degradation" (64–65). I should add that the mystification of the author also served the purposes of the ultimate proprietors of copyrights, the booksellers. The author might be represented as a noble or a conqueror or a conjurer, but in most cases the property he brought into being quickly passed into the hands of the booksellers, where it might increase greatly in value—as the Thomson properties did in Millar's hands, more than doubling over the thirty years he owned them.[3] Moreover, major literary properties were typically dispersed among many booksellers according to shares. A single author might be the fount of property for a large number of stationers, and the works of a major author such as Shakespeare or Milton would be, as Lord Kames remarked in *Hinton v. Donaldson*, "a vast estate."

At one point in the *Conjectures* Young seeks to demonstrate that "a spirit of *Imitation*" goes against the principles of nature. Nature "brings us into the world all *Originals*," he says: "No two faces, no two minds, are just alike; but all bear Nature's evident mark of Separation on them." Our birthright is distinctiveness, and yet this distinctiveness does not last: "Born *Originals*, how comes it to pass that we die *Copies*?" Unfortunately, we lose our native originality when "that medling Ape *Imitation* . . . snatches the Pen, and blots out nature's mark of Separation, cancels her kind intention, destroys all mental Individuality" (*Conjectures* 42). Nature, then, is a kind of author and we are her works: each of us is an original text produced by a creative genius; the visible mark of originality is the human face; and this in turn is the sign of the invisible distinctiveness of the mind. As an original text, the person produced by Nature's pen is destined to be an original author as well, until Imitation snatches the pen from Nature's hand and revises what she has written. Thus from "originals" we are reduced to "copies." Young's metaphorical fusion of textuality and personality, his equiva-

3. Millar purchased the Thomson copyrights in two lots, one directly from the author in 1729 and one in 1738 from John Mildan, for a total of £242 10s. After Millar's death the Thomson copyrights were sold in shares for £505 to a group of fifteen printers and booksellers. Becket was the senior shareholder, but all fifteen were technically respondents in *Donaldson v. Becket*. See *Cases of the Appellants and Respondents* 1–2.

lence of the making of books and the making of people, recalls the paternity trope, the book as the author's child. In this representation too, a continuity between author and work was posited—or, more precisely, an aspect of the author's essential "self" was conceived as somehow living in the text. Just so Milton in *Areopagitica* spoke of books as the "seasoned life of man preserved and stored up" (Hughes 720). What Young has done is to introduce the notion of original genius into the traditional discourse of authorship, thereby producing a representation in which the originality of the work, and consequently its value, becomes dependent on the individuality of the author. The Lockean discourse of property, let us note, was founded on a compatible principle—"Every Man has a *Property* in his own *Person*" was Locke's primary axiom—and thus the discourse of originality also readily blended with the eighteenth-century discourse of property. One logical point of connection between originality and property was *value;* another was *personality*—and of course the notions of value and personality were themselves deeply entwined.

Young's representation of personality as a text suggests the way in which a literary work in the eighteenth century was coming to be seen as something simultaneously objective and subjective. No longer simply a mirror held up to nature, a work was also the objectification of a writer's self, and the commodity that changed hands when a bookseller purchased a manuscript or when a reader purchased a book was as much personality as ink and paper. The emergence of this new commodity can be connected with the increasing tendency to read authors' works in the context of their biographies—Johnson's *Lives of the Poets* is the most prominent example—and with the rise of the novel, the literary form explicitly devoted to the display of character. *Pamela, Clarissa, Tom Jones, Tristram Shandy*—the very titles of the eighteenth-century novels suggested that what was changing hands in the purchase of reading matter was the record of a personality. Moreover, readers increasingly approached literary texts as theologians had long approached the book of nature, seeking to find the marks of the divine author's personality in his works. By 1827 Thomas Carlyle could remark in his "The State of German Literature" that the question with which the best critics were concerned was the discovery and delineation of "the peculiar nature of the poet from his poetry" (M. H. Abrams 226).

All the positing of original genius involved a major reassessment of the English canon, one in which such imitative writers as Ben Jonson and Alexander Pope were devalued. Interestingly, because of the pressure that the logic of literary property brought to bear on authorial personality, this reassessment was often cast in terms of the appraisal of character: "Such a one was Johnson, that he seems to have made it his study to cull out others sentiments, and to place them in his works as from his own mint. This surely is an odd species of improvement from reading, and savours very little of Invention or Genius: It borders nearly upon, if it is not really plagiarism" (Bowle 64). So wrote John Bowle, employing the suggestive metaphor of the author as the minter of money and presenting Ben Jonson as something of a criminal type assiduously at work gathering others' property. Young similarly associated Pope's imitative art with his Catholicism: "His taste partook the error of his Religion; it denied not worship to Saints and Angels" (*Conjectures* 67). Milton's art was also imitative, of course, but although for a time he stood accused of being a base plagiarizer, *Paradise Lost* could not be easily dismissed.[4] As Samuel Johnson represented him, it was by force of character that Milton rose above all previous imitators of Homer as the least indebted: "He was naturally a thinker for himself, confident of his own abilities, and disdainful of help or hindrance" (*Lives* 1:194).

Meanwhile, as Pope and Jonson's fortunes were declining and Milton's hung in the balance, Shakespeare, who had in fact participated in a mode of cultural production that was essentially collaborative, was being fashioned into the epitome of original genius. "*Shakespeare* gave us a *Shakespeare*, nor could the first in antient fame have given us more," Young exclaimed in tautological rapture, noting in a figure that, like that of the mint, suggestively associates authorship with exchange: "*Shakespeare* mingled no water with his wine, lower'd his Genius by no vapid Imitation" (*Conjectures* 78). Far less was known of Shakespeare than of Jonson, Pope, or Milton, and therefore "Shakespeare" had to be invented. Margreta de Grazia has shown how through three of Edmond Malone's projects—a chronology of the plays, an edition of the sonnets, and a documentary biography—Shakespeare was produced in the latter part of the eighteenth century as an individuated author. Yet even before the production of a coherent narrative of Shakespeare's

4. On the bizarre accusations leveled against Milton by the Jacobite William Lauder, see the studies by James Clifford and Michael Marcuse.

life and supposed experiences and thoughts, Shakespeare the individual had become an object of adulation. As early as the 1740s pilgrims began to visit Stratford on Avon in quest of Shakespearean relics. These were duly supplied by Thomas Sharpe, who purchased an old mulberry tree that Shakespeare was supposed to have planted and sold it off in pieces over a forty-year period. The climax of early bardolatry, however, came with David Garrick's great jubilee at Stratford in 1769. The *Gentleman's Magazine,* describing the forthcoming celebration, urged its readers to hurry to Stratford "as a pilgrim would to the shrine of some loved saint" in order to view "the humble shed, in which the immortal bard first drew that breath which gladdened all the isle" (Halliday 67). And at the celebration, Garrick toasted Shakespeare with a cup carved from the old tree that Thomas Sharpe had bought:

> Behold this fair goblet, 'Twas carv'd from the tree,
> Which, O my sweet Shakespear, was planted by thee;
> As a relic I kiss it, and bow at the shrine;
> What comes from thy hand must be ever divine.

During the three days of the jubilee, there was pageantry, feasting, and dancing, but not a single one of Shakespeare's plays was performed. The event was the canonization of the personality, not of the plays.

The Shakespeare jubilee was a commercial event through which the town of Stratford sought to exploit the connection with its famous son. Garrick made his living from Shakespeare, and anything he could do to encourage the cult of the bard was to his advantage. But the rhetorical excesses of the jubilee suggest that more than ordinary huckstering was at work. By the middle of the eighteenth century, the name "Shakespeare" had become in England the standard by which literary value was measured, the authorizing sign at the center of the entire galaxy of literary commodities. And underwriting the name "Shakespeare" was the notion that there had once lived a human being so extraordinary that all the value radiating from that galactic center was in turn the sign of his personal worth. In other words, the mystification of Shakespeare the man followed logically from the position of "Shakespeare" in the late eighteenth-century system of literary values. Indeed, there was a further step in the mystification of Shakespeare, the separation of the divine personality of the author of the plays from the human specificity of the actor-playwright-shareholder William Shakespeare.

Thus in the early 1780s the Reverend James Wilmot, rector of Barlow on the Heath, a village a few miles north of Stratford, first suggested that "Shakespeare" was Francis Bacon (see Nicoll 128). In the early years of the nineteenth century, the process of mystification was taken still further when John Keats, thinking of course of Shakespeare as the ultimate exemplar of the type, wrote to Richard Woodhouse that the essence of the "poetical Character" was that it had no essence, no self at all, but was "every thing and nothing" at once (*Letters* 1:386–387). Just so, in the Hebrew tradition the holy name "Jahweh," the guarantor of a universe of discourse, becomes successively "Adonai" and finally "Hashem" or, simply, "the name."

Thomas Becket's counsel in the Chancery case later appealed to the House of Lords was Francis Hargrave, a young lawyer who would make a name for himself as a legal scholar and barrister. Hargrave hoped to argue the respondents' case in the appeal and indeed drafted his speech. The speech was never delivered—Alexander Wedderburn and John Dunning, both of whom were more senior, were the pleaders—but Hargrave, as he explains in his Advertisement and Postscript, decided to publish it anyway as a pamphlet, hurrying it through the press so that it might have a chance to influence the case. In Hargrave's *Argument in Defence of Literary Property* the connections between property, originality, and personality are made explicit, and I want to turn now to a passage from this pamphlet that allows us to identify some of the evasions and ambiguities incorporated, along with these connections, into the notion of literary property.

What was the subject of literary property? Hargrave's answer is in Blackstone's vein—"The identity of a literary composition consists intirely in the *sentiment* and the *language;* the same conceptions, cloathed in the same words, must necessarily be the same composition" (2:406)—but it goes further in order, like Young, to invoke the distinctiveness of the human face as a proof of the individuality of each composition:

> The subject of the property is a *written composition;* and that one written composition may be distinguished from another, is a truth too evident to be much argued upon. Every man has a mode of combining

and expressing his ideas peculiar to himself. The same doctrines, the same opinions, never come from two persons, or even from the same person at different times, cloathed wholly in the same language. A strong resemblance of stile, of sentiment, of plan and disposition, will be frequently found; but there is such an infinite variety in the modes of thinking and writing, as well in the extent and connection of ideas, as in the use and arrangement of words, that a literary work *really* original, like the human face, will always have some singularities, some lines, some features, to characterize it, and to fix and establish its identity; and to assert the contrary with respect to either, would be justly deemed equally opposite to reason and universal experience. Besides, though it should be allowable to suppose, that there *may* be cases, in which, on a comparison of two literary productions, no such distinction could be made between them, as in a competition for originality to decide whether both were really original, or which was the original and which the copy; still the observation of the possibility of distinguishing would hold in *all other* instances, and the Argument in its application to them would still have the same force. (6–7)

The axiom with which Hargrave begins, "that one written composition may be distinguished from another," is in fact far from self-evident; indeed it begs the entire question of literary identity. How may one composition be distinguished from another? Does a composition have an essence that remains the same even if some of the language is changed? Are successive drafts of a composition still the same composition? Hargrave elaborates on the axiom by explaining that "every man has a mode of combining and expressing his ideas peculiar to himself" and that there exists an infinite variety of ways of thinking and writing. But this new proposition, that every man has a distinctive style, is not really an explanation of the axiom so much as a shift in focus from the composition to the writer. A blurring of categories has occurred, a slide from a statement about a property to one about a proprietor, and this conflation becomes explicit in the comparison of an original work to a unique human face. Like two faces, two compositions may resemble each other in various ways, but they will always have some distinguishing characteristics, some marks of individuality.

The effect of the analogy is to collapse the category of the work into that of the author and his personality. Hargrave's purpose has been to define the distinctiveness of the literary work, to show that its identity can be fixed and established. But he has demonstrated one kind of distinctiveness at the expense of another. If the individuality of the work is identical to that of the author, then the category of the work has been dissolved. Interestingly, this action traces in reverse the Lockean notion of the creation of property in which property originates when an individual's "person" is impressed on the world through labor:

> Though the Earth, and all inferior Creatures be common to all Men, yet every Man has a *Property* in his own *Person*. This no Body has any Right to but himself. The *Labour* of his Body, and the *Work* of his Hands, we may say, are properly his. Whatsoever then he removes out of the State that Nature hath provided, and left it in, he hath mixed his *Labour* with, and joyned to it something that is his own, and thereby makes it his *Property*. (*Two Treatises* 305–306)

Seeking to establish the distinctiveness of the literary work, what Hargrave has actually done is to retell the standard narrative of the creation of private property, a story in which the origins of the property are not located but deferred, transferred backward from the material possession to the individual's person.

There is an ambiguity too in Hargrave's use of the key term "original." Hargrave makes categorical statements about "every man" having "a mode of combining and expressing his ideas peculiar to himself," with an "infinite variety" of such modes of thinking and writing. But he does not state categorically that every literary composition has a distinct identity, saying only that "a literary work *really* original, like the human face, will always have some singularities, some lines, some features, to characterize it." In what sense is "original" used here? Does Hargrave mean merely a composition that has not been copied? Or does he mean one that is novel, that exhibits a certain freshness of character? If the sense is simply a work that has not been copied, then every composition produced by the writer will be distinct. But if the sense is "novel and fresh," then many compositions will not be original. The ambiguity on this point recurs in the long and obscure sentence that concludes the passage. Is Hargrave saying that in certain cases literary productions themselves are unindividuated, or is he saying simply that it is sometimes impossible to determine which is the original?

Hargrave's equivocal use of "original" reflects his indecision about whether every writer is an author. Pared to essentials, his argument is that since all men are distinct, all compositions must be distinct. But Hargrave is evidently not comfortable with a position that fails to distinguish between an original genius and a hack writer. So he hedges, asserting only that "a literary work *really* original" will always be distinguishable. Once qualified in this way, Hargrave's proposition is transformed, for it now appears that only some men—those blessed with at least modest powers of original genius—can produce distinct literary works. The two forms of the proposition are not compatible: one asserts that all literary compositions are individuated, the other that only some are individuated. Are we to infer that only some men have "personality"?

"The same doctrines, the same opinions, never come from two persons, or even from the same person at different times, cloathed wholly in the same language." With this statement Hargrave asserts the distinctiveness of personal styles and thus the distinctiveness of compositions as well. Note, however, that casually embedded in this affirmation of literary personality is the observation that just as authors differ from one another, so each author differs from himself from moment to moment in the form of his expression: not only will the same doctrines be expressed differently by different persons, they will be expressed differently by the same person at different times. Hargrave's casual comment is an implicit acknowledgment of the problem of personal identity that, as Christopher Fox has shown, had distressed British thinkers ever since John Locke in his *Essay Concerning Human Understanding* (1690) challenged tradition and located personal identity in consciousness. Thus David Hume reported in his *Treatise of Human Nature* (1739) that he could find no trace of any self inside himself other than the self that was constantly in the act of perceiving the world. Others might claim to find something more abiding in themselves, Hume said, but to him all of mankind was "nothing but a bundle or collection of different perceptions, which succeed each other with an inconceivable rapidity, and are in a perpetual flux and movement" (252). If so, where was the foundation that Hargrave might use to "fix and establish" the identity of literary property?

The ambiguities in *An Argument in Defence of Literary Property* do not reflect intellectual weakness on Hargrave's part, but rather preserve the gaps in the discourse of literary property as it developed over the eighteenth century. To his contemporaries, Hargrave's arguments would have seemed simple, direct, and solid—and indeed the *Argument* was commended for its "great clearness of thought and expression" (review of Hargrave, *Argument* 209). From a critical point of view, however, what the *Argument* reveals most clearly is the way in which the discourse of literary property was a complexly fabricated cultural artifact.

Property, originality, personality: the construction of the discourse of literary property depended on a chain of deferrals. The distinctive property was said to reside in the particularity of the text—"the same conceptions, cloathed in the same words"—and this was underwritten by the notion of originality, which was in turn guaranteed by the concept of personality. The sign of personality was the distinctiveness of the human face, but this was only the material trace of the genius of the immaterial self, and this when examined dissolved completely into contingency and flux. The attempt to anchor the notion of literary property in personality suggests the need to find a transcendent signifier, a category beyond the economic to warrant and ground the circulation of literary commodities. Thus the mystification of original genius, pressed to its logical extreme in the limiting case of Shakespeare, became bardolatry. Here was a transcendental signifier indeed. And yet the worship of Shakespeare resolved itself into the adoration of his relics, the plays of course but also the pieces of the old mulberry tree carved into goblets and other trinkets by the aptly named Thomas Sharpe who made, we must suppose, over the forty-year period of his industry, a very fair profit on the venture.

"But the property here claimed is all ideal," Joseph Yates protested in his opinion in *Millar v. Taylor,*

> a set of ideas which have no bounds or marks whatever, nothing that is capable of a visible possession, nothing that can sustain any one of the qualities or incidents of property . . . Yet these are the phantoms which the author would grasp and confine to himself: And these are what the defendant is charged with having robbed the plaintiff of. (*ER* 98:233)

Despite Yates's discomfort with the notion of immaterial property, the members of the Stationers' Company had, as they frequently insisted, long treated copies as property, and in *Pope v. Curll* Lord Chancellor Hardwicke explicitly acknowledged the immaterial nature of copyright.

We should not forget, however, that a majority of the Scottish judges in *Hinton v. Donaldson* and a significant minority of the English judges in *Donaldson v. Becket* agreed with Yates on this point. Still somewhat controversial, the idea of copyright as an immaterial property paralleled another eighteenth-century innovation, paper money. Currency had traditionally been solid and material: gold and silver refined to an established standard of purity and parceled into specified weights stamped into coins whose worth was measurable by any assayer. But coinage of this sort was inadequate to meet the needs of a developing commercial nation, and during the course of the century, banknotes, personal promissory notes, naval bills, and other forms of commercial paper were absorbed into the economic system as a legitimate form of currency (Ashton 167–200). Thus money also became fantasmic, a matter of the circulation of signs abstracted from their material basis. Furthermore, just as literary property was underwritten by the personality of the author, so the acceptability of commercial paper depended on the credibility of the note issuers and of the endorsers through whose hands they had passed.

It is interesting to observe that Lord Mansfield was an instrumental figure in establishing banknotes as a legitimate form of money. In *Miller v. Race* (1758) in which a defendant sought to avoid payment of a banknote by claiming it was not property but merely evidence of a debt, Mansfield said that the defendant's argument was based on a false comparison: notes were "treated as Money, as Cash, in the ordinary course and transaction of Business, by the general Consent of Mankind" (*ER* 97:398). Nor did Mansfield have difficulty with the abstractness of literary property. The author's property right was "equally detached from the manuscript, or any other physical existence whatsoever" (*ER* 98:251). Yates's protest against the immateriality of literary property was the voice of the past. In the advanced marketplace society of the eighteenth century, the solidity of apparently concrete referents was dissolving, replaced in many different but interconnected spheres by the circulation of signs.

8

⋄⋄⋄

Strange Changes

"The Courts of *Westminster* would be filled with Suits hitherto unheard of." So wrote the anonymous author of *An Enquiry in the Nature and Origin of Literary Property*, published in 1762 while *Tonson v. Collins* was still pending, as he predicted the dire consequences of recognizing literary property as a common-law right:

> Poet would commence his Action against Poet, and Historian against Historian, complaining of literary Trespasses. Juries would be puzzled, what Damage to give for the pilfering an Anecdote, or purloining the Fable of a Play. What strange Changes would necessarily ensue. The Courts of Law must sagely determine Points in polite Literature, and Wit be entered on Record. (13)

A few years later, Joseph Yates made a similar prediction, noting that if literary compositions were admitted into the law as property, "Disputes also might arise among authors themselves—'whether the works of one author were or were not the same with those of another author; or whether there were only colourable differences'" (*ER* 98:250). What damages should be awarded for pilfering an anecdote or purloining a plot? How many elements in two stories need to be similar before deeming them the same story? These are the kinds of questions that our law courts deal with every day, for we are the heirs of the institution of literary property created in the eighteenth century, and the strange changes predicted in *An Enquiry* are familiar to us.

A discussion of romantic aesthetic theory is outside the scope of this book. Nevertheless, as Martha Woodmansee has shown, German romantic theory formed in the context of a legal and economic struggle that in some of its concerns recalls the English debates. The German "debate over the book," which spanned two decades between 1773 and 1794, focused on the question of "whether or not the unauthorized reproduction of books [*Büchernachdruck*] should be prohibited by law" (442). Both writers and publishers were involved, and the theoretical questions taken up included such matters as whether a book was a material or an ideal object. One of the products of the debate over the book was the series of copyright laws enacted by the various German states beginning in 1794. Another was the articulation of elements of romantic theory, including Johann Gottlieb Fichte's concept of "form," which was crucial in establishing the philosophical grounds for German writers' claim to ownership of their work. What did a literary work consist of? Fichte distinguished between the material and the immaterial aspects of a book. He then divided the immaterial aspects into *content* and *form*. The content of the book, the ideas, could not be considered property. The form of the book, however, the specific way in which the ideas were presented, remained the author's property forever; as Fichte put it in his "Proof of the Illegality of Reprinting," each writer has "his own thought processes, his own way of forming concepts and connecting them" (Woodmansee 445).

Long before Fichte, Lord Chancellor Hardwicke in *Pope v. Curll* distinguished between the material and immaterial aspects of a composition; Blackstone argued in *Tonson v. Collins* that not ideas as such but "style and sentiment" were "the essentials of a literary composition" (*ER* 96:189); and Hargrave located the distinctiveness of literary property in the peculiar mode that each person has of expressing his ideas (6–7). Interestingly, in 1763, while *Tonson v. Collins* was pending, an anonymous journalist even used the term "form" in defining the nature of literary property, saying that it was an error to suppose that the doctrines contained in a book should be considered its "true and peculiar property." The true property in a book, this writer argued, "consists chiefly in the form and composition: at least, this being all that can be in any good degree ascertained, it is all the property capable of being legally secured" (review of *Vindication* 183). The eighteenth-century discourse of original genius can be understood as an anticipation of romantic doctrines of creativity. These anticipations of Fichte's distinctions between the material and immaterial aspects of a book and between content and form also suggest the continuity between the issues raised in the English debates and those raised by the German romantics. Why should an author have a property right in his work? What does that work consist of? How is a literary composition different from a mechanical invention? In representing the author as a specially gifted person able to produce from the depths of personal experience an organically unified work of art, romanticism provided codified theoretical answers to these critical legal questions.

We should also note the continuity between earlier literary-property debates and modern copyright doctrine. By 1774, the year in which the *Donaldson* decision resolved the issue of the perpetuity, all the essential elements of modern Anglo-American copyright law were in place. Most important, of course, was the notion of the author as the creator and ultimate source of property. This representation of authorship was at the heart of the long struggle over perpetual copyright; it survived the determination that literary property was limited in term; and it remains central to copyright today. "Copyright, in a word, is about authorship," writes Paul Goldstein. "Copyright is about sustaining the conditions of creativity that enable an individual to craft out of thin air, and intense, devouring labor, an *Appalachian Spring*, a *Sun Also Rises*, a *Citizen Kane*" (110). As suggested by Goldstein's invocation of a musical work and a film in addition to a literary text, the concept of authorship has been greatly extended since 1774—photographs, sculptures, sound recordings, and choreographic works are all, according to the current U.S. statute, defined as the work of authors and granted copyright protection—but the concept of authorship remains one that Edward Young and Lord Mansfield would recognize.

Along with the concept of the author as a creator and proprietor came that of the property itself, the "work" as an immaterial commodity. *Pope v. Curll* posed the question whether a letter belongs to the writer or the receiver, which Lord Chancellor Hardwicke answered by severing the spirit of the property from the body. Later, in response to the challenge from those who denied that ideas could be property, Blackstone worked out his influential representation of the original work as "the same conceptions, cloathed in the same words" (2:406), a formulation that anticipates the present-day distinction between idea and expression. Ideas are not protected, but expression is. But even if the notion of the work was in place by 1774, the implications of the concept were not yet clear, for the early rulings under the Statute of Anne focused on the author's labor and limited the property closely to the actual text at issue. Thus Lord Chancellor Macclesfield stated in *Burnett v. Chetwood* (1720) that a translation might be regarded as a new work (*ER* 35:1009), and in *Gyles v. Wilcox* (1740) Lord Chancellor Hardwicke stated that an abridgment would also qualify as new (*ER* 26:490). In the nineteenth century, however, the emphasis in litigation shifted to the abstract "work," which now came to be understood as equivalent, in the words of *Drone on Copyright,* the standard U.S. treatise of the period, to the "essence and value of a literary composition" rather than limited to the literal language of the text. The purchaser of a copyright now acquired, as Peter Jaszi puts it, "a general dominion over the imaginative territory of a particular literary or artistic production" (478).

The story of copyright since *Donaldson v. Becket,* then, can be understood as an exploration of two central reifications, the "author" and the "work." The narrative is one of steady expansion, of the enclosure of new territories, and this extension of dominion has occurred both at the level of the individual property—ownership of the work now includes the right to prepare all kinds of derivative products—and at the level of the basic commodity system as new technologies such as photography, cinema, and sound recording have been developed. I use the metaphor of territorial expansion advisedly, for, as Jaszi's comment about the copyright owner's general dominion over an "imaginative territory" suggests, the real-estate trope remains a vital part of contemporary thought about literary property. Thus Jessica Litman remarks in an article on public domain—a concept that is itself an import from the realm of real estate—that the model for copyright is real property. We "cast the author's rights in the mold of exclusive rights of control," Litman points out, and we treat invasion of these rights as "actionable on a strict liability basis, akin to the traditional formulation of trespass to land" (971). What copyright law relies on in place of physical borders to "divide the privately-owned from the commons and to draw lines among the various parcels in private ownership" is the notion of originality, but in fact, as Litman observes, cultural production is typically a matter of appropriation and transformation rather than creation (1000).

In copyright law, of course, "original" has been taken to mean merely that one work has not been copied from another. The classic formulation is Judge Learned Hand's puckish dictum in *Sheldon v. Metro-Goldwyn Pictures Corp.* (1936) about a hypothetical second author of Keats's "Ode on a Grecian Urn":

> Borrowed the work must indeed not be, for a plagiarist is not himself pro tanto an "author"; but if by some magic a man who had never known it were to compose anew Keats's Ode on a Grecian Urn, he would be an "author," and, if he copyrighted it, others might not copy that poem, though they might of course copy Keats's. (54)

One thinks of Borges' fable of "Pierre Menard, Author of the *Quixote*" in which a modern writer composes—writes anew from his own experience—several chapters of *Don Quixote*. Every word in Pierre Menard's *Quixote* is identical to Cervantes', and yet the text, Borges insists, is different.

But the problem raised by Learned Hand's Grecian Ode dictum is even knottier than at first appears, for how are we to know whether the second ode is really original? Litman poses the following variation on the theme:

> Two schoolboys encounter Keats' *Ode* when their teacher reads it aloud to them in class. Neither pays close attention. The first of the boys forgets the *Ode* utterly; the second has no conscious memory of the poem, but Keats' turns of phrase stick in his subconscious mind. Both boys grow up to be poets with no further contact with the works of Keats, and each composes the *Ode on a Grecian Urn* with no awareness that Keats has anticipated him. The similarities of the first poet's poem to that of Keats are sheer coincidence, and he is entitled to copyright his poem. The second poet, of course, relied unknowingly on his subconscious memory, and he is not entitled to a copyright because he copied his poem, albeit subconsciously, from Keats. (1000–1)

What we must determine, then, is whether the writer accused of plagiarizing Keats has "really" forgotten his exposure to the original text or only sincerely "thinks" he has forgotten that exposure. Litman's point is that the law purports to draw lines between works on the basis of facts that cannot be ascertained.

Jane Ginsburg also comments on copyright law's reliance on the notion of original authorship, noting that the law "comfortably embraces works manifesting a personal authorial presence" but "encounters far more difficulty accommodating works at once high in commercial value but low in personal authorship," such as a compilation of factual information (1866).[1] Thus in the recent case of *Feist Publications v. Rural Telephone Service Company* (1991) in which the U.S. Supreme Court ruled that the white pages of a telephone directory are not copyrightable, the decision, written by Justice Sandra Day O'Connor, reemphasizes the need for at least a minimal degree of "creativity" in having a work qualify for protection. "To be sure, the requisite level of creativity is extremely low; even a slight amount will suffice," Justice O'Connor writes. "The vast majority of works make the grade quite easily, as they possess some creative spark, 'no matter how crude, humble or obvious' it might be" (1287). Nevertheless, some creative spark there must be.

The persistence of the discourse of original genius implicit in the notion of creativity not only obscures the fact that cultural production is always a matter of appropriation and transformation, but also elides the role of the publisher—or, in the case of films, of the studio or producer—in cultural production. Thus it continues the tradition of the eighteenth-century arguments in which the booksellers appeared only as shadowy "assigns" of the author. Equally evident is the way that it elides the real means of cultural production. In the landmark case of *Burrow-Giles Lithographic Co. v. Sarony* (1884), for example, the U.S. Supreme Court decided that the crucial element in the making of the photograph in question—a studio portrait of Oscar Wilde—was simply the photographer's "intellectual invention" (282). Citing the finding of facts, which described the portrait as deriving entirely from the photographer's "original mental conception" (279), given visible form in the posing and lighting of the subject and the selection and arrangement of the draperies and other accessories, the court ruled that the

---

1. Ginsburg advocates discarding the current unitary system of copyright and having one for works high in personal authorship and a second for works low in personal authorship. She sees the modern focus on personality as a departure from earlier copyright history, when the emphasis was more on labor. I agree that the emphasis has changed, but, as Hargrave's *Argument* among other texts suggests, the eighteenth-century lawyers were also concerned with personality. Indeed, the Lockean doctrine of property depended on the notion of having property in one's "person."

portrait was indeed "an original work of art" and that the photographer Napoleon Sarony was its author. Thus not only did the camera disappear as a significant factor in the production of the photograph, but so did Oscar Wilde.

Because copyright is conceived as protecting original works of authorship, the products of new technologies such as photography must be represented as the work of authors in order to be brought under its umbrella. In a stimulating treatment of *Burrow-Giles,* Jane Gaines discusses how the photographer—rather than, say, the subject or, for that matter, nature itself in the form of light—came to be constructed as the author of the photographic image. And of course movies, television shows, textile designs, and pantomimes, as well as some lampbases, coinbanks, and stuffed animals, may have "authors." Moreover, in what Jaszi refers to as a "reverse-twist on individualistic 'authorship'" (487), the necessities of commerce have produced the work-for-hire doctrine, according to which the employer is defined as the author and thus "cast as the visionary" while the artist or music arranger or other cultural worker is treated as "a mere mechanic following orders" (489).

In the discourse of copyright, then, the goal of protecting the rights of the creative author is proudly asserted even as the notion of author is drained of content. This is because the legal concept of authorship is "simultaneously an artifact of the marketplace in commodity art *and* a throwback to early, pre-industrial ideas of the artist's relation to society" (Jaszi 502). But, like almost all the other elements in contemporary copyright discourse, this internal contradiction too was implicit in the moment of modern copyright's formation in the eighteenth century. The Scottish Lord Hailes fastened on it when he dyspeptically rejected the London booksellers' claim in *Hinton v. Donaldson* (1773) that the Reverend Thomas Stackhouse could be called an author:

> The London booksellers *enlarge* the common-law right by conferring the name of *original author* on every *tasteless compiler.*
>
> Hereof there is an apposite example in Stackhouse, the author of this day.
>
> He was as very a compiler as ever descended from a bookseller's garret.
>
> The incorporeal substance of Stackhouse's ideas is a non-entity.

And yet, in the opinion of *The Sages in St. Paul's Church-yard*, Stackhouse is no less an original author than Hooker or Warburton.

Here lies my first difficulty: were we to copy the judgment of the King's Bench in the case Miller *versus* Taylor; were we to find that the common-law right of authors in England could be made effectual in Scotland; were we even to find that literary property was established in the law of nature and nations; still we could not pronounce judgment for the pursuer, unless we were to hold Stackhouse to have been an original author; *this* I can never do. (Boswell, *Decision* 7–8)

And we recall the strategic equivocation in Francis Hargrave's *Argument in Defence of Literary Property* (1774) over whether all writings are genuinely original and whether every writer is an author.

Although condensations, compilations, and other works of a common nature were protected under the Statute of Anne, the arguments made for literary property still invoked the special claims of authorship. Recall, for instance, that Joseph Addison, lobbying for the statute at the start of the century, spoke of the author's life spent in "noble Enquiries," separated from the "rest of Mankind" in order to study "the Wonders of Creation, the Government of his Passions, and the Revolutions of the World" (*Tatler* 101, 1 Dec. 1709). Today the prestige of items of "high art"—*Appalachian Spring, The Sun Also Rises, Citizen Kane*—is also invoked to legitimate the protection of humbler products. The classic instance of this strategy is Justice Oliver Wendell Holmes's often-quoted opinion in *Bleistein v. Donaldson Lithographing Co.* (1903), which affirmed copyright protection for a circus advertising poster depicting acrobats performing on bicycles. The basis of Justice Holmes's decision was the notion of "personality." It was obvious, Holmes wrote, that even if the poster was a direct copy from a real performance, it would still be protected:

The opposite proposition would mean that a portrait by Velasquez or Whistler was common property because others might try their hand on the same face. Others are free to copy the original. They are not free to copy the copy. The copy is the personal reaction of an individual upon nature. Personality always contains something unique. It expresses its singularity even in handwriting, and a very modest grade of art has in it something irreducible, which is one man's alone. That something he may copyright. (299–300)

Thus Holmes presented the poster as if it were a minor Velasquez or Whistler. As Goldstein says, commenting on *Bleistein*, "A circus poster may not rise to the artistic level of a Mary Cassatt. But for authorship to flourish, those who seek to be authors must receive the same welcome as those who succeed as authors" (115–116).

"How is an author to be distinguished?" Joseph Yates asked in *Tonson v. Collins* (1760). "Some few may be known by their style; but the generality are not known at all" (*ER* 96:185). Yates's challenge to the discourse of proprietary authorship was fundamental. Can one really find much in the way of "the personal reaction of an individual upon nature" in the bulk of ordinary cultural productions such as formula fiction, television game shows, or newspaper advertisements—or even, for that matter, in certain extraordinary productions such as *Beowulf* or the Bayeux tapestry or the stained-glass windows at Chartres? These medieval examples, of course, embody the values and conceptions not of individuals but of entire societies, and remind us of the cultural and historical specificity of the very notion of "the personal reaction of an individual upon nature." It is significant that the defenders of literary property in the eighteenth century did not generally feel it necessary to respond to Yates's challenge. That one author might be distinguished from another was, as Francis Hargrave said, "a truth too evident to be much argued upon." And the same axiom is generally assumed in infringement cases today.

The eighteenth-century lawyers were certainly aware that drudges as well as genuine authors took shelter under the umbrella of literary property, but, after all, compilers such as Thomas Stackhouse had invested time and effort in their productions. If learning was to flourish, all those who labored to produce useful works had to receive the same welcome as Richard Hooker or William Warburton. Modern copyright lawyers are well aware that the author of a stuffed animal is not quite the same as the author of *Appalachian Spring*, and that the casting of the employer in the role of author in the case of work-for-hire is merely a legal convenience. What stabilizes the system, however, is the continuing conviction that though there may be exceptional cases, and though legal fictions may at times be useful, still there really are such beings as original authors, and these gifted creatures will express themselves in discrete works as readily distinguishable as individual human faces.

What finally underwrites the system, then, is our conviction about ourselves as individuals.

In 1890 Samuel Warren and Louis Brandeis published their famous *Harvard Law Review* essay arguing for the existence of a common-law right to privacy. This right could be discerned in the common-law protection of an author's unpublished writings, which should be properly understood not as a property right but as "an instance of the enforcement of the more general right of the individual to be let alone."

> It is like the right not to be assaulted or beaten, the right not to be imprisoned, the right not to be maliciously prosecuted, the right not to be defamed. In each of these rights, as indeed in all other rights recognized by the law, there inheres the quality of being owned or possessed—and (as that is the distinguishing attribute of property) there may be some propriety in speaking of those rights as property. But, obviously, they bear little resemblance to what is ordinarily comprehended under that term. The principle which protects personal writings and all other personal productions, not against theft and physical appropriation, but against publication in any form, is in reality not the principle of private property, but that of an inviolate personality. (205)

Warren and Brandeis chose as their epigraph a passage from Justice Edward Willes' opinion in *Millar v. Taylor* on the nature of the common law, and in one of the notes they invoke Justice Joseph Yates's opinion in the same case: "It is certain every man has a right to keep his own sentiments, if he pleases. He has certainly a right to judge whether he will make them public, or commit them only to the sight of his friends" (198n2). But their principal authority was the English Chancery case of *Prince Albert v. Strange* (1849)—as Daniel Tritter notes, this case was at the time the standard authority for common-law copyright before publication—in which the prince consort succeeded in securing an injunction prohibiting the printing or distribution of a catalogue of etchings he had executed.

Robert Post correctly points out that Warren and Brandeis' attempt to find a precedent for the right to privacy in *Prince Albert v. Strange* depended on a strained reading of the case. What is interesting to me, however, is the very fact that in their quest for a precedent Warren and Brandeis went to copyright law. Their instinct to look in this area was, I think, sound; copyright cases from the earliest days had mingled matters of privacy with matters of property. This is evident in *Burnet v. Chetwood* (1720), where Burnet's executor sued to prevent his book with its somewhat scandalous content from being widely distributed. But it is perhaps clearest in *Pope v. Curll* (1741), which was impelled by Pope's indignation about commercial intrusion into the private sphere.[2] Lord Mansfield, we recall, founded his conviction about the author's common-law right on principles of both propriety and property, arguing that an author should have the right to withhold a writing from publication—that is, to keep it private—and that he should be able to reap the profits of his labor. As Post remarks, the central thrust of Warren and Brandeis' article was "to disentangle privacy from property" (648). In effect, their task was to untie the knot that Mansfield had tied a century and a half earlier.

Warren and Brandeis' use of copyright as a precedent for the right to privacy draws attention to the fact that the institution of copyright stands squarely on the boundary between private and public. Understanding copyright in this way helps to explain its notorious duplicity: copyright is sometimes treated as a form of private property and sometimes as an instrument of public policy created for the encouragement of learning. Understanding copyright as a mediator between private and public also helps, as Peter Jaszi and James Boyle have observed, to explain why the private/public dichotomy reappears with uncanny regularity at every level of its operation. At the broadest level, copyright distinguishes between protected and unprotected works, thereby dividing the universe of cultural products into the private and the public. Not every aspect of a protected work is declared to be private property, however, because at this point the distinction between "expression" and "idea" comes into play, again calling for a division between the private and the public. Finally, at the third and narrowest

2. Did Pope's letters to Swift belong to the private sphere or the public? This was the question at the heart of the case. Pope maintained that his letters were private; Curll agreed, but argued from this that familiar letters did not fall under the statute, which was an act for the encouragement of learning. Lord Chancellor Hardwick's ruling was something of a paradox: since the letters were of public interest, Hardwicke ruled, they fell under the statute and therefore Pope had the right to keep them private.

level of adjudication, once "protected expression" has been determined, the concept of "fair use" comes into play, again calling for a division.

How does one determine what is a noninfringing fair use of a copyrighted work? Where does one draw the line between protected expression and unprotectable idea? Learned Hand's dictum on expression and idea delivered in *Nichols v. Universal Pictures Corp.* (1929)— "Nobody has ever been able to fix that boundary, and nobody ever can" (121)—is often quoted. And so is Justice Joseph Story's comment in *Folsom v. Marsh* (1841) about copyright determinations generally: "Patents and copyrights approach, nearer than any other class of cases belonging to forensic discussions, to what may be called the metaphysics of the law, where the distinctions are, or at least may be, very subtle and refined, and, sometimes, almost evanescent" (344). Much of the notorious difficulty of applying copyright doctrine to concrete cases can be related to the persistence of the discourse of original genius and to the problems inherent in the reifications of author and work. But much also has to do with copyright's role as mediator between private and public.

Let us note that what is private from one point of view (for example, the family room of a house seen from the street outside) will be public from another (the same family room considered from the privacy of one's bedroom in the house). That the meaning of private and public changes according to where one stands suggests that this dichotomy is not a part of the world, but a way of organizing the world. It belongs, we might say, not to geography but to cartography. There is no fixed boundary between the private and the public; it always waits to be drawn; and since significant interests are at stake in copyright questions, precisely where to draw the line is always a contest. Copyright does more, then, than govern the passage of commodified exchanges across the boundary between the private sphere and the public; it actually constitutes the boundary on which it stands. Change the rules of copyright—determine, say, that photographs have authors and are protected, or determine that fair use applies more restrictively to unpublished works than to published—and the demarcation between private and public changes. "Private" and "public" are radically unstable concepts, and yet we can no more do without them than we can do without such dialectical concepts as "inside" and "outside" or "self" and "other." Copyright law will consequently always remain a site of contestation and also a site of cultural production, a place where new maps are drawn and new entities such as the photographer-author are assembled. Always, that is, so long as copyright as an institution continues to exist. But *will* this unstable, problematic, often deeply frustrating institution continue to exist?

As we have seen, copyright is not a transcendent moral idea, but a specifically modern formation produced by printing technology, marketplace economics, and the classical liberal culture of possessive individualism. It is also an institution built on intellectual quicksand: the essentially religious concept of originality, the notion that certain extraordinary beings called authors conjure works out of thin air. And it is an institution whose technological foundation has recently turned, like a vital organ grown cancerous, into an enemy. Copyright developed as a consequence of printing technology's ability to produce large numbers of copies of a text quickly and cheaply. But present-day technology makes it virtually impossible to prevent people from making copies of almost any text—printed, musical, cinematic, computerized— rapidly and at a negligible cost.

Why, then, don't we abandon copyright as an archaic and cumbersome system of cultural regulation? Why don't we launch into the brave new world that Michel Foucault imagines at the end of "What Is an Author?" where the authorial function disappears and texts develop and circulate, as Foucault puts it, "in the anonymity of a murmur" (119). The institution of copyright is of course deeply rooted in our economic system, and much of our economy does in turn depend on intellectual property. But, no less important, copyright is deeply rooted in our conception of ourselves as individuals with at least a modest grade of singularity, some degree of personality. And it is associated with our sense of privacy and our conviction, at least in theory, that it is essential to limit the power of the state. We are not ready, I think, to give up the sense of who we are.

Appendix A

<o<o<o

Documents Related to *Pope v. Curll*

Pope's *Complaint* and Curll's *Answer*, which have not been previously printed, are transcribed from the originals in the Public Record Office, London. Each of these documents is written on a single piece of parchment, and each consists of a single largely unpunctuated sentence articulated in part by the use of capital letters at transitional moments. I have attempted to preserve this articulation but have also supplied punctuation. I have regularized accidentals and expanded abbreviations. Dates are presented in numerals instead of being written out in full. I am grateful to Robert Folkenflik, Traugott Lawler, and Ruth Warkentin for their assistance in deciphering parts of these documents. For convenience I have also reprinted Lord Chancellor Hardwicke's decision from *English Reports*.

Pope's Bill of Complaint

To the Right Honourable Philip Lord Hardwicke, Baron of Hardwicke in the County of Gloucester, Lord High Chancellor of Great Britain:

Humbly complaining, sheweth unto your lordship your orator Alexander Pope of Twickenham in the County of Middlesex, Esquire, that by an Act of Parliament made in the eighth year of the reign of her late majestie Queen Ann intitled An Act for Encouragement of Learning by Vesting the Copies of Printed Books in the Authors or Purchasers of such Copies During the Times therein Mentioned, it is among other things enacted that the author of any book or books composed on the 10th day of April 1710 and not printed and published, or that should thereafter be composed, and his assignee or assigns, should have the sole liberty of printing and reprinting such book and books for the term of 14 years to comence from the day of the first publishing the same as by the said Act of Parliament to which your orator craves leave to referr himself may appear: And your orator sheweth that he hath at different times, wrote several letters between the years 1714 and 1738, upon various subjects, addressed to the Reverend Doctor Swift, Dean of Saint Patrick's in the Kingdom of Ireland, bearing date respectively the 18th of June 1714, 20th of June 1716, 12th of January 1723, 14th of September 1725, 15th of October 1725, 10th of December 1725, 22nd of August 1726, 3rd of September 1726, 16th of November 1726, 8th of March 1726–7, 2nd of October 1727, 23rd of March 1727–8, 28th of June 1728, 12th of November 1728, 9th of October 1729, 28th of November 1729, 14th of April 1730, December the 5th 1732, 16th of February 1732–3, 2nd of April 1733, 28th of May 1733, 1st of September 1733, 6th of January 1734, 15th of September 1734, 19th of December 1734, 25th of March 1736, 17th of August 1736, 30th of December 1736, 23rd of March 1736–7: And your orator further sheweth that your orator was the sole author of the said letters, and having never disposed of the copy right of such letters to any person or persons whatsoever, and your orator had and has the sole and absolute right of printing, reprinting, vending, and selling the same as he should think fit: And your orator sheweth that your orator during the said period of time received several letters from the said Doctor Swift bearing date respectively the 28th of June 1715, 30th of August 1716, 20th of September 1723, 29th of September 1725, 26th of November 1725, 4th May 1726, 17th of November 1726, 5th of December 1726, 12th of October 1727, 30th of October 1727, 10th of May 1728, 1st of June 1728, 16th of July 1728, 13th of February 1728, 11th of August 1729, 31st of October 1729, 12th of June 1732, 1st of May 1733, 8th of July 1733, 1st of November 1734, 12th of May 1735, 3rd of September 1735, 21st of October 1735, 7th of February, 1735–6, 9th of February 1735–6, 22nd of April 1736, 2nd of December 1736, 31st of May 1737, 23rd of July 1737, 8th of August 1738: And your orator hoped that neither the said writings or letters whereof the property is vested in your orator as author thereof, nor those other letters which were sent and addressed to your orator, would have been printed, published, and sold without your orator's consent, but howso it is, may it please your lordship that Edmund Curl of the Parish of Saint Paul, Covent Garden, in the County of Middlesex, bookseller, combining and confederating with divers persons to your orator unknown (whose names, when discovered, your orator prays he may be at liberty to insert in this his bill of complaint and make them parties hereto with apt words to charge them) contrive and endeavour to defeat and defraud your orator in this behalf, and in order thereto, the said Edmund Curl, altho' he is well assured of your orator's right to the said writings or letters and all benefit thereof, has lately printed and published, or caused to be printed and published, a book with the following title, that is to say, Dean Swift's Literary Correspondence for Twenty-four Years from 1714 to 1738, Consisting of Original Letters to and from Mr Pope, Doctor Swift, Mr Gay, Lord Bolingbroke, Doctor Arbuthnott, Doctor Wotton, Bishop Atterbury, Duke and Dutchess of Queenbury. London. Printed for E. Curl, at Pope's Head in Rose Street, Covent Garden, MDCCXLI. Price: 4s Sewed, 5s Bound. And in the said book so published by the said Edmund Curl are contained the said writings or letters bearing date respectively as aforesaid composed by your orator and addressed to the said Doctor Swift, and also the said letters bearing date as aforesaid wrote by the said Doctor Swift and sent to your orator: And your orator charges that the said Edmund Curll and the rest of the confederates have and hath sold and disposed of a great number and quantity of the said surreptitious and pyrated edition of the said letters, and threaten that they will continue to sell and dispose of the same, in open defiance of the law and of your orator's just title to the said letters; in tender consideration whereof, and for that your orator is without remedy by the common law and cannot obtain a discovery of the numbers which have been printed and sold of such surreptitious and pyrated edition, nor get an account of the money which the said confederates have received for what they have respectively sold, nor restrain the said confederates from selling such writings so illegally printted, but by the aid of a court of equity: To the end therefore that the said Edmund Curl, and the rest of the confederates when discovered, may upon their respective corporal oaths true and perfect answer make to all and singular the premisses, and that as fully and particularly as if the same were herein again repeated and interrogated unto, your orator hereby leaving and disclaiming all penaltys and forfeitures whatsoever given or allowed by the said act, and may according to the best of their respective knowledge, information, remembrance, and belief set forth whether your orator

was not and is the sole author and proprietor of such part of the said book as purports to be letters written by your orator; and whether your orator has ever and when disposed of his right therein to any person or persons and whom; and whether your orator has not the sole and absolute right of printing and reprinting, vending, or selling such letters; and whether the said confederates, or any and which of them, or any other person or persons and who, with their or which of their privaty, knowledge, or procurement, have not printed and published or caused to be printed and published, any and what number of books under the aforesaid title of Dean Swift's Literary Correspondence for Twenty-four years from 1714 to 1738, Consisting of Original Letters to and from Mr Pope, Doctor Swift Mr Gay, Lord Bollingbrook, Doctor Arbuthnott, Doctor Wotton, Bishop Atterbury, Duke and Dutchess of Queensbury. London. Printed for E. Curll at Pope's Head in Rose Street, Covent Garden, MDCCXLI. Price: 4s Sewed, 5s Bound, or under any other and what title; and whether the said confederates do not know or beleive that your orator was and is the sole author and proprietor of the letters said to be wrote by your orator and contained in the said book so printed and published by the defendant as aforsaid; and whether the said confederates or any of them have ever had any licence or authority from your orator to print or publish any of your orator's said letters or any of the said letters sent by the said Doctor Swift to your orator in manner aforesaid or in any other manner whatsoever, and if not why they have done the same, and may set forth what right or title they or any of them have or pretend to have to your orator's letters, or the said letters wrote to your orator as aforesaid, or any part thereof, and how many books or copies of the said book so illegally printed and published by thesaid Edmund Curll as aforesaid have been at any time sold by the said confederates or any or which of them, and at and for what price and what profit they have made and gotten thereby, and may set forth all agreements made between the said confederates or any of them, or any other person or persons and whom, in relation to the printing any pyrated and illegal edition or the profits acruing thereby, and the names of all and every person and persons who are or have been any ways concerned aiding or assisting in the printing, publishing, buying, or selling thereof; and whether such proceedings of the said confederates are not or will be any and what

prejudice to your orator in preventing your orator from printing, publishing, and selling the said letters; and that the said confederates may set forth how many books or copies of the said pyrated or illegal edition remain unsold in the custody or power of them or any and which of them; and that the same and every of them may be delivered up to be disposed of as his lordship's court shall direct; and that the said defendants and their confederates may severally account with your orator for all profits and advantages which they or any of them have jointly or severally made or gotten by reason or means of the said pyrated and illegal edition, and may pay your orator the same, and may be restrained by the injunction of this honorable court from vending, selling, or disposing of any of the said books or copies of the said writings or letters whereof your orator is author or proprietor so by them or some of them illegally printed and published as aforesaid, and from printing, publishing, or selling any new or other edition thereof for the future; and that your orator may have such further and other releif in the premises as shall be agreeable to the nature of his case and the rules of equity and good conscience: May it please your lordship not only to grant unto your orator his majestie's most gracious writ of injunction to restrain the said Edmund Curll from vending, selling, or disposing of any of the said books or copies of the said writings or letters, but also his majestie's most gracious writ of subpoena to be directed to the said Edmund Curll, thereby comanding him at a certain day and under a certain pain therein to be limitted personally to be and appear before your lordship in this high and honourable court, then and there on his corporal oath true, direct, distinct, and perfect answer to make to all and singular the premisses, and further to stand to obey, abide, and perform such order, direction, and decree therein as to your lordship shall seem meet and your orator shall ever pray.

Curll's Answer

The Answer of Edmund Curll, Bookseller, to the Bill of Complaint of Alexander Pope, Esquire, Complainant:

This defendant, now and all times hereafter saving and reserving to himself all and all manner of benefit and advantage of exception that may be had and taken to the many untruths, uncertainties, and other insufficiencies in the complainant's said bill of complaint conteined, for answer thereunto, or unto so much thereof as he is advised is material for him to make answer unto, he answereth and saith that he admitts by an Act of Parliament made in the eighth year of the reign of her late majesty Queen Ann, intitled An Act for the Encouragement of Learning by Vesting the Copies of Printed Books in the Authors or Purchasers of such Copies during the Times therein Mentioned, it was among other things enacted to the intent and purport for that purpose set forth in the complainant's said bill: And this defendant further answereth and saith that he does not of his own knowledge know, nor can set forth, whether the complainant was not or is the sole author and proprietor of such part of the book in the complainant's said bill mentioned as purports to be letters written by the complainant and addressed to the Reverend Doctor Swift, Dean of Saint Patrick's in the Kingdom of Ireland, in the said bill named, bearing date the respective later in the said bill mentioned: And this defendant saith he doth not know, nor can set forth otherwise than as hereinafter is mentioned, whether the complainant has ever disposed of his right therein to any person or persons, or whether the complainant hath the sole and absolute right of printing and reprinting, vending, or selling such letters: But this defendant saith that all the letters mentioned in the complainant's said bill of complaint were, as this defendant verily believes, actually sent and delivered by and to the several persons by whom and to whom they severally purport to have been written and addressed; and therefore this defendant is advised and humbly insists that the complainant is not to be considered as the author and pro- prietor of all or any of the said letters: And this defendant is also advised and humbly insists that the said letters are not a work of that nature and sole right of printing whereof was intended to be preserved by the said statute to the author and his assignee or assigns, but this defendant doth admitt that he has printed, or caused to be printed, five hundred copies only of the said letters, together with several other peices under the title of Dean Swift's Literary Correspondence for Twenty-four Years from 1714 to 1738, Consisting of Original letters to and from Mr Pope, Doctor Swift, Mr Gay, Lord Bolingbroke and Letters from Dean Swift to the Duke and Dutchess of Queensbury, illustrated with explanatory notes and a key throughout, to which are subjoyned: first, philosophical letters between Doctor Arbuthnot and Doctor Wotton concerning the

Deluge and the case of marine bodies dug out of the earth; Second, classical letters written in exile from Bishop Atterbury to Doctor Friend; third, a letter from Doctor Crichton at Quincy concerning the climate of that country; Fourth, a letter from the late Barnham Goode, Esquire, to a lady who had great faith in fortune telling; fifth, Dean Swift's Present Case in verse; sixth, Epitaph for himself by Mr Pope, Printed for E. Curll, in Rose Street, Covent Garden; J. Jackson in Saint James Street; H. Chappelle in Grosvenor Street; and E. Cooke under the Royal Exchange; of which he has sold but sixteen copies, which were sold at the price of four shillings each to gentlemen purchasors, and three shillings and sixpence to booksellers; but this defendant hath been stayed in the sale of the rest of them by the injunction of this honourable court: And this defendant further answereth and saith that he never had any express lycence or authority to print or publish any of the complainant's said letters, or any of the said letters sent by the said Doctor Swift to the complainant, but this defendant saith he is informed and verily believes that the said letters were first printed at Dublin in the Kingdom of Ireland by Mr George Faulkener, bookseller there, and as it said by the direction of the said Doctor Swift to whom the said letters written by the complainant were addressed, and by whom the said letters addressed to the complainant were written, as this defendant believes: And this defendant is advised and humbly insists that all persons in this kingdom have a right to reprint such books as are first published in Ireland, and that such as are first published here may be lawfully reprinted in that kingdom; and this defendant is informed and believes that the practice of booksellers in both kingdoms hath been agreeable thereto; and as this defendant hath only reprinted the said letters from the said Dublin edition, he is advised and humbly insists he hath done nothing but what was lawfull for him to do: And this defendant saith that one third part of this defendant's said book consists of pieces not before published, composed by Doctor Arbuthnot, Doctor Wotton, Doctor Atterbury, the late Bishop of Rochester, Barman Goode, Esquire, and Doctor Crichton, some of which were given to and others purchased by this defendant, and in which this defendant hath the sole property; and that part of the said book which the complainant claims property in is no more than one-fifth part of the said book, being but four sheets out of twenty of which the book printed by this defendant consists; And this defendant does deny that he has made any agreement with any person or persons in relation to the printings of the said edition of this defendant's book or the profits arising thereby, except the agreement made by this defendant with the person who printed the same for this defendant; And this defendant saith that the complainant is not intitled, as he humbly apprehends and insists, to have any account of profitts from this defendant for the reason aforesaid, but humbly hopes that he shall be permitted to sell his said book, reprinted from the Dublin edition of the said letters as aforesaid; And this defendant denys all unlawfull combination and confederacy, as the said bill charged against him, without that that there is any other matter or thing in the complainant's said bill of complaint conteined material or effectual for this defendant to make answer unto and not herewith and hereby sufficiently answered unto, confessed or avoided, traversed or denyed, is true to the knowledge and beleif of this defendant; all which matters and things this defendant is ready to averr and prove as this honourable court shall award; And humbly prays to be hence dismissed with his reasonable costs and charges in this behalf unjustly by him susteined.

Lord Chancellor Hardwicke's Decision

Lord Chancellor,

The first question is, whether letters are within the grounds and intention of the statute made in the 8th year of Queen *Anne, c,* 19, intitled, An act for the encouragement of learning, by vesting the copies of printed books in the authors or purchasers of such copies.

I think it would be extremely mischievous, to make a distinction between a book of letters, which comes out into the world, either by the permission of the writer, or the receiver of them, and any other learned work.

The same objection would hold against sermons, which the author may never intend should be published, but are collected from loose papers, and brought out after his death.

Another objection has been made by the defendant's counsel, that where a man writes a letter, it is in the nature of a gift to the receiver.

But I am of the opinion that it is only a special property in the receiver, possibly the property of the paper may belong to him; but this does not give a licence to any person whatsoever to publish them to the world, for at most the receiver has only a joint property with the writer.

The second question is, whether a book originally printed in *Ireland*, is lawful prize to the booksellers here.

If I should be of that opinion, it would have very pernicious consequences, for then a bookseller who has got a printed copy of a book, has nothing else to do but send it over to *Ireland* to be printed, and then by pretending to reprint it only in *England*, will by this means intirely evade the act of parliament.

It has been insisted on by the defendant's counsel, that this is a sort of work which does not come within the meaning of the act of Parliament, because it contains only letters on familiar subjects, and inquiries after the health of friends, and cannot properly be called a learned work.

It is certain that no works have done more service to mankind, than those which have appeared in this shape, upon familiar subjects, and which perhaps were never intended to be published; and it is this makes them so valuable; for I must confess for my own part, that letters which are very elaborately written, and originally intended for the press, are generally the most insignificant, and very little worth any person's reading.

The injunction was continued by *Lord Chancellor* only as to those letters, which are under Mr. *Pope's* name in the book, and which are written *by him*, and not as to those which are written *to him*.

Appendix B

⭑⭑⭑

Justice Nares' Vote in *Donaldson v. Becket*

The standard legal and historical sources for *Donaldson v. Becket* give the judges' vote on the third question—whether the author's common-law right was taken away by the statute—as 6 to 5 against the author's right. But there is reason to believe that the vote was actually 6 to 5 in favor of the author's right. The crux of the matter is the vote of Justice George Nares of Common Pleas.

Nares, who delivered his opinion to the House of Lords on 15 February 1774, was the second most junior of the twelve common-law judges and therefore the second to speak, following Baron James Eyre of the Exchequer. Contemporary newspaper accounts of Nares' opinion indicate that he supported the author's right and did not believe it was taken away by the statute. The most important of these is William Woodfall's, published in the *Morning Chronicle* on 16 February 1774, the day after Nares' speech. Dubbed "Memory" Woodfall in testimony to his prodigious reportorial feats, Woodfall, who was editor and publisher of the *Morning Chronicle* as well as its regular parliamentary correspondent, was undoubtedly the most respected parliamentary reporter of his day. Indeed, Woodfall has been called possibly "the most gifted reporter in the whole history of the English Press" (Smith 356). According to Woodfall's account, Nares

> began by observing that the historical nature of the case had been so learnedly and fully agitated in the hearing of the house, that he should

wave entering into it, but should rather rest his opinion on general conclusions, deduced from principles which arose from fair argument. He stated to the House why he thought a Common Law right in Literary Property did exist, and why the statute of Queen Anne did not take it away. He observed that he was of Mr. Dunning's sentiments, that as it was admitted on all hands that an author had a beneficial interest in his own manuscript before publication, it was a most extraordinary circumstance that he should lose that beneficial interest the very first moment he attempted to exercise it. Mr. Justice Nares put several cases to support his argument, and the statute he said, did not take away the Common Law remedy, although it gave an additional one, as in the case of an action for maliciously suing out a commission of bankruptcy, although the statutes of bankruptcy have provided an additional penalty for that offence by the bond given to the Chancellor; after having spoke near an hour he concluded with answering the questions in a manner directly opposite to that of Mr. Baron Eyre.

After Nares' speech, Woodfall continued, Justice William Ashurst of King's Bench "rose, and accorded in the same opinion with Mr. Justice Nares." When Ashurst, who was a strong defender of the author's common-law right, concluded giving his own opinion, he informed the lords that Judge William Blackstone of King's Bench, also a strong supporter of the author's right, was at home ill with the gout. Blackstone had, however, written out his opinion and Ashurst read it to the house. Blackstone, reported Woodfall, "was of the same opinion with his brethren, Mr. Justice Nares, and Mr. Justice Ashurst."

According to Woodfall, then, Nares' vote on the crucial third question was the same as Ashurst's and Blackstone's; all three judges were agreed that there was a common-law right, that it survived publication, and that it was not taken away by the statute. Woodfall's report of Nares' vote is confirmed by other London newspapers, including the *Gazetteer,* the *London Chronicle,* the *London Evening Post,* and the *Public Advertiser.* The two accounts of the case published in pamphlet form shortly after the determination—*The Pleadings of the Counsel before the House of Lords in the Great Cause Concerning Literary Property,* derived in part from Woodfall, and *The Cases of the Appellants and Respondents in the Cause of Literary Property before the House of Lords*—also confirm Nares' vote, as does the account, derived in part from Woodfall, which appeared in the February, March, and April 1774 numbers of *Gentleman's Magazine*. The clerk of the House of Lords, however, both in his manuscript *Minute Book* and in the official *Journal of the House of Lords* reported Nares as voting against the author's right on the third question. And this report made its way into legal history through the brief notice of *Donaldson*—essentially the record of the case as it appeared in the *Minute Book*—that Sir James Burrow appended to his account of *Millar v. Taylor* in his 1776 collection of reports. Likewise, Josiah Brown's account in his 1783 collection of *Parliamentary Cases* reported Nares as voting against the common-law right; as did the account in the seventeenth volume of William Cobbett's *Parliamentary History of England*, published in 1813.

The clerk of the House of Lords did not take down the substance of the judges' opinions; he merely recorded their votes; and this tally was what both Burrow and Brown, neither of whom attempts to report the judges' speeches, relied on. Cobbett reprints the tally, but in addition he provides an account, derived in part ultimately from Woodfall, of the judges' speeches. Cobbett's report of Nares' position is thus completely contradictory. He first gives an account of Nares' opinion which repeats verbatim the one that first appeared in *The Morning Chronicle*—"He stated to the House why he thought a common law right in literary property did exist, and why the statute of queen Anne did not take it away"—and then he reports that Nares' opinion on the third question was that the common-law right was taken away by the statute (col. 976).

The contradiction in Cobbett's account of Nares' vote was first remarked by John Whicher, who also was the first to note the conflict between the two anonymous pamphlet accounts and the standard accounts by Burrow and Brown. More recently, Howard Abrams has studied the vote in the case in detail, basing his discussion also on the two pamphlet accounts and on Burrow, Brown, and Cobbett. He concludes, as do I, that "it appears that a majority of the judges actually took the position that common law copyright existed and was not 'impeached' or preempted by the Statute of Anne" (1166), but neither he nor Whicher is able to explain the discrepancy between the pamphlets and the tally in Burrow, Brown, and Cobbett. My own curiosity about this little historical puzzle has led me to the newspaper accounts, which confirm that the majority favored the survival of the author's right, and to the *Minute Book*, where the error in the recording of Nares' vote begins. But why did the clerk of the House of Lords err in recording Nares' vote?

Possibly the error was merely scribal. The clerk used standardized language for recording each judge's vote on each question. Perhaps in recording Nares' vote he inadvertently dropped the negatives from a passage that ought to have read "such action at Common Law is *not* taken away by the Statute 8th Anne and that an Author by the said Statute is *not* precluded from every Remedy except on the Foundation of the said Statute." But it is worth noting that the clerk was not the only person who misinterpreted Nares' vote on the third question. The London correspondent for the Donaldsons' paper *The Edinburgh Advertiser* in a summary article on the opinions of the first nine judges reported that Nares "thought a common law right did exist," but added that Nares "was clearly of opinion, that that common law right was taken away by the Statute of Queen Anne" (22 Feb. 1774). Of course the reporter for the *Edinburgh Advertiser* would have been motivated to understand Nares' opinion in this way. Still my suspicion is that there must have been something slightly confusing about the way Nares, who we are told by Woodfall spoke "near an hour," presented his opinion, something that allowed the correspondent for the *Advertiser* to hear what he wanted to hear and that also, perhaps, flustered the recording clerk.

At one time I thought I understood the source of the clerk's confusion, but now I am no longer so sure that I do. I can report, however, that keeping track of the judges' votes on the five questions is not easy—sometimes a vote in favor of the author's right is expressed as a negative and sometimes as a positive, according to the exact phrasing of the question; sometimes too the clerk would have to interpret a judge's statement in order to determine how his vote should be recorded. Abrams provides a useful appendix (1188–91) in which he tabulates each of the judges' votes as reported in the five sources he uses: Burrow, Brown, Cobbett, and the two pamphlets.

Substantively, the clerk's error was inconsequential: it was the vote of the House of Lords, not that of the judges, that determined the outcome of the appeal. Nevertheless, the clerk's error obscured the fact that the peers' vote did not follow the majority opinion of the judges. It allowed the vote to be understood as a confirmation of the majority opinion of the senior jurists of the land, which was not true. The clerk's error, in other words, contributed to a less than fully justified sense of closure to the literary-property question.

Works Cited

Primary Sources

Addison, Joseph. *The Spectator*. Ed. Donald F. Bond. Oxford: Clarendon, 1965. 5 vols.

———— *The Tatler*. Ed. Donald F. Bond. Oxford: Clarendon, 1987. 3 vols.

Arber, Edward, ed. *A Transcript of the Registers of the Company of Stationers of London: 1554–1640*. 1875–1894. New York: Peter Smith, 1950. 5 vols.

A Bill for the Encouragement of Learning and for Securing the Properties of Copies of Books to the Rightful Owners thereof. Text of first and second readings. 1710. MS Rawl. D.922, ff. 380–386. Bodleian Library, Oxford.

Blackstone, William. *Commentaries on the Laws of England*. Oxford, 1765–1769. Facsimile rpt. Chicago: U of Chicago P, 1979. 4 vols.

Blount, Charles. *Reasons Humbly Offered for the Liberty of Unlicens'd Printing*. London, 1693. Rpt. *Freedom of the Press: Four Tracts 1664–1693*. Ed. Stephen Parks. New York: Garland, 1975.

The Booksellers Humble Address to the Honourable House of Commons, In Behalf of the Bill for Encouraging Learning, etc. London, 1710.

Boswell, James. *The Decision of the Court of Session upon the Question of Literary Property in the Cause of Hinton against Donaldson*. Edinburgh, 1774. Rpt. *The Literary Property Debate: Six Tracts 1764–1774*. Ed. Stephen Parks. New York: Garland, 1975.

———— *The Life of Johnson*. 1799. Ed. George Birkbeck Hill, rev. L. F. Powell. Oxford: Clarendon, 1934–1964. 6 vols.

Bowle, John. *Reflections on Originality in Authors*. London, 1766.

Brown, Josiah. *Reports of Cases, Upon Appeals and Writs of Error, in the High Court of Parliament*. London, 1779–1783. 7 vols.

Burrow, James. *The Question Concerning Literary Property, Determined by the Court of King's Bench on 20th April, 1769, in the Cause Between Andrew Millar and Robert Taylor*. London, 1773. Rpt. *The Literary Property Debate: Seven Tracts 1747–1773*. Ed. Stephen Parks. New York: Garland, 1974.

The Case of Authors and Proprietors of Books. London, 1735. British Library copy [defective] rpt. *English Publishing, the Struggle for Copyright, and the Freedom of the Press: Thirteen Tracts 1666–1774*. Ed. Stephen Parks. New York: Garland, 1975.

The Case of the Booksellers and Printers Stated; with Answers to the Objections of the Patentee. London, n.d. Rpt. *English Publishing, the Struggle for Copyright, and the Freedom of the Press: Thirteen Tracts 1666–1774*. Ed. Stephen Parks. New York: Garland, 1975.

The Case of the Booksellers of London and Westminster. London, 1774.

The Case of the Booksellers Right to their Copies, or Sole Power of Printing their Respective Books, Represented to the Parliament. London, 1710.

The Cases of the Appellants and Respondents in the Cause of Literary Property, Before the House of Lords. London, 1774. Rpt. *The Literary Property Debate: Six Tracts 1764–1774*. Ed. Stephen Parks. New York: Garland, 1975.

Cervantes, Miguel de. *Don Quixote*. 1605. Trans. Walter Starkie. New York: Signet, 1964.

The Charter of the Company of Stationers of London. Rpt. Arber 1:xxviii–xxxii.

Considerations on the Nature and Origin of Literary Property. Attrib. John Maclaurin. Edinburgh, 1767. Rpt. *Freedom of the Press and the Literary Property Debate: Six Tracts 1755–1770*. Ed. Stephen Parks. New York: Garland, 1974.

Craigie, John, et al. *Reports of Cases Decided in the House of Lords, upon Appeal from Scotland, from 1726 to 1822*. Edinburgh, 1849–1856. 5 vols.

Curll, Edmund. *Answer to Alexander Pope's Bill of Complaint*. 1741. PRO C11/1569/29.

Defoe, Daniel. *An Essay on the Regulation of the Press*. London, 1704. Oxford: Basil Blackwell for Luttrell Society, 1948.

——— *The Little Review*. Rpt. Secord.

——— *The Review*. Rpt. Secord.

Dennis, John. *The Critical Works of John Dennis*. Ed. Edward Niles Hooker. 2 vols. Baltimore: Johns Hopkins UP, 1939–1943.

Dryden, John. *The Works of Virgil in English*. Berkeley: U of California P, 1987. Vol. 6 of *The Works of John Dryden*. 1697. Ed. William Frost and Vinton A. Dearing. 17 vols. 1956–.

Early English Newspapers. Microfilm collection.

The Edinburgh Advertiser. British Library.

The Eighteenth-Century Short Title Catalogue. Online database in RLIN.

Enfield, William. *Observations on Literary Property*. London, 1774. Rpt. *The Literary Property Debate: Eight Tracts, 1774–1775*. Ed. Stephen Parks. New York: Garland, 1974.

English Reports [*ER*]. Ed. A. Wood Renton. London: Stevens, 1900–1932. 178 vols.

An Enquiry into the Nature and Origin of Literary Property. Erroneously (?) attrib. William Warburton. London, 1762. Rpt. *Horace Walpole's Political Tracts 1747–1748 with Two by William Warburton on Literary Property 1747 and 1762*. Ed. Stephen Parks. New York: Garland, 1974.

Eyre, G. E. Briscoe, ed. *A Transcript of the Registers of the Worshipful Company of Stationers; from 1640–1708*. London: priv. print., 1913–14. 3 vols.

Fergusson, James, Lord Kilkerran. *Decisions of the Court of Session*. Edinburgh, 1775.

Fielding, Henry. *The Covent-Garden Journal*. Ed. Gerard Edward Jensen. New Haven: Yale UP, 1915. 2 vols.

———— *The History of Tom Jones.* 1749. Ed. Fredson Bowers. Middletown: Wesleyan
UP, 1975.

———— *The Jacobite's Journal and Related Writings.* Ed. W. B. Coley. Oxford:
Clarendon, 1974.

French, J. M., ed. *Life Records of John Milton.* New Brunswick: Rutgers UP, 1949–1958.
5 vols.

The Gazetteer. In *Early English Newspapers.*

Grant, Patrick, Lord Elchies. *Decisions of the Court of Session.* Edinburgh, 1813.

Hargrave, Francis. *An Argument in Defence of Literary Property.* 2nd ed. London,
1774. Rpt. *An Argument in Defence of Literary Property, 1774, Francis Hargrave;
Four Tracts on Freedom of the Press, 1790–1821.* Ed. Stephen Parks. New York:
Garland, 1974.

Hinman, Charlton, ed. *The First Folio of Shakespeare.* New York: Norton, 1968.

Home, Henry, Lord Kames. *Remarkable Decisions of the Court of Session from the
Year 1730 to the Year 1752.* Edinburgh, 1766.

Hughes, Merritt Y., ed. *John Milton: Complete Poems and Major Prose.* Indianapolis:
Odyssey, 1957.

The Humble Remonstrance of the Company of Stationers. Attrib. Henry Parker. 1643.
Rpt. Arber 1:584–588.

Hume, David. *A Treatise of Human Nature.* 1739–40. Ed. L. A. Selby-Bigge, 2nd ed.
rev. P. H. Nidditch. Oxford: Clarendon, 1978.

Johnson, Samuel. *Johnsonian Miscellanies.* Ed. George Birkbeck Hill. Oxford:
Clarendon, 1907. 2 vols.

———— *Johnson on Shakespeare.* New Haven: Yale UP, 1968. Vol. 7–8 of *The Yale
Edition of the Works of Samuel Johnson.* Ed. Arthur Sherbo. 16 vols. 1958–.

———— *Johnson's Lives of the Most Eminent Poets.* Ed. George Birkbeck Hill. 1905.
Rpt. New York: Octagon, 1967. 3 vols.

———— *The Rambler.* New Haven: Yale UP, 1969. Vol. 3–5 of *The Yale Edition of the
Works of Samuel Johnson.* Ed. W. J. Bate and Albrecht B. Strauss. 16 vols. 1958–.

Journals of the House of Commons [*CJ*].

Journals of the House of Lords [*LJ*].

Keats, John. *The Letters of John Keats, 1814–1821.* Ed. Hyder Edward Rollins. Cambridge: Harvard UP, 1958. 2 vols.

King, Peter. *The Life and Letters of John Locke.* London, 1884.

*A Letter from a Gentleman in Edinburgh to his Friend in London Concerning Literary
Property.* Edinburgh, 1769. Rpt. *Freedom of the Press and the Literary Property
Debate: Six Tracts 1755–1770.* Ed. Stephen Parks. New York: Garland, 1974.

*A Letter from an Author to a Member of Parliament Occasioned by a Late Letter
Concerning the Bill Now Depending in the House of Commons.* London, 1735.

*A Letter to a Member of Parliament Concerning the Bill Now Depending in the House
of Commons.* London, 1735.

Locke, John. *The Correspondence of John Locke and Edward Clarke.* Ed. Benjamin
Rand. Cambridge: Harvard UP, 1927.

———— *Memorandum.* King 202–209.

———— *Two Treatises of Government.* 1690. Ed. Peter Laslett. London: Cambridge
UP, 1967.

The London Chronicle. In *Early English Newspapers.*

The London Evening Post. In *Early English Newspapers*.

Macaulay, Catharine. *A Modest Plea for the Property of Copyright*. London, 1774. Rpt. *The Literary Property Debate: Eight Tracts 1774–1775*. Ed. Stephen Parks. New York: Garland, 1974.

Maugham, Robert. *A Treatise of the Laws of Literary Property*. London, 1828.

Milton, John. *Areopagitica*. 1644. Hughes 716–749.

——— *Eikonoklastes*. 1650. Hughes 781–815.

Minute Book. House of Lords. London.

More, John. *Strictures Critical and Sentimental on Thomson's Seasons*. London, 1777.

More Reasons Humbly Offer'd to the Honourable House of Commons, for the Bill for Encouraging Learning, and for Securing Property of Copies of Books to the Rightful Owners thereof. London, 1710.

The Morning Chronicle. In *Early English Newspapers*.

Murphy, Arthur. *Gray's-Inn Journal*. London, 1786. Vol. 5 of *The Works of Arthur Murphy, Esq*. 7 vols.

Observations on the Case of the Booksellers of London and Westminster. London, 1774.

Petitions and Papers Relating to the Bill of the Booksellers Now Before the House of Commons. London, 1774. Rpt. *The Literary Property Debate: Eight Tracts, 1774–1775*. Ed. Stephen Parks. New York: Garland, 1974.

The Pleadings of the Counsel Before the House of Lords in the Great Cause Concerning Literary Property. London, n.d. Rpt. *The Literary Property Debate: Six Tracts, 1764–1774*. Ed. Stephen Parks. New York: Garland, 1975.

Pope, Alexander. *Bill of Complaint*. 1741. PRO C11/1569/29.

——— *The Correspondence of Alexander Pope*. Ed. George Sherburn. Oxford: Clarendon, 1956. 5 vols.

——— *A Narrative of the Method by which Mr. Pope's Private Letters were Procured and Published by Edmund Curl, Bookseller*. *The Prose Works of Alexander Pope*. 1735. Ed. Rosemary Cowler. Oxford: Basil Blackwell for Shakespeare Head, 1986. 2:327–356.

——— *The Poems of Alexander Pope*. Ed. John Butt et al. London: Methuen, 1938–1968. 11 vols.

The Public Advertiser. In *Early English Newspapers*.

Records of the Court of the Stationers' Company, 1602 to 1640. Ed. William A. Jackson. London: Bibliographic Society, 1957.

Review of *An Argument in Defence of Literary Property* by Francis Hargrave. *Monthly Review* 51 (1774): 209–213.

Review of *A Vindication of the Exclusive Rights of Authors to their own Works: A Subject now under Consideration before the Twelve Judges of England*. *Monthly Review* 27 (1763): 176–191.

Richardson, Samuel. *An Address to the Public*. London, 1754.

——— *The Case of Samuel Richardson*. London, 1753. Rpt. *English Publishing, the Struggle for Copyright, and the Freedom of the Press: Thirteen Tracts 1666–1774*. Ed. Stephen Parks. New York: Garland, 1975.

A Second Letter from an Author to a Member of Parliament; Containing some Further Remarks on a Late Letter Concerning the Bill Now Depending in the House of Commons. London, 1735.

Secord, Arthur Wellesley, ed. *Defoe's Review Reproduced From the Original Editions*. New York: Columbia UP for Facsimile Text Society, 1938. 9 vols.

Shakespeare, William. *The Riverside Shakespeare*. Ed. G. B. Evans et al. Boston: Houghton Mifflin, 1974.

A Short State of the Publick Encouragement Given to Printing and Bookselling in France, Holland, Germany, and at London. London, 1735. Rpt. *English Publishing, the Struggle for Copyright, and the Freedom of the Press: Thirteen Tracts 1666–1774*. Ed. Stephen Parks. New York: Garland, 1975.

Sidney, Sir Philip. *The Countess of Pembroke's Arcadia*. 1598. Ed. Jean Robertson. Oxford: Clarendon, 1973.

———— *Defence of Poetry. Miscellaneous Prose of Sir Philip Sidney*. 1595. Ed. Katherine Duncan-Jones and Jan Van Dorsten. Oxford: Clarendon, 1973.

Some Thoughts on the State of Literary Property Humbly Submitted to the Consideration of the Public. London, 1764. Rpt. *The Literary Property Debate: Six Tracts 1764–1774*. Ed. Stephen Parks. New York: Garland, 1975.

Southey, Robert. "Inquiry into the Copyright Act." *Quarterly Review* 21 (Jan. 1819): 196–213.

Speeches or Arguments of the Judges of the Court of King's Bench in the Cause of Millar against Taylor. Leith, 1771. Rpt. *The Literary Property Debate: Seven Tracts 1747–1773*. Ed. Stephen Parks. New York: Garland, 1974.

The Statutes at Large, from the Tenth Year of King William the Third to the End of the Reign of Queen Anne. Ruffhead's Statutes. London: G. Eyre and A. Strahan, 1763–1800. 18 vols.

The Statutes of the Realm from Magna Carta to the End of the Reign of Queen Anne. 1810–1828. London: Dawsons, 1963. 11 vols.

"Summary of the Arguments of the Council and Judges in the Great Cause which Came on to be Heard before the House of Peers, on Friday the 4th instant, for ascertaining the Right of Literary Property." *Gentleman's Magazine* Feb. 1774:51–6; March 1774:99–104; April 1774:147–52.

Swift, Jonathan. *The Correspondence of Jonathan Swift*. Ed. Harold Williams. Oxford: Clarendon, 1963–1965. 5 vols.

Talfourd, Thomas Noon. *A Speech Delivered by Thomas Noon Talfourd, Sergeant at Law, in The House of Commons*. London, 1837.

A Vindication of the Exclusive Right of Authors to their own Works: A Subject now under Consideration before the Twelve Judges of England. London, 1762. Rpt. *Horace Walpole's Political Tracts 1747–1748 with Two by William Warburton on Literary Property 1747 and 1762*. Ed. Stephen Parks. New York: Garland, 1974.

Warburton, William. *A Letter from an Author to a Member of Parliament Concerning Literary Property*. London, 1747. Rpt. *Horace Walpole's Political Tracts 1747–1748 with Two by William Warburton on Literary Property 1747 and 1762*. Ed. Stephen Parks. New York: Garland, 1974.

Warren, Samuel D., and Louis D. Brandeis. "The Right to Privacy." *Harvard Law Review* 4 (1890): 193–200.

Wordsworth, William. *Letters of William and Dorothy Wordsworth*. 2nd ed. Ed. E. de Selincourt. Oxford: Clarendon, 1967–1988. 7 vols.

———— *The Prose Works of William Wordsworth*. Ed. W. J. B. Owen and Jane Worthington Smyser. Oxford: Clarendon, 1974. 3 vols.

Young, Edward. *Conjectures on Original Composition*. 1759. Leeds: Scolar, 1966.

———— *The Correspondence of Edward Young 1683–1765*. Ed. Henry Pettit. Oxford: Clarendon, 1971.

———— "On Lyric Poetry." 1728. *Eighteenth-Century Critical Essays.* Ed. Scott Elledge. 2 vols. Ithaca: Cornell UP, 1961. 1:410–415.

Secondary Sources

Abrams, Howard B. "The Historic Foundation of American Copyright Law: Exploding the Myth of Common Law Copyright." *Wayne Law Review* 29 (1983): 1119–91.

Abrams, M. H. *The Mirror and the Lamp.* New York: Oxford UP, 1953.

Altick, Richard D. *The English Common Reader: A Social History of the Mass Reading Public.* Chicago: U of Chicago P, 1957.

Armstrong, Elizabeth. *Before Copyright: The French Book-Privilege System, 1498–1526.* Cambridge: Cambridge UP, 1990.

Ashton, T. S. *An Economic History of England: The 18th Century.* London: Methuen, 1955.

Astbury, Raymond. "The Renewal of the Licensing Act in 1693 and its Lapse in 1695." *Library* 33 (1978): 296–322.

Barnard, John. "Dryden, Tonson, and Subscriptions for the 1697 *Virgil.*" *Papers of the Bibliographical Society of America* 57 (1963): 129–151.

Barney, Stephen A. "The Plowshare of the Tongue: The Progress of a Symbol from the Bible to *Piers Plowman.*" *Mediaeval Studies* 35 (1973): 261–293.

Barrell, John. *The Political Theory of Painting from Reynolds to Hazlitt.* New Haven: Yale UP, 1986.

Barthes, Roland. "The Death of the Author." Trans. Richard Howard. *The Rustle of Language.* New York: Hill and Wang, 1986.

Battestin, Martin C., with Ruthe R. Battestin. *Henry Fielding: A Life.* London: Routledge, 1989.

Belanger, Terry. "Publishers and Writers in Eighteenth-Century England." *Books and their Readers in Eighteenth-Century England.* Ed. Isabel Rivers. London: St. Martin's, 1982.

Bentley, G. E. *The Profession of Dramatist in Shakespeare's Time.* Princeton: Princeton UP, 1971.

Blagden, Cyprian. *The Stationers' Company: A History, 1403–1959.* London: Allen, 1960.

———— "Thomas Carnan and the Almanack Monopoly." *Studies in Bibliography* 14 (1969): 23–43.

Bloom, Edward A. "Johnson on Copyright." *JEGP* 47 (1948): 165–172.

Blum, Abbe. "The Author's Authority: *Areopagitica* and the Labour of Licensing." *Re-Membering Milton.* Ed. Mary Nyquist and Margaret W. Ferguson. London: Methuen, 1987.

Boyle, James. "A Theory of Law and Information: Copyright, Genes, Blackmail, and Insider Trading." Conference on Intellectual Property and the Construction of Authorship. Case Western Reserve University, April 1991.

Brady, Frank. *James Boswell: The Later Years 1769–1795.* New York: McGraw, 1984.

Brooks, Cleanth. *The Well Wrought Urn.* New York: Harcourt, 1947.

Brown, Cynthia. "Du manuscrit à l'imprimé en France: le cas des Grands Rhétoriqueurs." *Actes du Ve Colloque International sur le Moyen Francais*. 3 vols. Milan: Vita e pensiero, 1985. 1:103–123.

Brown, Horatio F. *The Venetian Printing Press, 1469–1800*. New York, 1891.

Bugbee, Bruce W. *Genesis of American Patent and Copyright Law*. Washington: Public Affairs, 1967.

Cardozo Arts and Entertainment Law Journal 10 (1992). Special number on "Intellectual Property and the Construction of Authorship."

Chartier, Roger. "The Practical Impact of Writing." Trans. Arthur Goldhammer. *A History of Private life III: Passions of the Renaissance*. Ed. Roger Chartier. Cambridge: Harvard UP, 1989.

Chavasse, Ruth. "The First Known Author's Copyright." *Bulletin of the John Rylands Library* 69 (1986): 11–37.

Clifford, James L. "Johnson and Lauder." *Philological Quarterly* 54 (1975): 342–356.

Cobbett, William. *Parliamentary History of England*. London, 1806–1820. 36 vols.

Collins, A. S. *Authorship in the Days of Johnson*. New York: Dutton, 1929.

Copinger, Walter Arthur, and E. P. Skone James. *Copinger and Skone James on Copyright*. 12th ed. London: Sweet, 1980.

Davis, Natalie Zemon. "Beyond the Market: Books as Gifts in Sixteenth-Century France." *Transactions of the Royal Historical Society* 5th ser. 33 (1983): 69–88.

Dawson, Giles E. "The Copyright of Shakespeare's Dramatic Works." *Studies in Honor of A. H. R. Fairchild*. Ed. C. T. Prouty. Columbia: U of Missouri P, 1956.

De Grazia, Margreta. *Shakespeare Verbatim: The Reproduction of Authenticity and the 1790 Apparatus*. Oxford: Clarendon, 1991.

Dock, Marie-Claude. *Etude sur le droit d'auteur*. Paris: Librairie générale de droit et de jurisprudence, 1963.

Donnelly, Lucy Martin. "The Celebrated Mrs. Macaulay." *William and Mary Quarterly* 3rd ser. 6 (1949): 172–207.

Dunn, John. *The Political Thought of John Locke: An Historical Account of the Argument of the "Two Treatises of Government"*. Cambridge: Cambridge UP, 1969.

Eagleton, Terry. *The Ideology of the Aesthetic*. Oxford: Blackwell, 1990.

Eaves, T. C. Duncan, and Ben D. Kimpel. *Samuel Richardson: A Biography*. Oxford: Clarendon, 1971.

Eeles, Henry S. *Lord Chancellor Camden and His Family*. London: Philip Allan, 1934.

Eilenberg, Susan. "Mortal Pages: Wordsworth and the Reform of Copyright." *ELH* 56 (1989): 351–374.

Eisenstein, Elizabeth. *The Printing Press as an Agent of Change*. Cambridge: Cambridge UP, 1980.

Feather, John. "The Book Trade in Politics: The Making of the Copyright Act of 1710." *Publishing History* 8 (1980): 19–44.

———— "Publishers and Politicians: the Remaking of the Law of Copyright in Britain 1775–1842. Part I: Legal Deposit and the Battle of the Library Tax. Part II: The Rights of Authors." *Publishing History* 24 (1988): 49–76; 25 (1989): 45–72.

———— "The Publishers and the Pirates: British Copyright Law in Theory and Practice, 1710–1775." *Publishing History* 22 (1987): 5–32.

Fifoot, C. H. S. *Lord Mansfield*. Oxford: Clarendon, 1936.

Foster, Donald W. "Master W. H., R.I.P." *PMLA* 102 (1987): 42–54.

Foucault, Michel. "What Is an Author?" *The Foucault Reader*. Ed. Paul Rabinow. New York: Pantheon, 1984.

Fox, Christopher. *Locke and the Scriblerians: Identity and Consciousness in Early Eighteenth-Century Britain*. Berkeley: U of California P, 1988.

Foxon, David. *Pope and the Early Eighteenth-Century Book Trade*. Ed. and rev. James McLaverty. Oxford: Clarendon, 1991.

Frye, Northrop. *Anatomy of Criticism*. Princeton: Princeton UP, 1957.

Gaines, Jane M. *Contested Culture: The Image, the Voice, and the Law*. Chapel Hill: U of North Carolina P, 1991.

Gallagher, Catherine. "George Eliot and *Daniel Deronda:* The Prostitute and the Jewish Question." *Sex, Politics, and Science in the Nineteenth-Century Novel*. Ed. Ruth Bernard Yeazell. Baltimore: Johns Hopkins UP, 1986.

Gerulaitis, Leonardas Vytautas. *Printing and Publishing in Fifteenth-Century Venice*. Chicago: American Library Association, 1976.

Gilbert, Sandra M., and Susan Gubar. *The Madwoman in the Attic*. New Haven: Yale UP, 1979.

Ginsburg, Jane. "Creation and Commercial Value: Copyright Protection of Works of Information." *Columbia Law Review* 90 (1990): 1865–1938.

Goldstein, Paul. "Copyright." *Journal of the Copyright Society of the U.S.A.* 38 (1991): 109–122.

Gray, W. Forbes. "Alexander Donaldson and His Fight for Cheap Books." *Juridical Review* 38 (1926): 180–202.

Greg, W. W. *The Shakespeare First Folio: Its Bibliographical and Textual History*. Oxford: Clarendon, 1955.

Halliday, F. E. *The Cult of Shakespeare*. New York: Yoseloff, 1960.

Harrison, Frank Mott. "Nathaniel Ponder: The Publisher of *The Pilgrim's Progress*." *Library* 4th ser. 15 (1934): 257–294.

Helgerson, Richard. *Self-Crowned Laureates: Spenser, Jonson, Milton, and the Literary System*. Berkeley: U of California P, 1983.

Hesse, Carla. "Enlightenment Epistemology and the Laws of Authorship in Revolutionary France, 1777–1793." *Representations* 30 (1990): 109–137.

——— *Publishing and Cultural Politics in Revolutionary Paris, 1789–1810*. Berkeley: U of California P, 1991.

Heward, Edmund. *Lord Mansfield*. Chichester: Barry Rose, 1979.

Holdsworth, Sir William. *A History of English Law*. 1938. London: Methuen and Sweet & Maxwell, 1966. 16 vols.

——— "The House of Lords, 1689–1783." *Law Quarterly Review* 45 (1929): 307–342, 432–458.

Hunter, David. "Copyright Protection for Engravings and Maps in Eighteenth-Century Britain." *Library* 6th ser. 9 (1987): 128–147.

——— "*Pope v. Bickham:* An Infringement of *An Essay on Man* Alleged." *Library* 6th ser. 9 (1987): 268–273.

Jaszi, Peter. "Towards a Theory of Copyright: The Metamorphoses of 'Authorship.'" *Duke Law Journal* 1991: 455–502.

Kaplan, Benjamin. *An Unhurried View of Copyright*. New York: Columbia UP, 1967.

Kennedy, Duncan. "The Structure of Blackstone's *Commentaries*." *Buffalo Law Review* 28 (1978): 205–382.

Kernan, Alvin. *Printing Technology, Letters and Samuel Johnson*. Princeton: Princeton UP, 1987.

Kirschbaum, Leo. "Author's Copyright in England before 1640." *Publications of the Bibliographical Society of America* 40 (1946): 43–48.

——— *Shakespeare and the Stationers*. Columbus: Ohio State UP, 1955.

Lieberman, David. *The Province of Legislation Determined: Legal Theory in Eighteenth-Century Britain*. Cambridge: Cambridge UP, 1989.

Lindenbaum, Peter. "Milton's Contract." *Cardozo Arts & Entertainment Law Journal* 10 (1992): 439–454.

Litman, Jessica. "The Public Domain." *Emory Law Journal* 39 (1990): 965–1023.

Loewenstein, Joseph. "The Script in the Marketplace." *Representations* 12 (1985): 101–114.

Macaulay, Thomas Babington. *History of England*. London: Dent, 1906. 4 vols.

Mack, Maynard. *Alexander Pope: A Life*. New York: Norton, 1985.

Macpherson, C. B. *The Political Theory of Possessive Individualism: Hobbes to Locke*. Oxford: Clarendon, 1962.

Marcus, Leah. *Puzzling Shakespeare: Local Reading and Its Discontents*. Berkeley: U of California P, 1988.

Marcuse, Michael J. "The Lauder Controversy and the Jacobite Cause." *Studies in Burke and His Time* 18 (1977): 27–47.

——— "'The Scourge of Imposters, the Terror of Quacks': John Douglas and the Exposé of William Lauder." *Huntington Library Quarterly* 42 (1978–79): 231–261.

McGill, Meredith L. "*Wheaton v. Peters* and the Materiality of the Text." Conference on Intellectual Property and the Construction of Authorship. Case Western Reserve University, April 1991.

McKillop, Alan D. "Richardson, Young, and the *Conjectures*." *Modern Philology* 22 (1925): 391–404.

McLaverty, James. "The First Printing and Publication of Pope's Letters." *Library* 6th ser. 2 (1980): 264–280.

——— "Lawton Gilliver: Pope's Bookseller." *Studies in Bibliography* 32 (1979): 101–124.

——— "Pope and Copyright." Foxon 237–251.

Miller, Edward Haviland. *The Professional Writer in Elizabethan England*. Cambridge: Harvard UP, 1959.

Moorman, Mary. *William Wordsworth: The Later Years*. Oxford: Clarendon, 1965.

Murray, Timothy. *Theatrical Legitimation: Allegories of Genius in Seventeenth-Century England and France*. New York: Oxford UP, 1987.

Nash, N. Frederick. "English Licenses to Print and Grants of Copyright in the 1640s." *Library* 6th ser. 4 (1982): 174–184.

Nicoll, Allardyce. "The First Baconian." *Times Literary Supplement* 25 Feb. 1932: 128.

Patterson, Lyman Ray. *Copyright in Historical Perspective*. Nashville: Vanderbilt UP, 1968.

——— "Free Speech, Copyright, and Fair Use." *Vanderbilt Law Review* 40 (1987): 1–66.

Paulson, Ronald. *Hogarth's Graphic Works*. Rev. ed. New Haven: Yale UP, 1970. 2 vols.

Plomer, Henry R. "A Lawsuit as to an Early Edition of the 'Pilgrim's Progress.'" *Library* 3rd ser. 5 (1914): 60–69.

Pocock, J. G. A. *The Machiavellian Moment: Florentine Political Thought and the Atlantic Republican Tradition.* Princeton: Princeton UP, 1975.

Pollard, A. W. *Shakespeare's Fight With the Pirates.* Cambridge: Cambridge UP, 1937.

Post, Robert C. "Rereading Warren and Brandeis: Privacy, Property, and Appropriation." *Case Western Reserve Law Review* 41 (1991): 647–680.

Prager, Frank D. "The Early Growth and Influence of Intellectual Property." *Journal of the Patent Office Society* 34 (1952): 106–140.

Putnam, George Haven. *Books and Their Makers During the Middle Ages.* 1896–97. New York: Hillary, 1962.

Quint, David. *Origin and Originality in Renaissance Literature.* New Haven: Yale UP, 1983.

Ransom, Harry. *The First Copyright Statute: An Essay on An Act for the Encouragement of Learning, 1710.* Austin: U of Texas P, 1956.

———— "From a Gentleman in Edinburgh: 1769, An Early Sidelight on Literary Property." *Sewanee Review* 44 (1936): 366–371.

Roeder, Martin A. "The Doctrine of Moral Right: A Study in the Law of Artists, Authors, and Creators." *Harvard Law Review* 53 (1940): 554–578.

Rogers, Pat. "The Case of *Pope v. Curll.*" *Library* 5th ser. 27 (1972): 326–331.

Ross, Ian Simpson. *Lord Kames and the Scotland of His Day.* Oxford: Clarendon, 1972.

Saunders, David, and Ian Hunter. "Lessons from the 'Literatory': How to Historicise Authorship." *Critical Inquiry* 17 (1991): 479–509.

Saunders, J. W. *The Profession of English Letters.* London: Routledge, 1964.

———— "The Stigma of Print: A Note on the Social Bases of Tudor Poetry." *Essays in Criticism* 1 (1951): 139–164.

Schlatter, Richard. *Private Property: The History of an Idea.* New Brunswick: Allen and Unwin, 1951.

Siebert, Fredrick Seaton. *Freedom of the Press in England, 1476–1776.* Urbana: U of Illinois P, 1952.

Smith, D. Nichol. "The Newspaper." *Johnson's England: An Account of the Life and Manners of his Age.* Ed. A. S. Turberville. 2 vols. Oxford: Clarendon, 1933. 2:331–367.

Smithers, Peter. *The Life of Joseph Addison.* Oxford: Clarendon, 1954.

Strauss, William. "The Moral Right of the Author." *Copyright Law Revision: Studies Prepared for the Subcommittee on Patents, Trademarks, and Copyrights of the Committee on the Judiciary, U.S. Senate.* Washington: GPO, 1960. Study 4, 109–142.

Streibich, Harold C. "The Moral Right of Ownership to Intellectual Property: Part I—From the Beginning to the Age of Printing." *Memphis State University Law Review* 6 (1975): 1–84.

Sutherland, James R. "*The Dunciad* of 1729." *Modern Language Review* 31 (1936): 347–353.

———— "'Polly' Among the Pirates." *Modern Language Review* 37 (1942): 291–303.

Swartz, Richard G. "Paternity, Patrimony, and the Figuration of Authorship in the Eighteenth-Century Literary Property Debates." Unpub. MS.

Thomas, P. D. G. *The House of Commons in the Eighteenth Century*. Oxford: Clarendon, 1971.

Tritter, Daniel F. "A Strange Case of Royalty: The Singular 'Copyright' Case of *Prince Albert v. Strange*." *Journal of Media Law and Practice* 4 (1983): 111–129.

Tucker, Irene. "Writing Home: *Evelina*, the Epistolary Novel and the Paradox of Property." Unpub. MS.

Tully, James. *A Discourse on Property: John Locke and His Adversaries*. Cambridge: Cambridge UP, 1980.

Turberville, A. S. *The House of Lords in the Eighteenth Century*. Oxford: Clarendon, 1927.

Vincent, Howard P. "Some *Dunciad* Litigation." *Philological Quarterly* 18 (1939): 285–289.

Walters, Gwyn. "The Booksellers in 1759 and 1774: The Battle for Literary Property." *Library* 29 (1974): 287–311.

Warner, William B. "The Institutionalization of Authorship: Richardson's Battle with the Irish Booksellers." Conference on Intellectual Property and the Construction of Authorship. Case Western Reserve University, April 1991.

Whicher, John F. "The Ghost of *Donaldson v. Beckett*." *Bulletin of the Copyright Society of the U.S.A.* 9 (1961–62): 102–151, 194–229.

Winn, James Anderson. *John Dryden and His World*. New Haven: Yale UP, 1987.

Woodmansee, Martha. "The Genius and the Copyright: Economic and Legal Conditions of the Emergence of the 'Author.'" *Eighteenth-Century Studies* 17 (1984): 425–448.

Zall, Paul M. "Wordsworth and the Copyright Act of 1842." *PMLA* 70 (1955): 132–144.

Zionkowski, Linda. "Territorial Disputes in the Republic of Letters: Canon Formation and the Literary Profession." *The Eighteenth Century: Theory and Interpretation* 31 (1990): 3–22.

Index

Charles I, king of England, 30
Chetwood, William, 49
Childe, Timothy, 58n
Clarke, Edward, 32
Clifford, James, 122n
Coalston, Lord, 84
Cobbett, William: *Parliamentary History of England,* 109n, 156
Coleridge, Hartley, 111
Collins, Benjamin, 74, 75
Common law rights of property transferrable by authors, 4–6, 7, 8, 13–14, 16, 18, 20, 22, 24, 25, 27, 28, 29, 38, 40, 44, 45, 47–48, 56–57, 69–70, 75, 78–91, 92–112
Condensations and compilations protected under Statute of Anne, 137
Considerations on the Nature and Origin of Literary Property, 94
Cop, Guillaume, 18–19
Copinger and Skone James on Copyright, 110n
Copy (stationers' term), 12, 14, 16, 58
Copyright: origin of term, 58, 58n, 65
Copyright Act of 1842, 111
Copyright term, 4, 34, 67, 92; in booksellers' relief bill, 93, 103, 108; in Copyright Act of 1842, 111; extension sought by booksellers, 54; ignoring limitation of, 52; Johnson's proposals for, 108, 110; Locke's proposals for, 45, 47; perpetual, 4–5, 24, 69, 74, 81, 85, 86, 88, 89, 91, 94, 95, 104, 112, 132; revised statute of 1814 extending, 110; in Statute of Anne, 45, 47; Talfourd's proposal for, 111
Court of Assistants. *See* Stationers' Company
Court of Star Chamber, 15, 22
Curll, Edmund, 59, 60, 61, 63, 64, 65, 149–152

Dalrymple, Sir John, 98, 103, 104
Daniel, Samuel: *History of England,* 11, 17
da Ravenna, Petro Francesco, 10
Davis, Natalie Zemon, 13–14
Defoe, Daniel, 40n, 56; *Essay on the Regulation of the Press,* 34–35, 36, 38, 40; *Review,* 35, 36, 37, 38, 39–40, 48; *Shortest Way with the Dissenters,* 34
De Grazia, Margreta, 122
Denbigh, Lord, 103
Dennis, John, 6
Deposit copies, 42–43

Dodsley, Robert, 59n6
Dodsley v. Watson, 59n6
Donaldson, Alexander, 74, 92–97, 113
Donaldson v. Becket (4 Burr 2408, 98 ER 257; 2 Bro PC 129, 1 ER 837 (1774)), 5, 7, 25n, 68, 69, 86, 87–88, 95–97, 97, 98, 102, 103, 107–108, 110, 112, 113, 120n, 129; Justice Nares' vote in, 154–157
Droit moral, 18n3, 82n
Drone on Copyright, 133
Dryden, John, 37n
Duke of Queensberry v. Shebbeare (2 Eden 329, 28 ER 924 (1758)), 79
Dunning, John, 78, 98, 124

Eagleton, Terry, 119–120
Edinburgh Advertiser, The, 93, 96, 101, 157
Effingham, Lord, 86, 102
Eilenberg, Susan, 112n
Eisenstein, Elizabeth, 3–4
Elizabeth I, queen of England, 13
Engraving Copyright Act, 52n
Enquiry into the Nature and Origin of Literary Property, An, 87n, 130
Erskine, Andrew, 93
Eyre, Baron James, 87–88
Eyre v. Walker (cited 1 Black W 331, 96 ER 184; 4 Burr 2325, 98 ER 213 (1735)), 51

Fair use, 141
Faulkner, George, 63
Feather, John, 36, 42n, 45n, 52
Feist Publications v. Rural Telephone Service Company (111 S Ct 1282 (1991)), 135
Fichte, Johann Gottlieb, 131
Fielding, Henry, 115, 118; *Jacobite's Journal,* 115, 116; *Joseph Andrews,* 115; *Tom Jones,* 115–116
Fifoot, C. H. S., 68
Filmer, Sir Robert, 41n6
Folsom v. Marsh (9 F Cas 342 (CCD Mass 1841) (No 4901)), 141
Form as basis of literary property, 130–133
Forrester, Alexander, 59n5
Forrester v. Waller (cited 4 Burr 2331, 98 ER 216 (1741)), 59n5
Foucault, Michel, 1, 142
Fox, Christopher, 127
Frye, Northrop, 2

Gadbury's Almanac, 23
Gaines, Jane, 136

London Booksellers, 68, 97; actions against pirated editions, 69–71, 74–78, 93; as author's agents and assigns, 53, 70; *The Booksellers Humble Address to the Honourable House of Commons, In Behalf of the Bill for Encouraging Learning*, 43; *The Case of Authors and Proprietors of Books*, 53, 58n; *The Case of the Booksellers Right to their Copies*, 44; House of Lords opposition to booksellers' monopolies, 102; *The Humble Remonstrance of the Company of Stationers to the High Court of Parliament*, 15, 18n4; injunctions against other booksellers, 51; *More Reasons Humbly Offer'd to the Honourable House of Commons*, 44; petition for relief, 93, 103, 108; petition to make 1710 Act more effectual, 52–58; response to Lord Mansfield's silence, 101

London Chronicle, 155

London Evening Post, 155

Lyttleton, Lord, 101–102

Macaulay, Catherine, 105–107, 119

Macaulay, Thomas Babington, 31–32, 32n, 33

Macclesfield, Lord Chancellor, 50, 51, 133

Maclaurin, John, 95n2

Mahon, Lord, 111

Malone, Edward, 122

Mansfield, Lord, 59, 62, 68, 69 70, 71, 71n3, 74, 75, 76, 78–79, 80, 82, 84, 99–100, 101, 104, 109, 129, 140

Manutius, Aldus, 10

Marcuse, Michael, 122n

Mary I, queen of England, 13

McGill, Meredith, 86n7

McLaverty, James, 60

Metaphors of authorship, 38–41

Midwinter v. Hamilton. See Millar v. Kinkaid

Millar, Andrew, 95

Millar v. Donaldson (2 Eden 328, 28 *ER* 924 (1765)), 93

Millar v. Ilive (PRO C 12/307/62; C41/51/66; C/33/380/I.1, 113 (1742)), 115

Millar v. Kinkaid, (Home, *Remarkable Decisions* 154; Grant, *Decisions* 2:251; Fergusson, *Decisions* 96; Craigie, *Reports* 1:48; cited 4 Burr 2319, 98 *ER* 210 (1750)), 67–68, 69, 72, 76, 83, 92, 93

Millar v. Taylor (4 Burr 2303, 98 *ER* 201 (1769)), 5, 7, 63, 71n3, 78–83, 86, 95, 98, 99, 101, 108, 113, 114, 128, 139, 156

Miller v. Race (2 Keny 189, 96 *ER* 1151; 1 Burr 452, 97 *ER* 398 (1758)), 129

Milton, John, 105; accused of plagiarism, 122; *Aeropagitica*, 16, 28–30, 32n, 81, 81n, 121; contract for *Paradise Lost*, 27–28, 37n; *Eikonoklastes*, 30; "Lycidas," 105; *Paradise Lost*, 51, 71, 105, 122

Mitchell, J. Forbes, 110

Moral rights. See *Droit moral*

More, John, 113–114

Morning Chronicle, The, 96, 97, 101, 102, 154–155, 156

Motte, Benjamin, 58n

Muret, Marc-Antoine, 20

Murphy, Arthur, 7, 8, 78, 98, 103

Murray, William. See Mansfield, Lord

Nares, George, 154–157

Nash, N. Frederick, 17

Natural rights, 5–6, 69

Nelson, Robert, 51

New works: abridgments as, 51; printing privileges and, 10–11; translations as, 51, 133

Nichols v. Universal Pictures Corp. (34 F 2d 145 (2nd Cir 1929)), 141

Nivelle, Nicolas, 20

Northington, Lord Chancellor, 93–94

O'Connor, Sandra Day, 135

Original genius and personality as basis of literary property, 2, 6, 114–129, 135, 136, 137–138

Original works of authorship, in modern copyright law, 133–139

Osborne v. Donaldson (2 Eden 328, 28 *ER* 924 (1765)), 93

Parlement of Paris, 18, 19, 20

Parliament. *See* House of Commons; House of Lords

Parliamentary edict of 1642, 22

Patents, 10, 11, 12, 45; relation between literary property and, 73, 88

Patronage, 4, 13, 16, 17

Patterson, Lyman Ray, 14, 27, 48–49

Pavier, Thomas, 21

Perrin v. Blake (1 Black W 672, 96 *ER* 392; 4 Burr 2579, 98 *ER* 355 (1769)), 79n

Photographers as authors, 135–136

Piracy, 12, 35, 40, 42, 49, 55; foreign piracy, 53, 56n; London booksellers' actions against, 69–71, 74–78, 93

Pocock, J. G. A., 85

Ponder v. Braddill (cited 4 Burr 2303, 2317, 98 ER 201, 209 (1679)), 22–23

Pope, Alexander, 6, 56n, 59, 122; Bill of Complaint in *Pope v. Curll*, 62, 145–146; *Epistle to Dr. Arbuthnot*, 61; publication of letters of, 60–65, 140n; use of "copyright" by, 58n

Pope v. Bickham (PRO C 11/626/30, C 31/104/986 and 987, C 33/382, f. 179 (1744)), 59n6

Pope v. Curll (2 Atk 342, 26 ER 608 (1741)), 59n6, 59–60, 62, 68, 73, 79, 82, 128, 131, 132, 140; Curll's Answer, 63, 149–152; Lord Chancellor Hardwicke's decision, 152–153; Pope's Bill of Complaint, 62, 145–149

Post, Robert, 139–140

Pratt, Charles. *See* Camden, Lord

Precedent, value of, 99–100, 102

Prince Albert v. Strange (2 DeG & Sm 652, 64 ER 293 (1849)), 139–140

Printing privileges, in fifteenth-century Venice, 9–12, 17

Privacy, right to, 139–142

Property rights. *See* Common law rights of property transferrable by authors

Propriety, 18n4, 50, 51, 82

Public Advertiser, 100, 101, 102, 103, 104, 106n, 155

Quarterly Review, 107, 110

Quint, David, 6

Ransom, Harry: *The First Copyright Statute*, 42n

Registration of copyrights, 46. *See also* Stationers' Company

Rex v. Woodfall (Lofft 776, 98 ER 914 (1774)), 99n

Richardson, Samuel, 117; *An Address to the Public*, 116; *The History of Sir Charles Grandison*, 116

Rogers, Pat, 63n8

Rolls, Serjeant, 24

Royal prerogative, 12, 20, 23, 34, 71, 76

Sabellico, Marc' Antonio, 10, 17

Saunders, J. W., 21

Scotland, action under Statute of Anne in, 46

Scottish booksellers: counterpetition against London booksellers' petition for relief, 103

Scottish law, 5, 67–68, 69, 83–85, 129

Second Letter from an Author, A, 54n2

Shakespeare, William, 21, 25–26, 118, 122–124, 128

Sharpe, Thomas, 123, 128

Sheldon v. Metro-Goldwyn Pictures Corp. (81 F 2d 49 (2d Cir 1936)), 134

Short State of the Publick Encouragement, A, 54n2

Sidney, Sir Philip, 13, 30, 38

Simmons, Samuel, 27, 28

Some Thoughts on the State of Literary Property Humbly Submitted to the Consideration of the Public, 74, 93

Southey, Robert, 107, 110, 111, 112

Speeches or Arguments of the Judges of the Court of King's Bench in the Cause of Millar against Taylor, 83

Stackhouse, Thomas, 83, 136–137, 138

Stackhouse's Bible, 95

Stationers' Company, 4, 12, 15, 31, 33, 35–36, 48, 76, 78, 128; charter of, 12, 13, 43; continuity of Statute of Anne with guild copyright, 55; Court of Assistants, 12, 21, 22; *The Humble Remonstrance of the Company of Stationers*, 40n; *Register Book*, 14, 42, 46

Stationers' Company v. Carnan (2 Black W 1004, 96 ER 590 (1775)), 25n

Stationers' Company v. Patentees (Carter 89, 124 ER 842 (1666)), 23–24, 57

Stationers' Company v. Seymour (1 Mod 256, 86 ER 865; 3 Keble 792, 84 ER 1015 (1677)), 23

Statute of Anne (8 Anne c. 19), 5, 36, 64, 133; action under statute in Scotland, 46; bill for improving, 52–58; condensations and compilations protected under, 137; legal standing of author under, 49; legislative history of, 42–48; penalties in, 62–63, 64–65, 69–70; plaintiff's right to sue at common law during statutory term, 109–110; protection of letters under, 60–65; relation to common-law property rights, 5; term of copyright in, 5, 45, 47; as trade regulation act, 81

Statute of monoplies (21 Jac. I c. 3), 45, 47

Steele, Sir Richard, 75

Story, Joseph, 141

Strahan, William, 108

Streater v. Roper (cited Skin 233, 90 ER 107 (1688)), 24–25, 25n

Swift, Jonathan, 101; *Dean Swift's Literary Correspondence,* 60; *A Modest Proposal,* 39–40

Talfourd, Thomas Noon, 110–111
Taylor, Robert, 94
Tegg, Thomas, 111
Thomson, James: *Dramatic Works,* 94; ownership of Thomson copyrights, 120n; *The Seasons,* 78, 93, 94, 95, 113–114; *Works,* 94
Thurlow, Edward, 75, 76, 77, 78, 87, 98, 103
Tonson, Jacob, 37n, 51, 58n, 74, 75
Tonson, Richard, 74, 75
Tonson v. Collins (1 Black W 301, 96 *ER* 169 (1761)), 5, 51, 67, 68, 71n3, 79, 81, 82, 86n8, 87, 89, 90, 91, 93, 94, 98, 103, 119, 130, 131, 138
Tonson v. Walker (cited 1 Black W 331, 96 *ER* 184 (1739)), 93
Tonson v. Walker (3 Swans. 672, 36 *ER* 1017 (1752)), 69, 71, 76
Translator as author, 51, 133
Tucker, Irene, 65

United States copyright statute, 132

Venice, system of printing privileges in, 9–12, 17, 20–21

Vergier d'honneur, 19
Vindication of the Exclusive Rights of Authors, A, 87n

Walker, Jeffrey, 51
Walthoe v. Walker (cited 1 Black W 331, 96 *ER* 184 (1736)), 51
Warburton, William, 71, 76, 88n, 138; *A Letter from an Author to a Member of Parliament,* 54–55, 56–58, 71–74, 76, 87, 88n, 119
Warren, Samuel, 139–140
Webb v. Rose (cited 1 Black W 330, 96 *ER* 184 (1732)), 59n5
Wedderburn, Alexander, 75, 76 98, 103, 124
Wheaton v. Peters (33 US 591 (1834)), 86n7
Whicher, John, 156
Willes, Edward, 62–63, 75, 79, 139
Wilmot, Reverend James, 124
Woodfall, William, 97, 154–155
Woodhouse, Richard, 124
Woodmansee, Martha, 130–131
Wordsworth, William, 110, 111, 112, 112n
Wortley, Edward, 42, 43

Yates, Sir Joseph, 75, 77, 78, 79, 79n, 83, 86, 86n8, 87, 89, 90, 102, 128, 129, 130, 138, 139
Young, Edward, 6, 117–118, 119, 120–121, 122

Zionkowski, Linda, 118, 119